THE UNIVERSE

THE UNIVERSE

THE ULTIMATE GUIDED TOUR OF THE COSMOS FROM THE FORMATION OF STARS TO THE FARTHEST REACHES OF THE UNIVERSE

Bath · New York · Cologne · Melbourne · Delhi
Hong Kong · Shenzhen · Singapore · Amsterdam

This edition published by Parragon Books Ltd in 2014 and distributed by

Parragon Inc.
440 Park Avenue South, 13th Floor
New York, NY 10016
www.parragon.com

Consultant: Lee Pullen

ISBN 978-1-4723-4675-9

Printed in China

Based on an idea by Editorial Sol 90.
Editorial coordination Marta de la Serna
Design Susana Ribot
Editing Mar Valls
Graphic editing Alberto Hernández
Layout María Beltrán, María Nolis
Copy Editor Stuart Franklin
Infographics Sol90Images
Photography Corbis, ESA, Getty Images, AGE Fotostock, Graphic News, NASA, National Geographic,
Science Photo Library

CONTENTS

EAGLE NEBULA
This nebula, located 7,000 light years from Earth, got its name from its shape, resembling an eagle with outstretched wings.

Introduction

Since the dawn of time, humans have been curious about what the heavens have to hide. It was this curiosity that led to the construction of telescopes and spacecraft, which have enabled blurry, distant objects to be viewed with precision. According to physics and mathematical calculations, the Milky Way contains up to four hundred billion stars. Our Sun is a resident of this galaxy, as is the Earth, which rotates around the Sun and is the only planet currently known to support life. Thanks to scientific and technological advances, human beings have been able to explore the far reaches of the Solar System and even beyond its boundaries. In doing so, some of the secrets of the Universe have been uncovered: its governing forces, its composition, its creation, the birth and death of stars, the features of black holes, the makeup of invisible dark matter that surrounds the galaxies, and so much more.

MAN ON THE MOON

An astronaut from the *Apollo 16* mission walks on the surface of the Moon, in a digitalized image made by Roger Ressmeyer from the original flight film.

However, although space observation dates back to time immemorial, the history of space exploration is much shorter. The first satellite was launched into space in 1957. More recently astronomers have started to observe other icy worlds, much smaller in size than planets, in a region known as the Kuiper Belt. Scientists affirm that the Kuiper Belt represents one of the most interesting moments in the exploration of the Solar System, given that a significant number of discoveries are now being made. Orbiting spacecraft like *Mars Odyssey* and *Mars Express* have confirmed the existence of ice deep inside Mars. The sending of exploration spacecraft to Saturn is another prestigious accomplishment, demonstrating humankind's capacity to dream of new worlds, as is the exploration of the outer limits of the Solar System by *New Horizons*. However, the search has only just begun; there is still a great deal to discover. For some time now, astronomers have been searching the Universe for other worlds similar to Earth, where life could be sustained. Perhaps one will be found farther away than we could imagine. Or perhaps, as some creative minds would like to think, the coming decades will see the project to colonize other planets come to fruition. For now, the best candidate is Mars. For the time being, however, this remains just a dream—similar to the one made reality on July 21, 1969, when man set foot on the Moon.

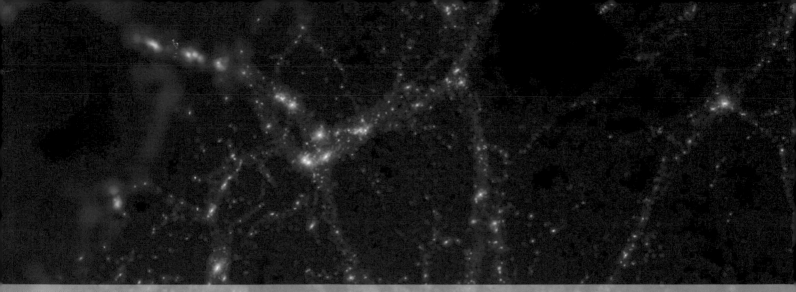

1

DARK MATTER
Dark matter accounts for 84.5 percent
of the total matter in the Universe. As
it does not emit radiation, it is invisible
to telescopes. This simulation has
been generated by a supercomputer.

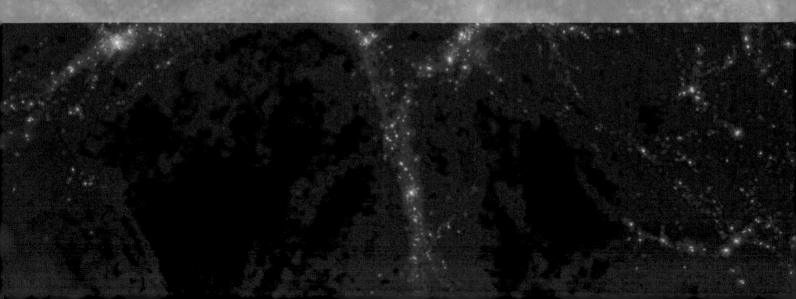

WHAT IS THE UNIVERSE?

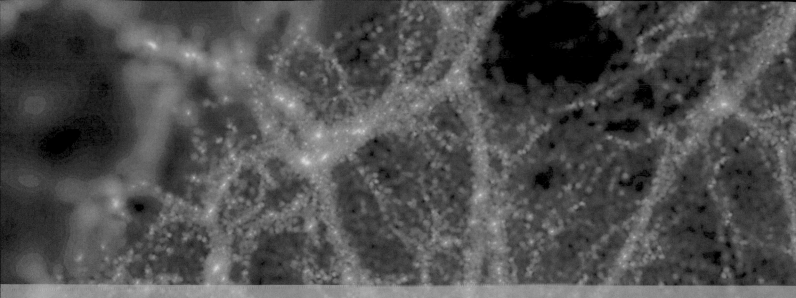

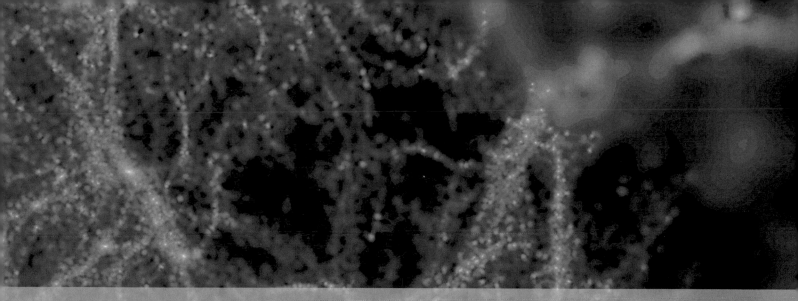

The Universe is everything that exists—from the smallest to the very largest particles, combined with all existing matter and energy. This includes both visible and invisible objects, such as "dark matter," the cosmos's greatest secret component. The search for dark matter is currently one of the most important tasks pursued in the field of cosmology. Matter literally determines the density of all of space and, it could also be claimed, the future of the Universe. Did you know that since the Universe was created almost 14 billion years ago, it has not stopped growing? The question that astronomers ask themselves, and what most concerns them, is how much longer will it continue to grow like a balloon until it turns into something cold and dark?

Radiography of the Cosmos

The Universe, or cosmos, is a series of at least one hundred billion galaxies. In turn, each of these galaxies, which tend to join together in large groups, contains billions of stars. These galactic concentrations are surrounded by empty spaces, or "cosmic gaps."

1 **Earth**
Created along with the Solar System when the Universe was already nine billion years old.

The Universe

Dating back almost 14 billion years to a gigantic explosion, it is impossible to render an idea of the current size of the Universe. And the number of stars and galaxies remaining continues to expand. For many years, astronomers believed the Milky Way represented the entire Universe. However, during the twentieth century, it was discovered that not only is space much more vast than originally thought, but that it was located within an expanse of extraordinary dimensions.

Capricornus Supercluster

Sculptor Supercluster

Pisces-Cetus Superclusters

750

1,000

Horologium Superclusters

2 **Nearby stars**
Located between 4.37–20 light years from the Sun in all directions, they form a local neighborhood of stars.

G51-15
Ross 128
Lalande 2185
Wolf 359
Struve 2398
Procyon
12.5
7.5
90°
Luyten's Star
2.5
SUN
Barnard's Star
61 Cygni
Alpha Centauri
Sirius
Groombridge 34
Ross 248
270°
0°
Ross 154
Epsilon Eridani
L726-8
L372-58
Epsilon Indi
L789-6
Tau Ceti
L725-32
Lacaille 9352

3 **Neighbors**
The Milky Way and its nearest galaxies are within one billion light years.

Sextans Dwarf
L789-6
180°
Ursa Minor Dwarf
Draco Dwarf
MILKY WAY
0.12
Canis Major
0.25
Sagittarius Dwarf
0.37
0°
0.5
Large Magellanic Cloud
Carina Dwarf
Small Magellanic Cloud

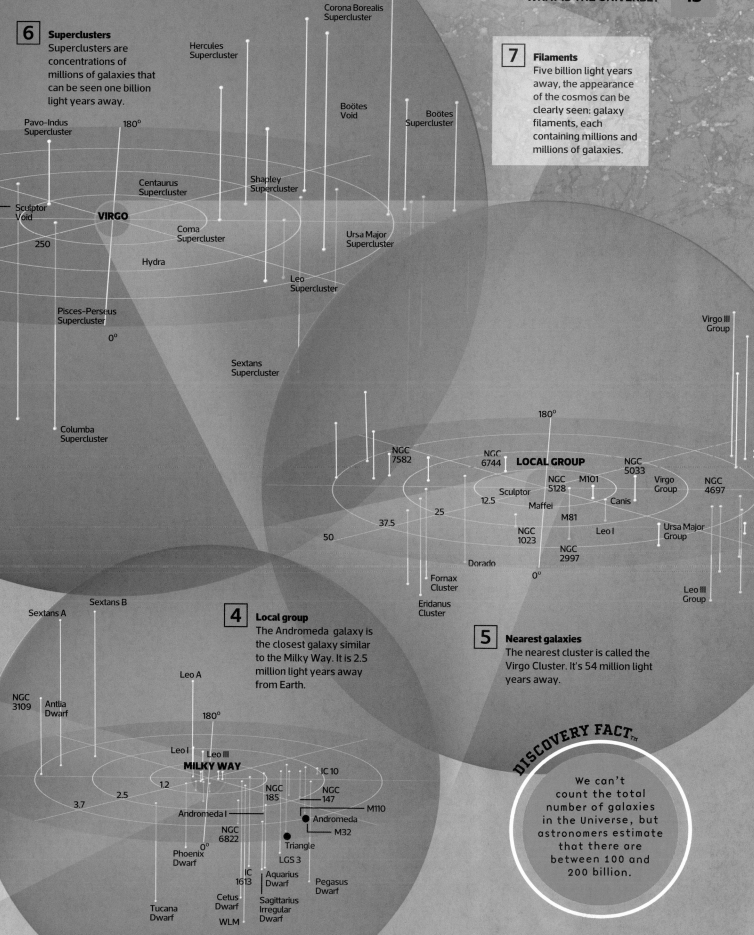

6 Superclusters
Superclusters are concentrations of millions of galaxies that can be seen one billion light years away.

7 Filaments
Five billion light years away, the appearance of the cosmos can be clearly seen: galaxy filaments, each containing millions and millions of galaxies.

Corona Borealis Supercluster

Hercules Supercluster

Boötes Void

Boötes Supercluster

Pavo-Indus Supercluster

180°

Centaurus Supercluster

Shapley Supercluster

Sculptor Void

VIRGO

250

Coma Supercluster

Ursa Major Supercluster

Hydra

Leo Supercluster

Pisces-Perseus Supercluster

0°

Sextans Supercluster

Columba Supercluster

Virgo III Group

180°

NGC 7582

NGC 6744

LOCAL GROUP

NGC 5033

Sculptor

NGC 5128

M101

Virgo Group

NGC 4697

12.5

Maffei

Canis

25

M81

37.5

NGC 1023

Leo I

Ursa Major Group

50

NGC 2997

Dorado

0°

Leo III Group

Fornax Cluster

Eridanus Cluster

5 Nearest galaxies
The nearest cluster is called the Virgo Cluster. It's 54 million light years away.

Sextans B

Sextans A

4 Local group
The Andromeda galaxy is the closest galaxy similar to the Milky Way. It is 2.5 million light years away from Earth.

Leo A

NGC 3109

Antlia Dwarf

180°

Leo I

Leo III

MILKY WAY

1.2

IC 10

3.7

2.5

NGC 185

NGC 147

M110

Andromeda I

Andromeda

M32

Phoenix Dwarf

0°

NGC 6822

Triangle

Tucana Dwarf

IC 1613

Aquarius Dwarf

Pegasus Dwarf

Cetus Dwarf

Sagittarius Irregular Dwarf

WLM

LGS 3

DISCOVERY FACT™

We can't count the total number of galaxies in the Universe, but astronomers estimate that there are between 100 and 200 billion.

The Moment of Creation

It is not known with any level of accuracy how, from nothing, the Universe was born. Initially, according to the Big Bang theory—the most commonly accepted theory among the scientific community—an infinitely small and dense hot ball appeared, which gave rise to space, matter, and energy. This happened 13.7 billion years ago, although what generated it is unknown to this day.

DISCOVERY FACT™

British astronomer Fred Hoyle (who disagreed with the theory) came up with the name "Big Bang" when discussing it on a radio program in 1949.

Energetic radiation

The hot ball that gave rise to the Universe was a permanent source of radiation. Subatomic particles and antiparticles annihilated one another. The high density spontaneously created and destroyed matter. Having remained in this state, the Universe would never have experienced the growth that, as is believed, occurred as a result of "cosmic inflation."

HOW IT GREW
The inflation caused each region of the young Universe to grow. The galactic neighborhood appears uniform: the same types of galaxy, the same background temperature.

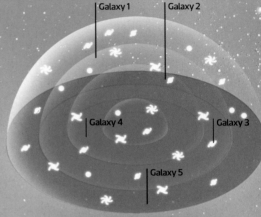

Galaxy 1　Galaxy 2
Galaxy 4　Galaxy 3
Galaxy 5

Time	0	10^{-43} seconds	10^{-38} seconds
Temperature	–	$10^{32°}$ C	$10^{29°}$ C

1 According to the theory, everything that currently exists was compressed into a space smaller than the nucleus of an atom.

2 At the moment closest to hour "zero," which physics has been able to identify, the temperature is immensely high. A superforce governs the Universe.

3 The Universe is unstable and grows 100 trillion trillion trillion trillion trillion times. Inflation starts and the forces separate.

ELEMENTARY PARTICLES
Initially, the Universe was a "hodgepodge" of particles that interacted with others due to high levels of radiation. Later, once the Universe had inflated, quarks formed the nuclei of the elements, and with electrons, atoms were formed.

Photon
Light elementary particle with no mass.

Electron
Negatively charged elementary particle.

Graviton
A particle believed to transfer gravity.

Gluon
Responsible for interactions between quarks.

Quark
Light elementary particle.

The cosmic inflation theory

Big Bang theorists have been unable to understand with any level of certainty why the Universe has grown so quickly throughout its evolution. In 1979, physicist Alan Guth resolved this problem with his Inflation Theory. In an extremely short space of time (less than a thousandth of a second), the Universe grew 100 trillion trillion trillion trillion trillion times.

WMAP (WILKINSON MICROWAVE ANISOTROPY PROBE)
NASA's WMAP project makes it possible to see the Universe's background radiation. In the picture, hotter (red-yellow) and colder (green-blue) areas can be seen. WMAP makes it possible to establish the amount of dark matter.

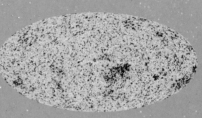

HOW IT DIDN'T GROW
If there had been no inflation, the Universe would have comprised a series of clearly distinguishable regions. It would comprise "remnants," each of which would contain certain types of galaxy.

Region 1
Region 3
Region 2
Region 4
Region 5

SEPARATION OF FORCES
Before the inflation, there was just a single force that governed all interactions. The first to separate was gravity, then electromagnetic force, and finally nuclear interaction. As the forces separated, matter was created.

GRAVITY
STRONG NUCLEAR
WEAK NUCLEAR
ELECTROMAGNETIC FORCE
SUPERFORCE
INFLATION

10^{-12} seconds 10^{-4} seconds   1 second   3 minutes

$10^{15°}$ C

4 The Universe experiences an immense cooling process. Gravity becomes separated, electromagnetic force appears, and nuclear interaction begins.

$10^{12°}$ C

5 Protons and neutrons are born, formed by three quarks each. The Universe is still dark: light is trapped in the mass of particles.

$5 \times 10^{9°}$ C

6 Electrons and positrons annihilate one another, until the positrons disappear. The remaining electrons go on to form atoms.

$10^{9°}$ C

7 They create the nuclei of the lightest elements: helium and hydrogen. Each nucleus comprises protons and neutrons.

1 second Neutrinos decouple as a result of neutron disintegration. With a very small mass, neutrinos go on to form most of the Universe's dark matter.

FROM PARTICLE TO MATTER
Quarks interacted with others thanks to the force transferred by gluons. Later, along with neutrons, they formed nuclei.

Quark
Gluon

1 A gluon interacts with a quark.

2 Quarks join gluons to form protons and neutrons.

Proton
Neutron

3 Protons and neutrons join to form nuclei.

The transparent Universe

The creation of atoms and general cooling allowed the Universe, which was dense and opaque, to become transparent. Photons, light particles with no mass, were free to roam space; radiation lost its crown as governor of the Universe and matter was able to carve out its own destiny under the forces of gravity. Gaseous accumulations grew, and over hundreds of millions of years formed protogalaxies; thanks to gravity, they became the first galaxies, and in denser regions, the first stars began to fuse hydrogen and release energy. The great, lingering mystery was why the galaxies took on their current shape. Dark matter—an intergalactic empty space—could hold the key; it was responsible for their expansion and can only be detected indirectly.

1 Gas cloud
The first gases and dust generated by the Big Bang formed a cloud.

2 First filaments
As a result of dark matter's gravity, gases joined together to form filaments.

DARK MATTER
Dark matter, invisible to the most powerful telescopes, comprises 84.5 percent of the Universe's matter. Galaxies and stars move as a result of the gravitational effects of dark energy and matter.

EVOLUTION OF MATTER
The Big Bang initially produced a gas cloud that was uniformly dispersed. Three million years later, the gas started to organize itself into the shape of filaments. Today, the Universe can be seen as networks of galactic filaments with enormous spaces between them.

TIME	380,000 years	500 million
TEMPERATURE	4,892° F (2,700° C)	−405° F (−243° C)

8 Atoms are born. Electrons orbit around the nuclei, attracted by protons. The Universe becomes transparent. Photons travel throughout space.

9 Galaxies acquire their definitive shape: "islands" with billions of stars and masses of gas and dust. Stars explode, as supernovas, and scatter heavier elements such as carbon.

FIRST ATOMS
Helium and hydrogen were the first elements to be joined at an atomic level. They are the main components of stars and planets, and the most common throughout the Universe.

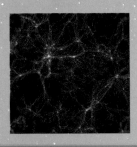

NUCLEUS 1 — Proton

Electron

Neutron

NUCLEUS 2

1 Hydrogen
An electron is attracted and orbits around a nucleus, which contains a proton.

2 Helium
As the nucleus has two protons, two electrons are attracted.

3 Carbon
Over time, more complex elements like carbon (six protons and six electrons), were formed.

3 Networks of filaments
The Universe can be seen as filaments with billions of galaxies.

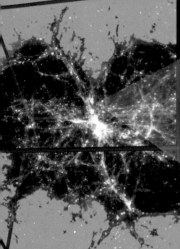

The Universe today

Irregular galaxy

Barred spiral galaxy

Spiral galaxy

Elliptical galaxy

Nebula

Star

Quasar

Galaxy cluster

9.1 billion

THE EARTH IS CREATED
Like all the other planets in our Solar System, the Earth was formed from material left over from the creation of the Sun.

9 billion

–432° F (–258° C)

10 Nine billion years after the Big Bang, the Solar System is born. A mass of gas and dust collapses, giving rise to the creation of the Sun. Then, with the remaining material, a planetary system is brought together.

13.7 billion

–454° F (–270° C)

11 Currently, the Universe continues expanding, with a vast number of galaxies separated by dark matter. The predominant energy is also an unknown: dark energy (74 percent).

DISCOVERY FACT™

Located in a 1-mile deep former gold mine in South Dakota, the Large Underground Xenon (LUX) experiment is designed to detect dark matter.

COSMIC CALENDAR

In an attempt to make the magnitudes of time related to the Universe more tangible, U.S. writer Carl Sagan introduced the concept of the "Cosmic Calendar." On January 1 of that imaginary year, at 12:00 a.m., the Big Bang occurred. *Homo sapiens* would appear at 11:56 p.m. on December 31, with Columbus discovering America (1492) at 11:59 p.m. that same day. One second in the Cosmic Calendar is representative of 500 years.

Big Bang
Occurred on the first second of the first day of the year.

JANUARY

The Solar System
Created on August 24 of the Cosmic Calendar.

Columbus arrives in America
This would occur on the last second of December 31.

DECEMBER

The End of the Universe

To predict the future of the Universe, its total mass first needs to be discovered; up to now, this piece of data has eluded humankind. According to the latest observations of astronomers, it is likely that the Universe's mass is significantly lower than the mass required to slow down its expansion. Thus, the current rate of growth is just a stepping-stone on the path to complete destruction—and then total darkness.

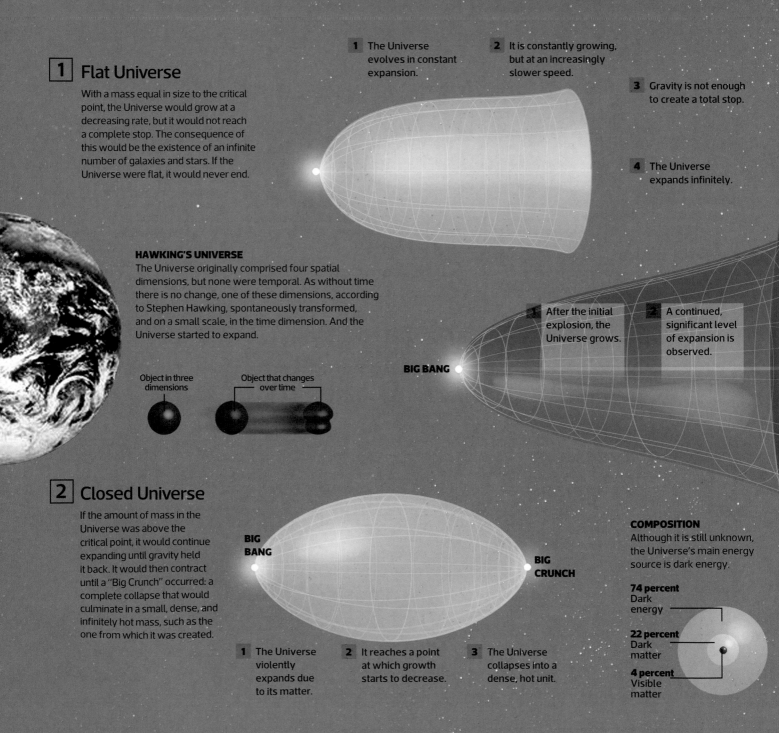

1 Flat Universe

With a mass equal in size to the critical point, the Universe would grow at a decreasing rate, but it would not reach a complete stop. The consequence of this would be the existence of an infinite number of galaxies and stars. If the Universe were flat, it would never end.

1 The Universe evolves in constant expansion.

2 It is constantly growing, but at an increasingly slower speed.

3 Gravity is not enough to create a total stop.

4 The Universe expands infinitely.

HAWKING'S UNIVERSE

The Universe originally comprised four spatial dimensions, but none were temporal. As without time there is no change, one of these dimensions, according to Stephen Hawking, spontaneously transformed, and on a small scale, in the time dimension. And the Universe started to expand.

Object in three dimensions

Object that changes over time

BIG BANG

1 After the initial explosion, the Universe grows.

2 A continued, significant level of expansion is observed.

2 Closed Universe

If the amount of mass in the Universe was above the critical point, it would continue expanding until gravity held it back. It would then contract until a "Big Crunch" occurred: a complete collapse that would culminate in a small, dense, and infinitely hot mass, such as the one from which it was created.

BIG BANG

BIG CRUNCH

1 The Universe violently expands due to its matter.

2 It reaches a point at which growth starts to decrease.

3 The Universe collapses into a dense, hot unit.

COMPOSITION

Although it is still unknown, the Universe's main energy source is dark energy.

74 percent Dark energy

22 percent Dark matter

4 percent Visible matter

DISCOVERIES

The key discovery, which supported the existence of a Big Bang, was made by Edwin Hubble, who discovered that the galaxies are in constant expansion. Twenty years later, George Gamow proposed the existence of original background radiation. At the Bell Labs in New Jersey, Arno Penzias and Robert Wilson accidentally detected a constant signal throughout space at a temperature of -454 °F: a fossil of the Universe's early radiation.

1920s—Edwin Hubble
He noted a deviation toward red on the spectrum and was able to establish that galaxies moved away from one another.

1940s—George Gamow
Russia's Gamow was the first to propose the Big Bang theory. He maintained that the early Universe was a "melting pot" of particles.

1965—Penzias and Wilson
They discovered that, regardless of where they aimed, their antenna picked up a constant signal: background radiation.

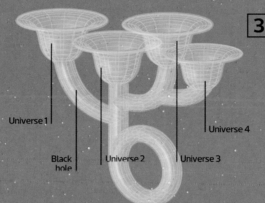

Universe 1
Black hole
Universe 2
Universe 3
Universe 4

3 Self-regenerating Universes

A less commonly accepted theory is that universes generate themselves. In this instance, there would be several universes that are continuously recreating themselves. Self-regenerating universes could be transmitted by supermassive black holes.

A point arrives at which everything dies and life comes to an end.

4 Open Universe

The most accepted theory on the future of the cosmos is that the Universe's mass is lower than the critical point. The latest measurements seem to indicate that the current moment of expansion is just one phase prior to death. One day, the Universe will be extinguished for good.

BLACK HOLES

It is believed that by traveling through a black hole, it may be possible to travel through space and get to know other universes. This would be possible owing to antigravity effects.

Black hole

Turning point

New universe

5 Baby Universes

According to this theory, universes continually give rise to other universes. However, in this case, a universe would be created after the death and disappearance of another universe, which would create a supermassive black hole; it would be from this that another universe is born. This process could be repeated indefinitely and it would be impossible to determine the number of universes in existence.

The Forces of the Universe

The four main forces that inhabit space are those that cannot be explained using more basic forces. Each one participates in different processes and each interaction involves different types of particles. Gravity, electromagnetic force, strong nuclear force, and weak nuclear force are indispensable in the understanding of how the objects in the Universe behave.

General theory of relativity

The main contributions to understanding how the Universe works were formulated by Albert Einstein in 1915. Einstein thought of space as being connected to a dimension that nobody had previously considered: time. And gravity, which to Newton was the force that generated the attraction between two objects, was proposed by Einstein as the consequence of what he called the "space-time curvature." According to his theory of relativity, the Universe is curved by the presence of objects with different masses. And so, gravity is a spatial distortion, which establishes that one object "pulls" toward another, depending on whether the curve is greater or smaller.

DISCOVERY FACT™

Using ideas such as string theory, a major aim of physicists is to find a way to fit all four basic forces into a fundamental "theory of everything."

Real position

What we see

LIGHT TRAJECTORY

Positive pole

SUN

EARTH

Negative pole

1 Gravity

The first to separate itself from the original super force. It is an attraction force that is currently perceived as set out by Einstein: as an effect of the space-time curvature. If you were to think of the Universe as a cube, the presence of any object with mass would generate a deformation in that cube. Gravity has the special feature of being able to act from a significant distance (like electromagnetism); however, it always exerts an attraction force.

$E = mc^2$

As part of Einstein's equation, energy and mass are interchangeable. If an object increases its mass, its energy content also increases.

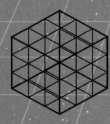

If the Universe contained no objects with mass, it might look like this.

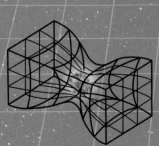

The Universe is permanently undergoing deformations due to the masses of objects.

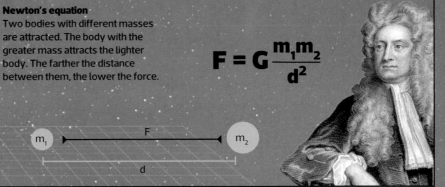

UNIVERSAL GRAVITATION

Gravitation, as proposed by Newton, is the mutual attraction between two bodies of certain masses. Newton's Law, a paradigm accepted until Einstein's time, did not take into account either time or space as an essential part of the interaction between two objects. Attraction was caused by mass: objects with a greater mass attract objects with an inferior mass. And this was attributable solely to the intrinsic nature of objects. Nonetheless, the Law of Universal Gravitation was the pillar of Einstein's theory.

Newton's equation

Two bodies with different masses are attracted. The body with the greater mass attracts the lighter body. The farther the distance between them, the lower the force.

$$F = G \frac{m_1 m_2}{d^2}$$

m_1 — F — m_2

d

3 Strong nuclear force

It keeps the components of atomic nuclei together. Gluons are the particles responsible for transporting strong nuclear force and their immensity allows quarks to join together to form nuclear particles: protons and neutrons.

1 Quarks and gluons
The strong interaction is transmitted when the gluon interacts with the quarks.

Nucleus

Quark
Force
Gluon

2 Union
Quarks join together and form nuclear protons and neutrons.

2 Electromagnetic force

The force that affects electrically charged bodies. It participates in the chemical and physical transformations of atoms and molecules that form part of different elements. It is more intense than gravitational force and is active on two fronts, or poles: positive and negative.

Attraction

Two atoms are attracted and the electrons rotate around the new molecule.

Hydrogen

Helium

Force

Electron

Positive pole

Nucleus

Negative pole

MOLECULAR MAGNETISM

Electromagnetic force is the predominant force in atoms and molecules. Charged atoms attract one another.

LIGHT CURVES

Light also curves due to the space-time curvature. Seen from a telescope, the real position of an object is distorted. What the telescope sees is a false location, generated by the curve of light. It is not possible to witness the true position of the object.

4 Weak nuclear force

The least intense force compared with all other forces. A weak interaction is active in the disintegration of a neutron, during which a proton and a neutrino are released; this later transforms into an electron. This force is active in natural radioactive phenomena, which occur in the atoms of certain particles.

1 Hydrogen
A hydrogen atom interacts with a light and weak particle (Wimp). A Down quark in the neutron becomes an Up quark.

HYDROGEN ATOM

HELIUM ISOTOPE

Electron

Proton

Proton

Electron

2 Helium
The neutron becomes a proton. An electron is released and a helium isotope is created, with no nuclear neutrons.

Neutron   WIMP

ETA CARINAE NEBULA
With a diameter of over 200 light years, it is one of the biggest and brightest nebulae in our galaxy.

2

HOW
IS IT
FORMED?

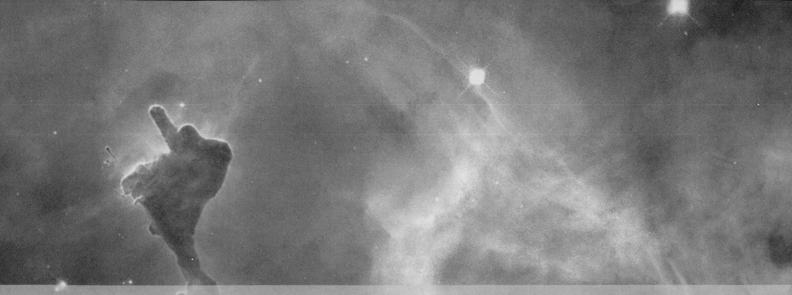

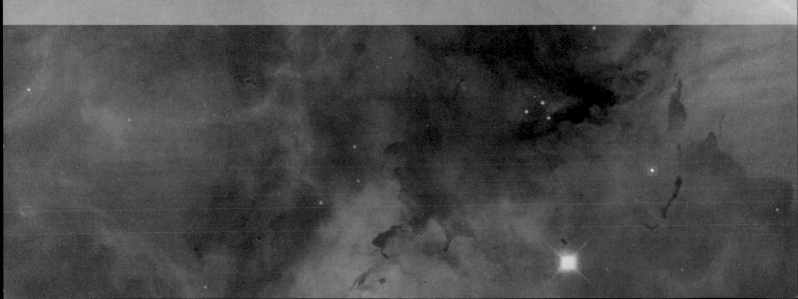

For the most part, the Universe is populated by superclusters of galaxies, which comprise filaments that encompass empty spaces. Occasionally, galaxies come so close together that they collide, sparking intense rates of star formation. These stars then live long lives, until they exhaust their fuel supply and gradually fizzle out, or explode as supernovae. Throughout the vast cosmos, there are also quasars, pulsars, and black holes. Thanks to modern technology, it is also possible to appreciate the array of light silhouettes and shadows that comprise some nebulae, made up of filaments of hot, fluorescent gases. Although we still have not discovered all the objects that exist in the Universe, it is possible to assert without doubt that the majority of the atoms that form our bodies were born among the stars.

The Stars

For a long time, stars were a mystery to humankind. Today, it is known that they are enormous spheres of plasma, mostly hydrogen with a smaller amount of helium. Based on the light they emit, experts can ascertain their brightness, color, and temperature. Given their huge distance from Earth, they can only be seen as dots of light, even with the most powerful telescopes.

GLOBULAR CLUSTER
Around 10 million stars join together to form a huge band: Omega Centauri.

OPEN CLUSTER
The Pleiades are a formation of around 1,000 stars that will scatter throughout space in the future.

Hertzsprung-Russell Diagram

The H-R diagram groups stars according to their visual brightness, the spectral type that corresponds to the wavelengths of light they emit, and their temperature. Stars in the Main Sequence with a greater mass tend to be brighter—such as blues, red giants, and red supergiants. Stars live 90 percent of their lives in the Main Sequence.

Light years and parsecs

In order to measure the immense distance between stars, the terms light year (ly) and parsec (pc) are used. A light year is the distance light travels in one year: almost 6 trillion miles (9.5 trillion km). A pc is the distance between a star and Earth, if its parallax angle is one arc second. One pc equals 3.26 ly, or 19.3 trillion miles (31 trillion km).

DISCOVERY FACT™

The hottest stars (O-, B-, and A-spectral type) are blue-white in color. The coldest (G-, K-, and M-type) stars, are yellow, orange, and red.

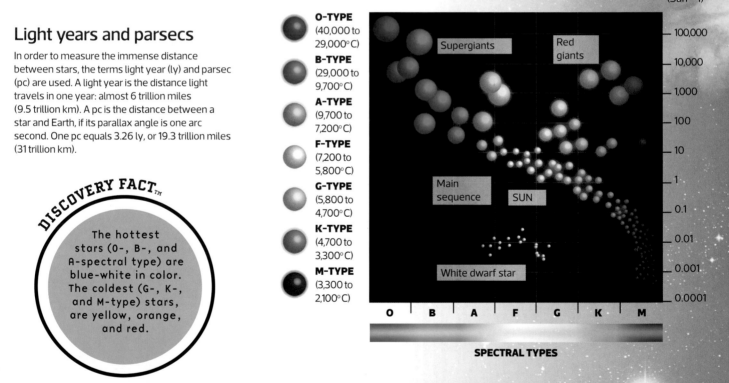

O-TYPE (40,000 to 29,000°C)

B-TYPE (29,000 to 9,700°C)

A-TYPE (9,700 to 7,200°C)

F-TYPE (7,200 to 5,800°C)

G-TYPE (5,800 to 4,700°C)

K-TYPE (4,700 to 3,300°C)

M-TYPE (3,300 to 2,100°C)

VISUAL BRIGHTNESS (Sun = 1)

Supergiants

Red giants

Main sequence

SUN

White dwarf star

100,000 — 10,000 — 1,000 — 100 — 10 — 1 — 0.1 — 0.01 — 0.001 — 0.0001

O B A F G K M

SPECTRAL TYPES

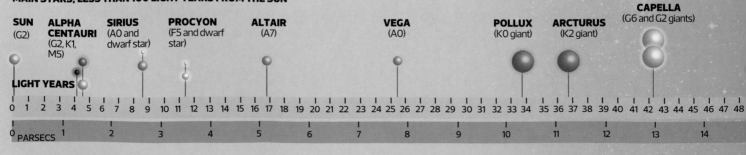

MAIN STARS, LESS THAN 100 LIGHT YEARS FROM THE SUN

SUN (G2)

ALPHA CENTAURI (G2, K1, M5)

SIRIUS (A0 and dwarf star)

PROCYON (F5 and dwarf star)

ALTAIR (A7)

VEGA (A0)

POLLUX (K0 giant)

ARCTURUS (K2 giant)

CAPELLA (G6 and G2 giants)

LIGHT YEARS

0 1 2 3 4 5 6 7 8 9 10 11 12 13 14 15 16 17 18 19 20 21 22 23 24 25 26 27 28 29 30 31 32 33 34 35 36 37 38 39 40 41 42 43 44 45 46 47 48

0 PARSECS 1 2 3 4 5 6 7 8 9 10 11 12 13 14

Measuring distance

When the Earth orbits the Sun, the closest stars appear to move over a background of more distant stars. The angle that results from the movement of a star within the Earth's six-month rotation period is known as the "parallax angle." The closer a star is to Earth, the larger the parallax.

The parallax angle of star A is small. Therefore, it is a long way from Earth.

The parallax angle of star B is greater than that of A. B is therefore closer to Earth.

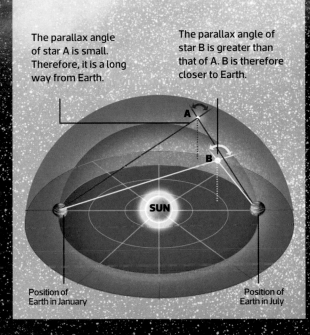

A

B

SUN

Position of Earth in January

Position of Earth in July

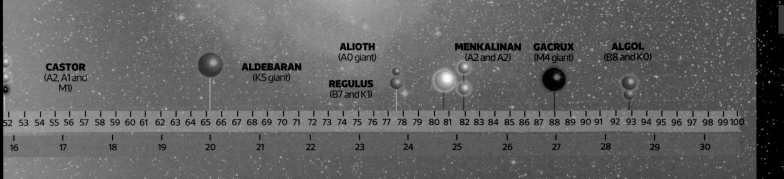

CASTOR
(A2, A1 and M1)

ALDEBARAN
(K5 giant)

ALIOTH
(A0 giant)

REGULUS
(B7 and K1)

MENKALINAN
(A2 and A2)

GACRUX
(M4 giant)

ALGOL
(B8 and K0)

52 53 54 55 56 57 58 59 60 61 62 63 64 65 66 67 68 69 70 71 72 73 74 75 76 77 78 79 80 81 82 83 84 85 86 87 88 89 90 91 92 93 94 95 96 97 98 99 100

16   17   18   19   20   21   22   23   24   25   26   27   28   29   30

The Evolution of Stars

Stars are born in nebulae, enormous gas clouds, mainly comprising hydrogen and dust, that float in space. They can live for millions, or even billions, of years. Often, their size can provide clues about their age: smaller stars tend to be younger, while larger stars are closer to perishing, soon to cool down or explode as supernovas.

Massive star

More than eight solar masses

1 Protostar
Comprising a dense, gaseous core surrounded by a dust cloud.

2 Star
The star is born. Hydrogen fuses to form helium during the main sequence.

Nebula

A cloud of gas and dust collapses because of the effects of gravity; it heats up and divides into smaller clouds that may form protostars.

Low-mass star

Fewer than eight solar masses

The life cycle of a star

The evolution of a star depends on its mass. Low-mass stars, like the Sun, have much longer, more modest lives. When they run out of hydrogen, they turn into a red giant and, eventually, end their lives as white dwarves until they completely burn out. Stars with a greater mass eventually explode: all that is left of one is a hyper-dense remnant—a neutron star. Significantly more massive stars eventually form black holes.

1 Protostar
Formed by the release of gas and dust. Its core rotates owing to the effects of gravity.

2 Star
It shines and slowly consumes its hydrogen reserves. It fuses helium while it grows in size.

3 **Red supergiant**
The star expands and heats up, forming a heavy iron core.

4 **Supernova**
When the star is no longer able to fuse more elements, the core collapses, leading to a large release of energy.

5 **Neutron star**
If the initial mass ranges between 8 and 20 suns, the resulting star is a neutron star.

5 **Black hole**
If the initial mass is greater than 20 suns, the core is even denser and forms a black hole, with a highly intense gravitational pull.

6 **Black dwarf star**
If it completely burns out, the white dwarf star turns into a black dwarf star. They cannot be seen in space.

5 **White dwarf star**
The star is encompassed by the gases and loses brightness.

4 **Planetary nebula**
Having run out of fuel, the core condenses and the outer layers are detached. The gases released form gas clouds.

3 **Red giant**
The star continues to grow. The core heats up. As it runs out of helium, it fuses carbon and oxygen.

Approximately 95 percent of stars end their lives as white dwarf stars. Other, more massive stars can explode as supernovas, illuminating entire galaxies for weeks.

Red Giants

When a star exhausts its hydrogen reserves, it starts to die. When this happens the core turns into a ball of helium, and reactions begin to cease. The helium stays bright and luminous, until it consumes itself and the core contracts. The outer layers of the star dilate until it becomes a red giant, before finally cooling down.

THE LIFE CYCLE OF A STAR

Red giant

Spectacular dimensions

When the star exhausts its hydrogen, it can grow to 200 times the diameter of the Sun. It then starts to fuse helium, and its diameter changes further. Its growth stabilizes at this point until, after billions of years, it dies. In the case of supergiants, they collapse before exploding.

CORE REGION

The core of a red giant is ten times smaller than the original core, as it shrinks due to a lack of hydrogen.

1 Hydrogen
It keeps fusing outside the core when the core has run out of hydrogen.

2 Helium
This is produced after the hydrogen is fused.

3 Carbon and oxygen
Produced during helium combustion, they fuse at the core of the red giant.

4 Temperature
While the helium fuses, the core reaches 100 million degrees Celsius.

CONVECTION CELLS
They transfer heat toward the surface. Currents of rising and descending gas move from the core to the surface. Certain elements formed at the core of the star are also transported to the surface.

1 percent

The size of the Sun's diameter compared to a typical red giant.

HEAT SPOTS
These appear when large currents of incandescent plasma reach the surface. They can be seen on the surface of neighboring red giants.

GRAINS OF DUST
They condense in the outer atmosphere and then scatter by means of stellar winds. The dust is dispersed throughout interstellar space, where new generations of stars are formed.

White dwarf star

After experiencing a period as a red giant, stars like the Sun lose their outer layers, giving rise to a planetary nebula. At its heart is a white dwarf star, an extremely hot (180,032° F/100,000° C) and dense object. When it completely extinguishes, it becomes a black dwarf star.

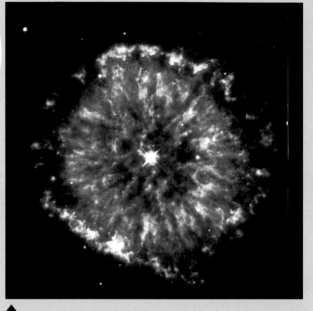

▲ Nebula NGC 6751

The future of the Sun

Like any typical star, the Sun fuses hydrogen. It will take another five billion years to exhaust its reserves; only then will it become a red giant. Its luminosity will multiply, and it will expand until it swallows Mercury and even Earth. Once it stabilizes, it will remain as a giant for two billion years, until it turns into a white dwarf star.

6 billion

years: this is how long it will take the Sun to swallow up the Earth.

4 Red giant
The Sun's radius reaches the Earth's orbit.

93 million miles (150 million km)

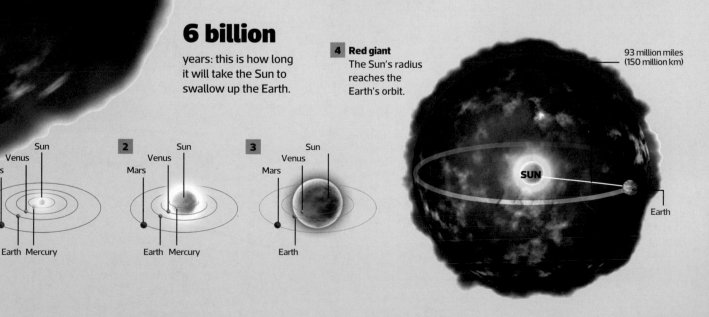

Sun
Venus
Mars
Earth Mercury

2
Sun
Venus
Mars
Earth Mercury

3
Sun
Venus
Mars
Earth

SUN

Earth

Planetary Nebulae

When low-mass stars die, all that is left of them are enormous shells of expanding gas; these are known as "planetary nebulae." When early astronomers viewed them through telescopes they could see disks that looked like planets; the name has stuck ever since. In general, they are symmetrical and spherical objects. When viewed through a telescope, a white dwarf star can be seen at the center of several nebulae—a remnant of the original star.

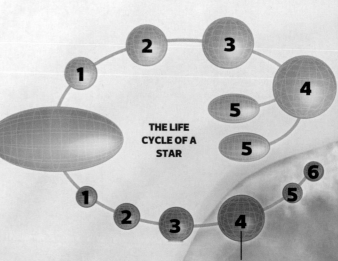

THE LIFE CYCLE OF A STAR

Planetary nebula

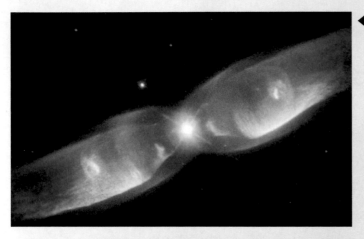

◄M2–9

The Minkowski's Butterfly contains two stars that orbit around one another within a disk of gas that measures ten times the size of the orbit of Pluto. It is 2,100 light years from Earth.

CONCENTRIC CIRCLES
Spheres of gas form an onion-layer structure around the white dwarf. The mass of each white dwarf is greater than all the masses of the Solar System's planets combined.

DISCOVERY FACT™

The surface temperature of a white dwarf star is twice that of the sun. This is why it appears white, despite its brightness being a thousand times less.

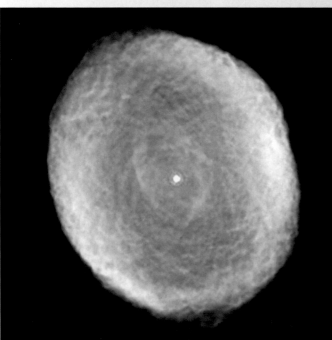

◄IC 418

The Spirograph Nebula has a hot and bright core that stimulated neighboring atoms, making them glow. Located 2,000 light years from Earth, it measures 0.3 light years in diameter.

HYDROGEN
Constantly expanding gaseous masses contain hydrogen for the most part, in addition to helium, and to a lesser extent, oxygen, nitrogen, and other elements.

3 tons

Equals the weight of one spoonful of a white dwarf star. Although the size is similar to a spoonful of cream, its mass is vastly different. While the spoonful of cream weighs very little, the weight of one spoonful of white dwarf star is 3 tons. The mass of a white dwarf star is immense, despite its diameter (9,300 miles/15,000 km) being comparable to the Earth's diameter.

NGC 7293 ▶

The Helix is a planetary nebula created at the end of the life of a star similar to our Sun. It is 700 light years from Earth.

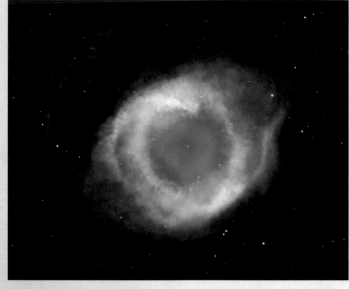

MYCN 18 ▶

Two rings of gas form the silhouette of the Hourglass Nebula. The red color corresponds to nitrogen, and the green color to hydrogen. This nebula is 8,000 light years from Earth.

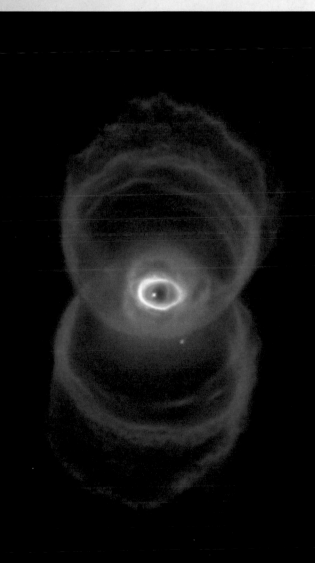

WHITE DWARF STAR
The remainder of the red giant can be found at the heart of the nebula. The star cools down and, at some stage, completely extinguishes; as a result, it becomes a black dwarf star and can no longer be seen.

GREATER DIAMETER
Less massive white dwarf

SMALLER DIAMETER
More massive white dwarf

Density of a white dwarf

The density of a white dwarf is one million times greater than the density of water. In other words, one cubic meter (35.3 cu ft) of a white dwarf star would weigh one million metric tons. The mass of a star varies, and is indirectly proportional to its diameter. A white dwarf star, with a diameter 100 times smaller than the diameter of the Sun, has a mass 70 times greater.

Supernova

The explosion of stars toward the end of their lives is extraordinary; there is a sudden increase in their brightness and an enormous release of energy. This is a "supernova," and it releases, in just ten seconds, ten times more power than the Sun releases in its entire life. After the star's detonation a gaseous remnant remains, and this expands and shines for millions of years throughout the galaxy.

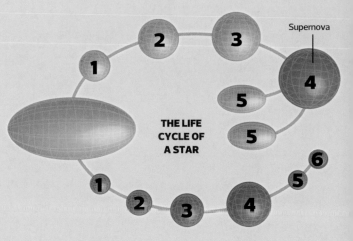

THE LIFE CYCLE OF A STAR

Supernova

A star's decline

The explosion that sees the end of a supergiant's life is attributable to its extremely heavy iron core no longer being able to support its own gravitational pull. As internal fusions are no longer possible, the star collapses in on itself, expelling the remaining gases outward; these then expand and shine for millennia. The expelled elements provide the interstellar medium with new material, which is capable of giving rise to new generations of stars.

CORE
Divided into different layers, each one corresponds to the different elements generated as a result of nuclear fusion. The final element created prior to the collapse is nuclear iron.

DISCOVERY FACT™

It is estimated that two supernovas explode each century in the Milky Way, but the last one visible with the naked eye occurred in 1604.

Fusion
The nuclear reactions happen more quickly than those of a red giant.

DENSE CORE

SUPERGIANT
Once the star swells, it is capable of measuring more than 1,000 times the diameter of the Sun. The star is capable of producing elements heavier than carbon and oxygen.

OTHER ELEMENTS
When the iron core becomes so dense that it is unable to withstand its own weight, it collapses in on itself. Elements that are heavier than iron, such as gold and uranium, then start to fuse.

EXPLOSION
The star ends its life with an immense explosion. In the weeks following the explosion, the supernova continues releasing large amounts of energy; sometimes, the amount of energy released is greater than the energy released by the galaxy to which it belongs. Its brightness can illuminate the galaxy for weeks.

The end
A neutron star, or a black hole, is created; this depends on the initial mass of the star that has died.

Stellar remnants

When the star explodes as a supernova, it leaves a series of the heavy elements (carbon, oxygen, iron) contained in its core during its time in space prior to the explosion. These remnants may form nebulae, like the Crab Nebula, at the center of which can be found a pulsar that rotates 33 times per second and that emits X-rays; as a result, it is a very powerful source of radiation.

Gaseous filaments
Expelled by the supernova, they expand outward at a rate of 620 miles/sec (1,000 km/sec).

◀ CRAB NEBULA (M1)
Created by a supernova seen for the first time in China in 1054. It is 6,500 light years from Earth and is six light years in diameter. The star that gave rise to this nebula may have had an initial mass of around ten solar masses.

The Death of a Star

The final stage in the evolution of a star's core is the formation of a very compact object, the nature of which depends on the mass that collapses. More massive stars end up as black holes; these strange objects have such intense gravity that not even light can escape.

THE LIFE CYCLE OF A STAR

1 2 3 4

Black hole

5

5

Neutron star

6

5

1 2 3 4

Black holes

Black holes have intense gravity, and nothing that gets too close—not even light—can escape. This means they are very difficult to detect, although measuring unusual effects on nearby objects gives clues that a black hole may be present.
1) Objects orbiting or spiraling into a black hole provide mass estimates. 2) Intense gravity from a black hole can bend light, known as gravitational lensing. 3) Material falling into a black hole heats up and forms an accretion disk, which glows so brightly that it can be detected from Earth.

X-rays
Gas enters the black hole and is heated up. This results in the emission of X-rays.

LIGHT RAYS

ACCRETION DISK
An accumulation of gases that a black hole absorbs from neighboring stars. The gas spins at an extremely high speed and, in areas very close to the black hole, this results in the emission of X-rays.

Darkness
Like any object, if it passes very close to the core, light is trapped.

Neutron star

When the initial star has a mass of between 10 and 20 solar masses, its final mass will be greater than that of the Sun. Despite having lost significant amounts of matter during the nuclear reaction process, the star ends up with a very dense core, resulting in the creation of a "neutron star."

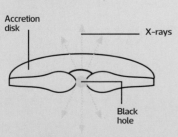

1 billion tons

is the weight of one spoonful of a neutron star. Although the size is similar to the spoonful shown (left), its mass is vastly different. While a spoonful of chocolate spread weighs very little, the weight of one spoonful of neutron star is 1 billion tons. It has a compact and dense core, with an intense gravitational pull.

1 Red giant
Its diameter is 100 times greater than the diameter of the Sun.

2 Supergiant
It grows and quickly fuses elements. It produces carbon and oxygen until it finally forms iron.

3 Explosion
The iron core collapses. Protons and electrons annihilate one another to form nuclear neutrons.

4 Dense core
Its exact composition is unknown. It contains interacting particles, most of which are neutrons.

Full escape
When light passes very far from the center, it follows its natural course.

Close to the limit
Light has still not crossed the event horizon, the limit between what is and what is not absorbed, and it maintains its brightness.

SHINING GASES
As the accretion disk feeds on the gases that spin at extremely high speed, the part closest to the core shines intensely. Toward the edges, it has a colder and darker appearance.

Pulsars

The first pulsar, a neutron star that emits radio waves, was discovered in 1967. Pulsars rotate between 30–716 times per second and have a very intense magnetic field. A pulsar emits waves from both its poles as it spins. If it absorbs gas from a neighboring star, it generates a heat spot on its surface that emits X-rays.

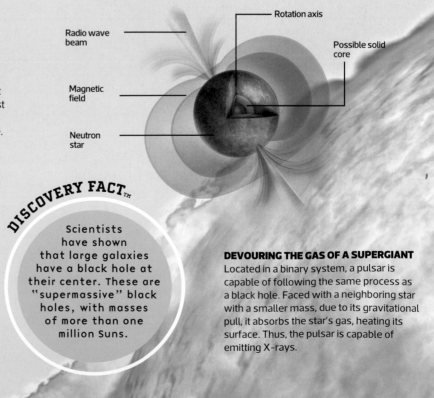

Radio wave beam

Rotation axis

Possible solid core

Magnetic field

Neutron star

CROSS SECTION

Accretion disk

X-rays

Black hole

DISCOVERY FACT™

Scientists have shown that large galaxies have a black hole at their center. These are "supermassive" black holes, with masses of more than one million Suns.

DEVOURING THE GAS OF A SUPERGIANT
Located in a binary system, a pulsar is capable of following the same process as a black hole. Faced with a neighboring star with a smaller mass, due to its gravitational pull, it absorbs the star's gas, heating its surface. Thus, the pulsar is capable of emitting X-rays.

Anatomy of the Galaxies

Galaxies are groups of stars, gas, and dust that are constantly in rotation. The oldest known galaxy was formed 380 million years after the Big Bang; today, there are billions throughout space. They take on very different shapes, with the greatest number of stars accumulating at their core. Galaxies tend to group together in space because of the effects of gravity; in doing so, they form clusters of hundreds or thousands of galaxies, with varying and different forms.

▼ Sombrero Galaxy

This galaxy is located 28 million light years from Earth and its name is attributable to the special shape of its spiral arms, which encompass a shining, white core.

Collision

Located 300 light years away from Earth, these two colliding galaxies form part of the so-called "Mice" galaxies. Their name is attributable to the large tails of stars and gas that emanate from each galaxy. Over time, they will fuse into a single, larger galaxy.

Galactic collisions

In 1924, scientist Edwin Hubble proposed the existence of faraway galaxies; just five years later, he confirmed that they were moving away from the Milky Way, demonstrating that the Universe was constantly expanding. However, galaxies tend to find one another and "galactic collisions" cause galaxies to merge and result in a clash over gaseous matter. The future of the Universe will be made up of fewer, much larger, and much more dense galaxies.

1 **1.2 billion years ago,** the Antennae Galaxies (NGC 4038 and NGC 4039) are two separate spiral galaxies.

Hubble's classification of the galaxies

ELLIPTICAL GALAXIES
Galaxies with old stars in the form of an ellipse. They contain a small amount of dust and gas. Their masses vary in size.

SPIRAL GALAXIES
A core of old stars is encompassed by a flat disk of stars with two or more spiral arms.

IRREGULAR GALAXIES
Galaxies with no defined form are classified as irregular galaxies. They are abundant in gas and dust clouds.

Subclassifications

Galaxies are subdivided into different categories, depending on whether they are more or less circular (in the case of elliptical galaxies, which range from E0 to E7) and depending on whether their arms and axis are larger or smaller (in the case of spiral galaxies, which run from Sa to Sc).

An E0 galaxy is an almost circular galaxy, while an E7 has a flatter, oval shape. An Sa galaxy has a large central axis and distinctly curved arms, whereas an Sc has a smaller axis and more spread-out arms.

E0   E3   E5   E7

Sa   Sb   Sc

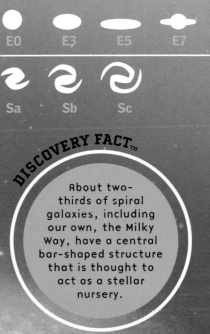

DISCOVERY FACT™

About two-thirds of spiral galaxies, including our own, the Milky Way, have a central bar-shaped structure that is thought to act as a stellar nursery.

2 **300 million years later,** the galaxies start to interact; they charge toward one another at high speed.

3 **300 million years** pass until a mutual cross is generated, as part of which the shapes of the galaxies change.

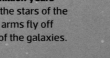

4 **300 million years later,** the stars of the spiral arms fly off each of the galaxies.

5 **In its present state,** two jets of expelled stars extend away from the original galaxies.

Active Galaxies

There is a small proportion of galaxies that are different from the others, distinguished by their high level of energetic activity. This could be attributable to the presence of black holes at their core, formed as a result of the death of supermassive stars. It is very likely that these cores of the first galaxies are "quasars," which can be seen today at a remote distance.

Gas
Two jets are expelled from the core and emit radio waves. If they cross paths with intergalactic gas clouds, they form huge clouds capable of emitting X-rays or radio waves.

Energetic activity

It is believed that active galaxies are direct descendants of the early stages of the Universe. After the Big Bang, these galaxies would have been left with a significant amount of energetic radiation. Quasars, small, dense, and luminous, comprise the cores of this type of galaxy. In certain cases, X-rays may be emitted, but in others, radio waves.

Central ring
The core is covered by a ring of dust and gas, dark on the inside and shiny on the outside. It is a potent energy source.

1 THE FORCE OF GRAVITY
Vast amounts of hot gas clouds start to join together. The clouds attract one another and collide. As part of these collisions, stars are created. A large amount of gas accumulates at the center of the galaxy. The gravitational force increases until it reaches such a level of intensity that a massive black hole grows at the core.

2 THE CORE'S QUASAR
It expels two jets of particles that reach a speed close to the speed of light. The gas and stars generated by the jets sent into space are swallowed in the form of a spiral by the black hole, creating an accretion disk and a quasar.

GAS CLOUDS
Formed as a result of the gravitational collapse of immense masses of gas during the first stages of the Universe. Later, in their interior, stars were formed.

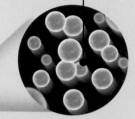

1 Dark gas and dust clouds are located on its outer edge. They are gradually swallowed by the hole.

2 The gas moves inward, gradually heating up.

4 Its core is so strong that it emits charged particles.

3 The disk's strong gravitational pull attracts and destroys stars.

Particles
Expelled from the black hole, they contain intense magnetic fields and charged particles. The jets travel at speeds close to the speed of light.

Accretion disk
Formed by interstellar gas and the remnants of stars, it is capable of emitting X-rays given the extreme levels of heat at the center.

3 **BLACK HOLE**
It swallows all gas that starts to surround it. It forms a gaseous, hot spiral that also emits jets at high speed. Its magnetic field dumps charged particles around the black hole. The outside of the disk feeds on interstellar gas.

4 **STABLE GALAXIES**
It is commonly accepted that most galaxies are formed from the progressive inactivity of nuclear quasars. As gases gather together to form stars, the quasars are left with no further gas left to swallow and so they are rendered inactive.

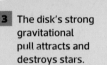

The Milky Way

For a long time our galaxy, the Milky Way, so named because of its milky, bandlike appearance, was a true mystery. It was Galileo Galilei who, in 1610, directed his telescope on it and saw that the weak cloudy-white band comprised thousands and thousands of stars, practically stuck to one another. Gradually, astronomers started to realize that all the stars, and our Sun, formed part of one large entity: a galaxy, our huge stellar home.

Structure of the galaxy

Our galaxy has two spiral arms that rotate around the core. It is on these arms that the youngest objects in our galaxy can be found, and where interstellar gas and dust are most abundant. On the Sagittarius Arm, one of the brightest stars in the Universe can be found—Eta Carinae. Our Solar System is located on the inner border of the Orion Arm, between the Sagittarius and Perseus Arms.

ROTATION

The speed at which the Milky Way rotates varies depending on the distance from the core of the galaxy. Between the core and edge, where most stars can be found, the speed is much greater, as objects feel the attraction of billions of stars.

155 MPH (250 KM/H)

0°

136 MPH (220 KM/H)

30°

142 MPH (230 KM/H)

130 MPH (210 KM/H)

60°

90°

CENTRAL BULGE

3KPC ARM

NORMA ARM

120°

SAGITTARIUS ARM

Eagle Nebula

Eta Carinae star

ORION ARM

210°

SOLAR SYSTEM

6,000 light years

Orion Nebula

PERSEUS ARM

Cassiopeia A

Crab Nebula

150°

180°

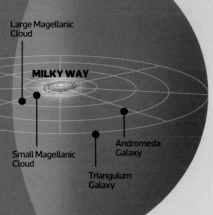

Large Magellanic
Cloud

MILKY WAY

Small Magellanic
Cloud

Triangulum
Galaxy

Andromeda
Galaxy

Hot gases
Emitted from the surface
of the central part. They
may be the result of
violent explosions on
the accretion disk.

Shining stars
They are created from
gas that is not swallowed
by the black hole. Most
are young.

Gaseous vortexes
From the center outward, the
gas is stuck and concentrated by
a gravitational force that may be
attributable to a black hole.

Black hole
One is believed to occupy the center
of the galaxy. It attracts gas through its
gravitational pull and keeps it in orbit.

Magnetism
The heart of the galaxy is
encompassed by a region
with strong magnetic fields,
perhaps resulting from a
rotating black hole.

DISCOVERY FACT™

Obscured
by gas and
dust clouds,
the shape of the
galaxy's center was
not clearly known until
the 1990s, when it
could be viewed
using infrared
radiation.

Sagittarius B2
The largest dark cloud in
the central area.

CARINA ARM

Outer ring
A ring of smoke and dark dust
and molecule clouds expands
as a result of a huge explosion.
It is suspected that this was
attributable to a small object
toward the center.

240°

OUTER ARM

Central region

The central axis of the galaxy contains old stars, dating back around
14 billion years, and exhibits an intense level of activity at its interior.
Here, two hot gas clouds can be found: Sagittarius A and B. In the
central region, although outside the core, a giant cloud contains 70
different types of molecule. These gas clouds are attributable to
violent activity at the center of the galaxy. The heart of the Milky Way
can be found in the depths of Sagittarius A and B.

100–400
billion

stars inhabit the Milky
Way. The number of suns
it contains is so high that
they cannot be separated
in this image.

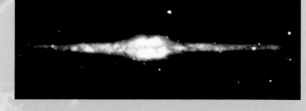

◄ The appearance of the
Milky Way

From the side, our galaxy looks like a flattened
disk with a bulge toward the center. Around
the disk there is a spherical region, called the
"halo"; here, there are globular clusters of stars
and dark matter.

3

OLYMPUS MONS ON MARS
The largest volcano in the Solar System: its height is three times the size of Mount Everest and it is as wide as the chain of Hawaiian islands.

THE SUN AND ROCKY PLANETS

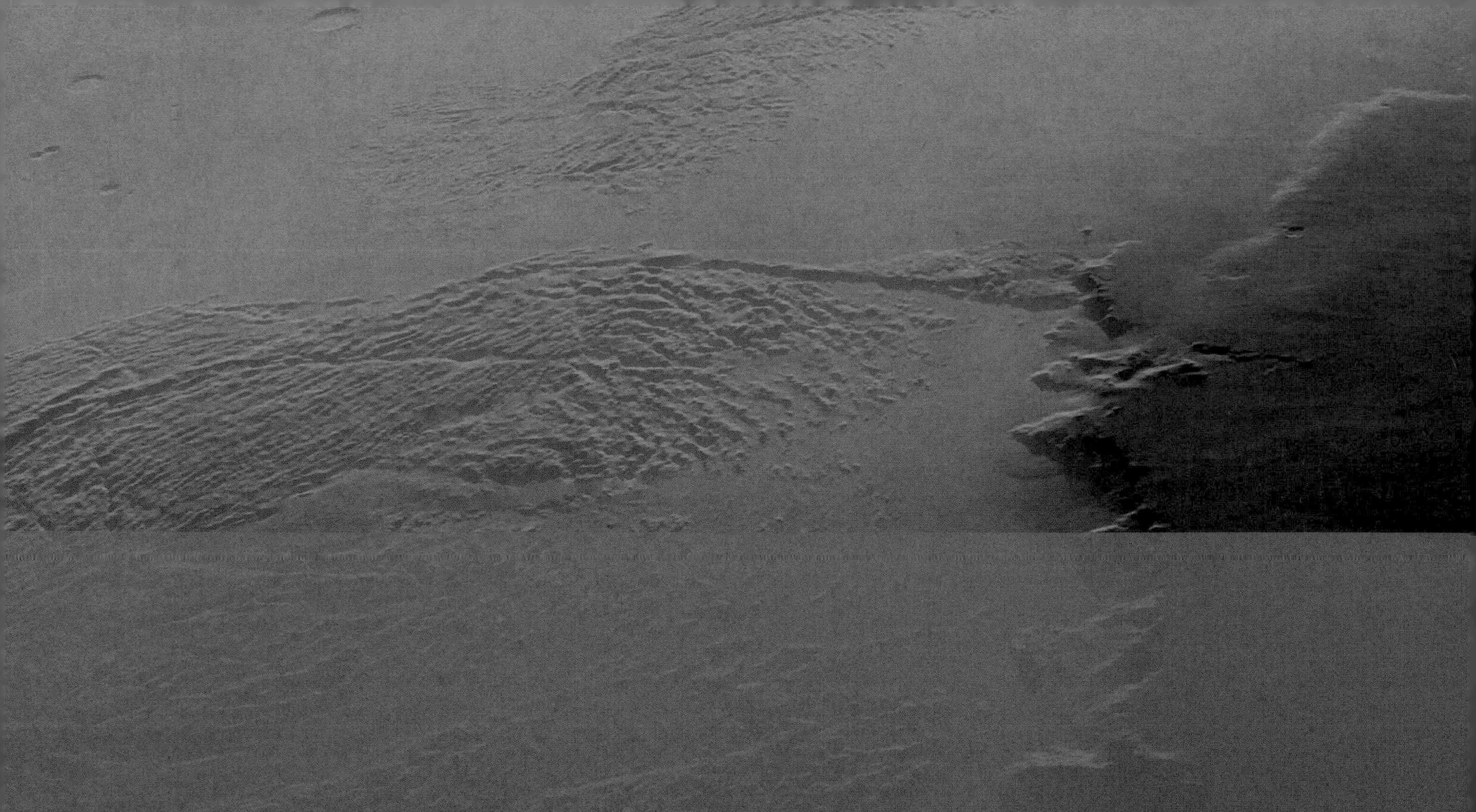

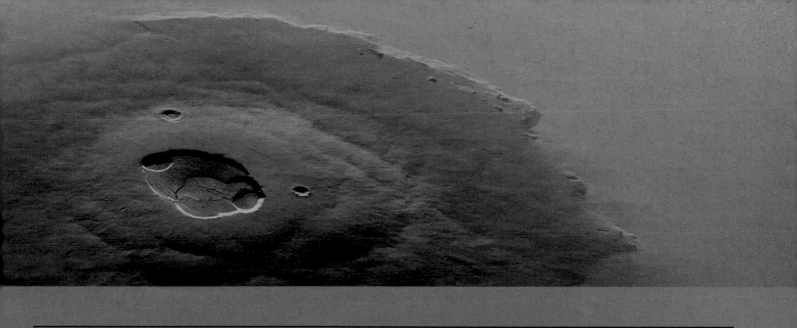

Among the billions of stars that form our galaxy, there is one important average-size star, located on an arm of the Milky Way spiral: our Sun. To ancient man, it was a god; to us, it is an energy center that generates heat and helps to maintain life. This star, together with the planets and other bodies that orbit it, comprise the Solar System, formed around 4.6 billion years ago. The planets that orbit the Sun are attracted by its gravitational pull; they do not have their own light source, but reflect the light of the Sun. The four planets closest to the Sun are all rocky planets: Mercury, Venus, Earth, and Mars. Among them, Mars is the most similar and the closest to Earth; as a result, it is also the most explored planet—after Earth itself. It is home to Olympus Mons, which is three times taller than Mount Everest.

The Solar System

The planets, satellites, asteroids, other rocky objects, and the vast number of comets that circle the Sun comprise the Solar System; its diameter is often considered to be in the region of two light years. The elliptical paths of the planets around the Sun are known as "orbits." Today, thanks to advances in astronomy, over 1,000 extrasolar planets have been confirmed, and there are doubtless many more waiting to be discovered.

Types of planet

Our Solar System is home to eight planets that orbit a single star: the Sun. The closest are rocky, smaller planets, whereas the most distant are gaseous, larger planets.

Outer planets

Planets located outside the asteroid belt. They are huge balls of gas with small, solid cores. Their temperatures are extremely low, due to the huge distance that separates them from the Sun. The greatest in size is Jupiter, into which Earth would fit 1,300 times.

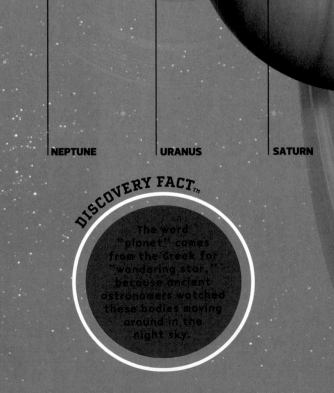

NEPTUNE **URANUS** **SATURN**

The creation of the planets

The first proposals suggested that the planets were gradually formed by hot dust particles that joined together. Today, scientists believe that they were generated by the collision and merger of two or more larger bodies, known as "planetesimals."

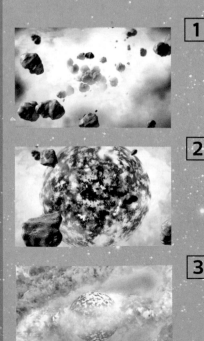

1 Origins
The remnants from when the Sun was created generate a disk of gas and dust, from which planetesimals form.

2 Collision
When they collide together, the different size planetesimals join together with other objects that have a greater mass.

3 Heat
These collisions generate a significant amount of heat inside the planets, depending on their distance from the Sun.

DISCOVERY FACT™

The word "planet" comes from the Greek for "wandering star," because ancient astronomers watched these bodies moving around in the night sky.

SOLAR GRAVITY
The Sun's gravitational pull on the planets does not just keep them within the confines of the Solar System, it also influences the speed at which they orbit. Those closest to the Sun orbit more quickly than those farther away.

Inner planets

They are solid bodies inside which inner geological phenomena take place, such as volcanism, capable of changing their surface. Almost all have a palpable atmosphere, although these differ in thickness; this plays a key role in the surface temperatures of each planet.

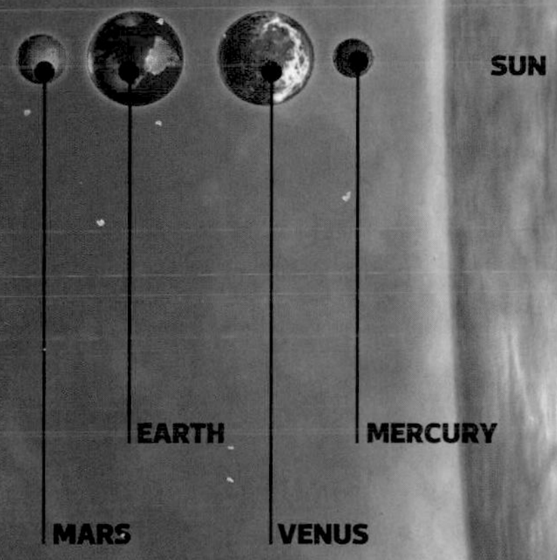

SUN

EARTH

MERCURY

MARS

VENUS

JUPITER

Asteroid belt

The boundary between the inner and outer planets is defined by an assembly of millions of rocky fragments of different sizes, which form a ring known as the "asteroid belt." Its movement is seen to be influenced by the gravitational pull exercised by Jupiter.

The Sun

The Sun is an enormous ball of plasma (superheated gas). It is mainly hydrogen (90 percent) and helium (9 percent), with traces of elements such as carbon, nitrogen, and oxygen, among others. To humankind, it is a vital source of light and heat; this energy is produced by the fusion of hydrogen atomic nuclei.

**27,000,000° F
(15,000,000° C)**

CONVENTIONAL PLANETARY SYMBOL FOR SUN

ESSENTIAL DATA

Average distance from Earth 93 million miles (150 million km)	
Diameter at the equator 865,000 miles (1.4 million km)	
Orbital speed 135 miles/sec (220 km/sec)	
Mass (Earth = 1) 332,900	
Gravity (Earth = 1) 28	
Density 0.255 g/cm³	
Average surface temperature 9,950° F (5,500° C)	
Atmosphere Dense	
Moons No	

CONNECTIVE ZONE
This extends from the base of the photosphere to a depth of around 15 percent of the solar radius. Here, energy is transported outward by (convective) currents of gas.

RADIATIVE ZONE
Particles from the nucleus cross this zone. A proton can take a million years to cross it.

**14,400,000° F
(8,000,000° C)**

NUCLEUS
It occupies just 2 percent of the Sun's total volume; however, it is responsible for around half of its total mass. Given the intense pressures and temperature, thermonuclear fusions are generated here.

Positron
Proton
Neutron
1

Neutrino

Deuterium

2

Photon

NUCLEAR FUSION

1 **Nuclear collision**
Two hydrogen nuclei (two protons) collide and join together. One transforms into a neutron and forms deuterium, releasing a neutrino, a positron, and a significant amount of energy.

2 **Photons**
The deuterium formed collides with a proton. As a result of this collision, a gamma ray photon is released. The photon is full of energy and needs 30,000 years to reach the photosphere.

3 **Helium nucleus**
A group of two protons and a neutron collide with one another. A helium nucleus is formed, and a couple of protons are released.

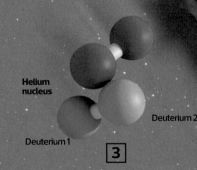

Helium nucleus

Deuterium 2

Deuterium 1

3

Proton 1

Proton 2

Surface and atmosphere

The visible portion of the Sun is a ball of light, comprising boiling gases that emanate from its core. The flares of gas form plasma that crosses this layer. Then, they penetrate a vast layer of gases called the "solar atmosphere"; here, two strata, the chromosphere and the corona, overlap. The energy generated by the Sun's core moves throughout the surface of the photosphere and the atmosphere for thousands of years.

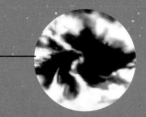

Sunspots
These comprise areas of gas that are colder (7,000° F /4,000° C) than the photosphere (9,950° F/ 5,500° C); as a result, they are darker in appearance.

CHROMOSPHERE
Above the photosphere, and with a much smaller density, this 3,000-mile (5,000-km) thick layer can be found. Its temperature ranges from 8,000° F to 900,000° F (4,500° C–500,000° C) depending on the distance from the core.

900,000° F
(500,000° C)

Spicules
These rising vertical jets of gas are attributable to the chromosphere. They often reach 6,000 miles (10,000 km) in height.

Macrospicules
These types of vertical jet are similar to spicules, but they often reach a height of 25,000 miles (40,000 km).

CORONA
Located above the chromosphere. It reaches millions of miles into space and extremely high temperatures.

1,800,000° F
(1,000,000° C)

Solar prominences
Clouds and layers of gas from the chromosphere that reach the corona. As a result of the activity of the magnetic fields to which they are subjected, they take on the form of an arc or a wave.

9,950° F
(5,500° C)

PHOTOSPHERE
This is the visible surface of the Sun, a boiling, thick tide of gases in a state of plasma. Density decreases while transparency increases in its outermost stratum. Thus, solar radiation escapes into extrasolar space in the form of light.

Solar flares or protuberances
These jets are released from the solar atmosphere and are capable of interfering with radio communication on Earth.

DISCOVERY FACT™
The Sun is an almost perfect sphere, and its mass makes up 99.86 percent of the total mass of the solar system.

Mercury

Mercury is the closest planet to the Sun, and as a result areas of the surface can reach a temperature of 800 degrees Fahrenheit. It moves at a high speed, orbiting the Sun every 88 days. It has practically no atmosphere and its surface is dry and harsh, plagued by craters caused by the impact of meteorites and numerous faults.

CORE
Dense, large, and made of iron. Its diameter is believed to measure between 2,200 and 2,400 miles (3,600 and 3,800 km).

300 miles (500 km)

2,200 miles (3,600 km)

A scar-covered surface

On Mercury's surface, it is possible to find craters of different sizes, flatlands and hills. Recently, evidence of frozen water was found in the polar regions of Mercury. The polar ice may be located at the bottom of very deep craters, preventing the ice from interacting with sunlight.

Caloris Basin
Measuring 960 miles (1,550 km) in diameter, it is one of the largest craters in the entire Solar System. The largest is Utopia Planitia on Mars, with a diameter of 2050 miles (3,300 km).

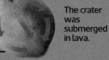

The crater was submerged in lava.

When the projectile that formed the crater made impact, Mercury was still being formed: the expansive waves created hills and mountains.

Rembrandt
The planet's second biggest basin is 445 miles (715 km) in diameter.

MEAGER ATMOSPHERE
Mercury's atmosphere is almost nonexistent: it consists of a very fine layer that is unable to protect the planet from the Sun or meteorites. As a result, temperatures during the day and at night vary enormously.

During the day, the Sun directly heats the surface.

At night, the surface quickly loses heat and the temperature drops.

883° F
(473° C)

−315° F
(−193° C)

Composition and magnetic field

Like Earth, Mercury also has a magnetic field, although it is much weaker (around 1 percent). The magnetism is attributable to its huge core, composed of solid iron. The mantle that encompasses the nucleus is made from a fine layer of liquid iron and sulfur.

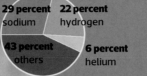

29 percent sodium

22 percent hydrogen

43 percent others

6 percent helium

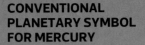

CONVENTIONAL PLANETARY SYMBOL FOR MERCURY

ESSENTIAL DATA

Average distance from the Sun 36 million miles (57.9 million km)	
Solar orbit (Mercurial year) 88 days	
Diameter at the equator 3,032 miles (4,880 km)	
Orbital speed 29.75 miles/sec (47.87 km/sec)	
Mass (Earth = 1) 0.06	
Gravity (Earth = 1) 0.38	
Density 5.43 g/cm³	
Average temperature 333° F (167° C)	
Atmosphere Almost nonexistent	
Moons None	

AXIAL TILT

0.1°
One rotation lasts 59 days

MANTLE
This mantle mostly comprises silicate-based rocks.

CRUST
Made from silicate rocks. Similar to Earth's crust and mantle. It ranges between 300 and 375 miles (500 and 600 km) thick.

Rotation and orbit

Mercury spins slowly on its axis and takes approximately 59 calendar days to complete a full turn, but needs just 88 to travel its orbit. To an observer on Mercury, the combination of these two movements would result in an interval of 176 days between two sunrises.

MERCURY'S ORBIT AROUND THE SUN

Each number corresponds to a position of the Sun in the sky, as seen from Mercury.

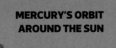

3 It reaches its zenith (midday) and stops.

4 It moves backward slightly.

VIEW OF THE SUN FROM MERCURY

6 It resumes its path until it reaches the horizon.

5 It stops again.

2 It climbs and its size increases.

7 It falls toward the sunset.

1 The sun rises.

HORIZON OF MERCURY

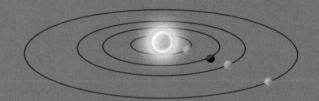

Venus

Venus is the second closest planet to the Sun. Similar in size to Earth, it has a volcanic surface and a hostile atmosphere, and is ruled by the effects of carbon dioxide. Four billion years ago, the atmospheres on Earth and Venus were similar; today, the air pressure on the surface of Venus is 92 times that of the Earth. Its sulfuric acid and dust clouds are so thick and dense that it would be impossible to see the stars from the planet's surface.

The effects of its thick atmosphere

The predominant carbon dioxide content in Venus's atmosphere generates a greenhouse effect that elevates the planet's surface temperature to around 864° F (462° C). Consequently, Venus is hotter than Mercury, despite being farther from the Sun, and with the fact that only 20 percent of sunlight reaches its surface (due to its dense atmosphere). Pressure on Venus is 92 times greater than the pressure on Earth.

CONVENTIONAL PLANETARY SYMBOL FOR VENUS ♀

ESSENTIAL DATA

Average distance from the Sun 67 million miles (108 million km)	
Solar orbit (Venusian year) 224 days 17 hours	
Diameter at the equator 7,520 miles (12,100 km)	
Orbital speed 21.76 miles/sec (35.02 km/sec)	
Mass (Earth = 1) 0.8	
Gravity (Earth = 1) 0.9	
Density 5.25 g/cm3	
Average temperature 860° F (460° C)	
Atmosphere Very dense	
Moons No	

AXIAL TILT

117°
One rotation takes 243 days

50 miles
(80 km)

is the thickness of Venus's atmosphere.

MANTLE
Comprising molten rock, it is responsible for trapping solar radiation.

CORE
Believed to be similar to Earth's core, with metallic (iron and nickel) and silicate elements. It has no magnetic field, perhaps due to its slow rotating speed.

97 percent carbon dioxide

3 percent nitrogen and remnants of other gases

ATMOSPHERE
Its glowing appearance is attributable to its thick, suffocating atmosphere, made up of carbon dioxide and sulfur clouds that reflect the Sun's light.

Phases of Venus

While Venus orbits the Sun, its visibility from Earth is more or less apparent depending on its position compared with the Sun and our planet. That is to say, it has "phases" like those of the Moon. It is brightest during elongations (the angle between the Sun and the planet, as viewed from Earth) when it is farthest from the Sun in the sky. As a result, it can be seen after the Sun sets or before it rises.

Waxing crescent   First quarter   Waxing gibbous   Waning gibbous   Last quarter   Waning crescent

EARTH   VENUS   SUN

The "New" and "Full" phases are not visible from Earth.

3,700 miles (6,000 km)

3,700 miles (6,000 km)

Surface

Venus's surface has not remained the same since its creation. Its current surface is 500 million years old and this rocky surface is attributable to intense volcanic activity. The entire planet is characterized by wide plains, enormous rivers of lava, and a number of mountains. The shine on the surface is attributable to its metallic compounds.

14,500° F
(8,000° C)

is the core temperature.

Ishtar Terra
This elevated plateau is similar in size to Australia. It has four main mountain ranges, named as the Maxwell Montes, Freyja Montes, Akna Montes, and Danu Montes.

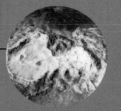

Aphrodite Terra
Larger in size than Ishtar Terra, it measures more or less the same as Africa. It comprises mountainous areas to the east and west, separated by lowlands.

CRUST
Comprising silicates, it is thicker than Earth's crust.

Mars

Known as the "Red Planet," as its surface is covered in iron oxide, Mars's atmosphere is thin and not particularly dense; it is essentially composed of carbon dioxide. Its orbital period, tilt axis, and internal structure are all similar to those of Earth. Its poles house ice pockets, and although no water can be seen on its surface, it is believed that the planet's water content was high during past times, and that there may be water in the subsurface.

Martian orbit

Mars's orbit is more elliptical than Earth's; as a result, its distance from the Sun varies more. At its closest point, Mars receives 45 percent more solar radiation than at its farthest point. Surface temperatures vary between –220° F and 63° F (–140° C and 17° C).

–220° F (–140° C)
in winter

63° F (17° C)
in summer

MANTLE
Molten rock, the density of which is greater than Earth's surface.

Moons

Mars has two moons, Phobos and Deimos, both of which are more dense than Mars and are pockmarked with craters. They are made up of carbon-rich rock. Deimos orbits Mars in 30.3 hours, whereas Phobos, which is closer to the red planet, does so in just 7.66 hours. Astronomers believe that the moons were asteroids attracted by Mars's gravity.

DEIMOS
Diameter 9.3 miles (15 km)
Distance from Mars 14,627 miles (23,540 km)

PHOBOS
Diameter
16.8 miles (27 km)
**Distance
from Mars**
5,840 miles (9,400 km)

DISCOVERY FACT™
The diameter of Mars is 4,222 miles (6,794 km), making it almost half the size of Earth and the second smallest planet in the Solar System.

ATMOSPHERE
Its thin atmosphere comprises carbon dioxide and features clouds, climates, and prevailing winds.

95.3 percent
carbon dioxide

2.6 percent
nitrogen

2.1 percent
oxygen, carbon monoxide, water vapor, and other gases

POLAR ICE CAPS
At the North Pole, the layer of frozen water is 600 miles (1,000 km) in diameter and 2 miles (3 km) thick. It is covered by a layer of dry ice (CO_2).

Surface

Mars's surface was created as a result of volcanic activity, meteorite impacts, floods, and winds, and is home to neither vegetation nor water. It features enormous volcanoes and flatlands flooded by volcanic lava. In the southern hemisphere, mountains prevail; in the north, flatlands are predominant.

CORE
Relatively small and most probably made of iron.

1,950 miles (1,700 km)

2,047 miles (3,294 km)

Olympus Mons
The giant inactive volcano is the largest on Mars and in the entire Solar System.

Olympus Mons

Everest	Olympus
29,029 ft (8,848 m)	72,178 ft (22,000 m)

Tharsis Montes

Valles Marineris

Solis Lacus

South Pole

CONVENTIONAL PLANETARY SYMBOL FOR MARS ♂

ESSENTIAL DATA

Average distance from the Sun 142 million miles (227.9 million km)	
Solar orbit (Martian year) 1.88 years	
Diameter at the equator 4,222 miles (6,794 km)	
Orbital speed 14.99 miles/sec (24.13 km/sec)	
Mass (Earth = 1) 0.107	
Gravity (Earth = 1) 0.38	
Density 3.93 g/cm³	
Average temperature –81° F (–63° C)	
Atmosphere Very thin	
Moons 2	

AXIAL TILT

25.2°
One rotation takes 24 hours and 40 minutes

CRUST
Thin and comprising solid rocks, it is 30 miles (50 km) thick.

Valles Marineris
The origins of the Valles Marineris valley system may be attributable to the effects of water erosion and tectonic activity.

4

JUPITER
A digitally generated image of the
Solar System's largest planet, as
seen from the surface of Io, one of
its moons.

THE GAS
GIANTS

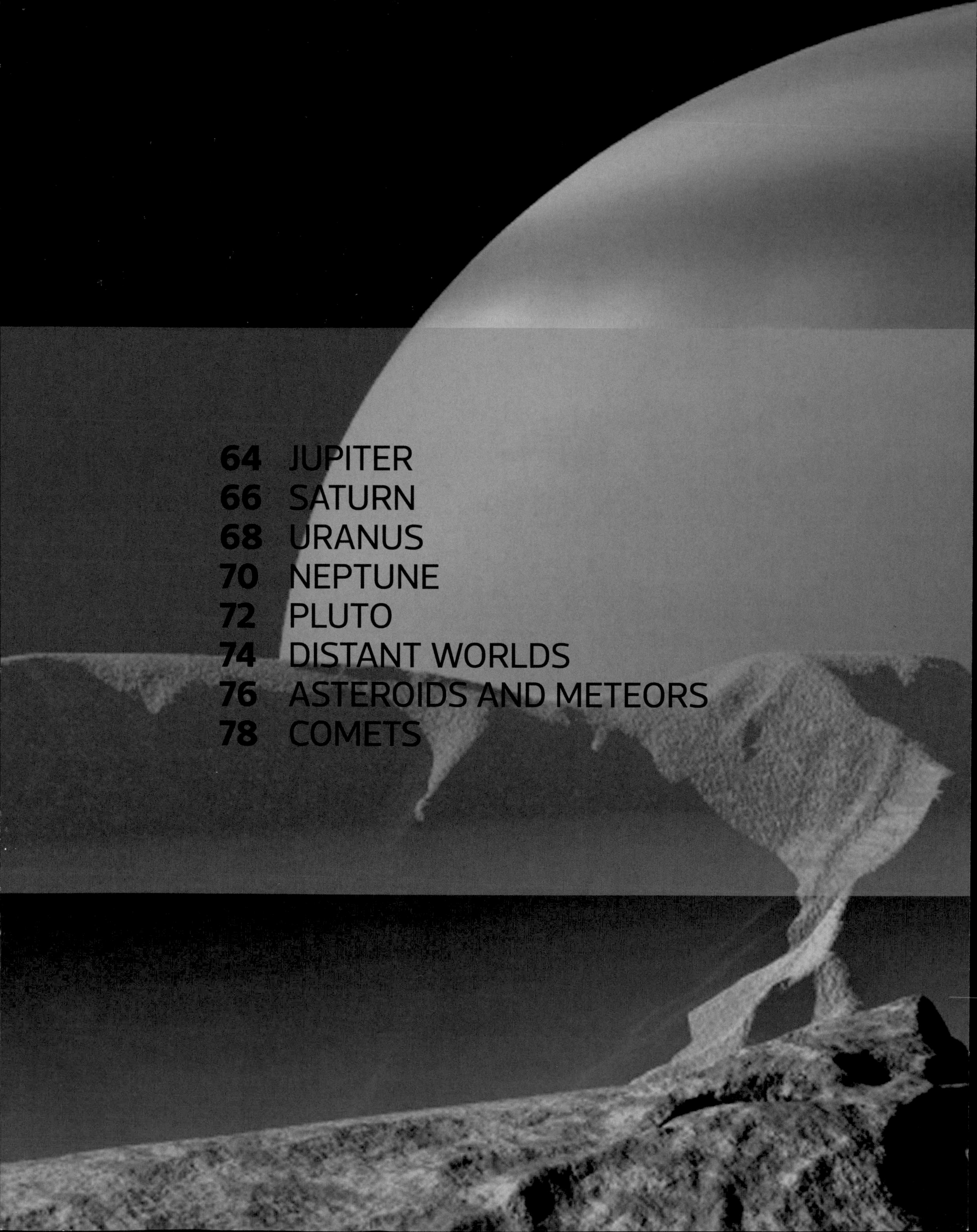

Separated from the rocky planets by the asteroid belt, the Solar System's large, gas planets reign supreme. The presence of planetary rings is a unique feature of these planets, and each one is orbited by varying numbers of moons. Beyond Neptune, the planet farthest from the Sun, a vast number of bodies eccentrically orbit the Sun. Among these is Pluto, which prior to 2006 was considered the Solar System's ninth planet. However, astronomers now consider this body a dwarf planet, given its small size and eccentric orbit. Recently, many other dwarf planets have been discovered beyond Saturn and within the confines of the Solar System, in addition to a vast number of icy planetesimals that have the potential to become comets.

Jupiter

The largest planet in the Solar System. Its diameter is eleven times greater than Earth's, its mass is 300 times greater and it spins at a speed of 24,850 miles (40,000 km) per hour. One of the most distinctive features of its atmosphere is the so-called "Great Red Spot," an enormous area of high-pressure turbulence. The planet has several satellites and a fine ring of particles that orbit around it.

Composition

Jupiter is a huge mass of hydrogen and helium, compressed in liquid form. Little is known about its core, and it has not been possible to measure its size; however, it is believed to be a metallic solid with a high density.

CONVENTIONAL PLANETARY SYMBOL FOR JUPITER ♃

ESSENTIAL DATA

Average distance from the Sun 483 million miles (778 million km)	
Solar orbit (Jovian year) 11 years 312 days	
Diameter at the equator 88,730 miles (142,800 km)	
Orbital speed 8.12 miles/sec (13.07 km/sec)	
Mass (Earth = 1) 318	
Gravity (Earth = 1) 2.36	
Density 1.33 g/cm³	
Average temperature –184° F (–120° C)	
Atmosphere Very dense	
Moons 67	

AXIAL TILT

3.1°
One rotation takes 9 hours and 55 minutes

CRUST
It is 620 miles (1,000 km) thick.

23,400 miles (37,700 km)

16,800 miles (27,000 km)

CORE

INNER MANTLE
Comprising metallic hydrogen, an element that can only be found at very high temperatures and pressures.

OUTER MANTLE
Comprising liquid hydrogen and helium. The outer mantle merges with the planet's atmosphere.

So far, 67 moons have been discovered, plus an additional dozen "temporary" moons whose nature and orbits have yet to be confirmed.

ATMOSPHERE
It encompasses the inner liquid and solid core layers.

89.8 percent hydrogen

10.2 percent helium with traces of methane and ammonia

Galilean moons

Of Jupiter's many moons, four can be seen from Earth with the use of binoculars. They are known as the Galilean moons, in honor of their discoverer, Galileo Galilei. Io is the most volcanically active world in our Solar System, and Europa may be home to an ocean beneath its ice crust.

EUROPA
1,990 miles
(3,200 km)

GANYMEDE
3,273 miles
(5,268 km)

IO
2,264 miles
(3,643 km)

CALLISTO
2,986 miles
(4,806 km)

Winds

The planet's surface winds blow in opposite directions and in contiguous bands. The slight variations in their individual temperature and chemical composition are responsible for the planet's colored bands. The inclement environment—winds can exceed 370 mph (600 km/h)—are capable of causing storms, such as the Great Red Spot. It is believed to comprise mainly ammonia gas and ice clouds.

RINGS
Formed by dust released by the planet's four inner moons.

16,150 miles
(26,000 km)

is the length of the "Great Red Spot."

404,000,000 miles
(650,000,000 km)

Jupiter produces the largest planetary magnetosphere in the Solar System. It varies in size and shape depending on its interaction with solar winds (matter released by the Sun every second).

The magnetism of Jupiter

Jupiter's magnetic field is 20,000 times more intense than Earth's. The planet is surrounded by an enormous magnetic bubble—the magnetosphere. Its magnetotail extends beyond Saturn's orbit.

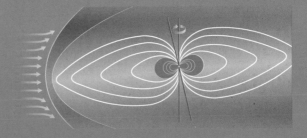

Saturn

Just like Jupiter, Saturn is a huge ball of gas that encompasses a small solid core. To an onlooker, it would seem like just another yellow-tinted star; however, with the help of a telescope, its rings can be clearly distinguished. Ten times farther from the Sun than Earth, it is the least dense of all the planets, and would even be able to float in the sea.

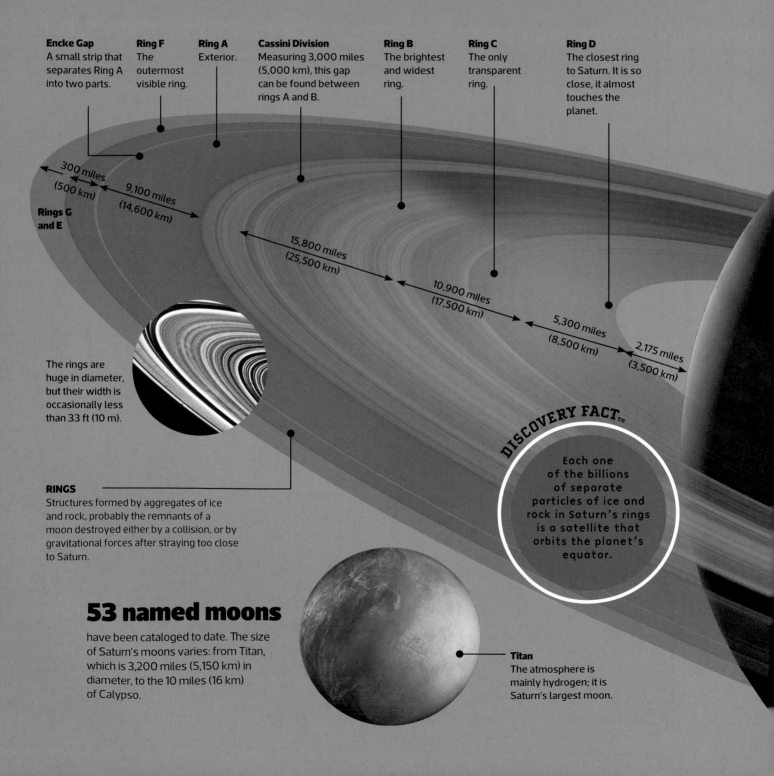

Encke Gap
A small strip that separates Ring A into two parts.

Ring F
The outermost visible ring.

Ring A
Exterior.

Cassini Division
Measuring 3,000 miles (5,000 km), this gap can be found between rings A and B.

Ring B
The brightest and widest ring.

Ring C
The only transparent ring.

Ring D
The closest ring to Saturn. It is so close, it almost touches the planet.

300 miles (500 km)

9,100 miles (14,600 km)

Rings G and E

15,800 miles (25,500 km)

10,900 miles (17,500 km)

5,300 miles (8,500 km)

2,175 miles (3,500 km)

The rings are huge in diameter, but their width is occasionally less than 33 ft (10 m).

RINGS
Structures formed by aggregates of ice and rock, probably the remnants of a moon destroyed either by a collision, or by gravitational forces after straying too close to Saturn.

DISCOVERY FACT™

Each one of the billions of separate particles of ice and rock in Saturn's rings is a satellite that orbits the planet's equator.

53 named moons

have been cataloged to date. The size of Saturn's moons varies: from Titan, which is 3,200 miles (5,150 km) in diameter, to the 10 miles (16 km) of Calypso.

Titan
The atmosphere is mainly hydrogen; it is Saturn's largest moon.

Surface

Saturn has a surface of clouds, which form bands attributable to the rotation of the planet on its axis. Saturn's clouds are calmer and less colorful than those of Jupiter. Temperatures in the highest (white) clouds reach -220° F (-140° C) and a layer of fog extends over them.

Fog

White clouds

Deep, orange clouds

Blue clouds

ATMOSPHERE
Mainly composed of hydrogen and helium. The remainder is made up of sulfurs (responsible for its yellowy tones), methane, and other gases.

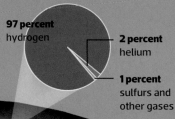

97 percent hydrogen

2 percent helium

1 percent sulfurs and other gases

CONVENTIONAL PLANETARY SYMBOL FOR SATURN ♄

ESSENTIAL DATA

Average distance from the Sun 887 million miles (1,427 million km)	
Solar orbit (Saturnian year) 29 years 154 days	
Diameter at the equator 74,940 miles (120,600 km)	
Orbital speed 6 miles/sec (9.66 km/sec)	
Mass (Earth = 1) 95	
Gravity (Earth = 1) 0.92	
Density 0.69 g/cm³	
Average temperature -193° F (-125° C)	
Atmosphere Very dense	
Named Moons 53	

AXIAL TILT

26.7°
One rotation takes 10 hours and 39 minutes

Winds
Wind speeds of up to 225 mph (360 km/h) can be reached at the equator. The planet can experience torrid storms.

18,650 miles (30,000 km)

MANTLE
The planet is externally covered by a mantle of liquid hydrogen and helium that extends into its gaseous atmosphere.

8,700 miles (14,000 km)

HYDROGEN LAYER
Liquid hydrogen encompasses the outer core.

19,900 miles (32,000km)

CORE
Comprising rock and metallic elements such as silicates and iron. On the inside, it is similar to Jupiter.

21,600° F (12,000° C)

OUTER CORE
Water, methane, and ammonia encompass the hot rocky core.

is the core temperature.

Uranus

At first glance, Uranus seems like just another star at the farthest limits of the naked eye's reach. It is almost four times larger than Earth and is unique in that its rotation axis is tilted to almost 98 degrees relative to its orbital plain, meaning one of its poles is always facing the Sun. Uranus's orbit is so large that the planet takes 84 years to orbit the Sun just once.

Magnetic field

Uranus's magnetic field is 50 times greater than Earth's and is tilted 60 degrees compared to its rotation axis. On Uranus, magnetism is generated by the mantle and not the core.

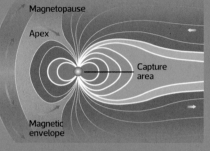

Magnetopause

Apex

Capture area

Magnetic envelope

Some scientists have suggested that Uranus's strange magnetic field may be attributable to the fact that there is no convection at its core because of cooling, or that it is magnetically inverted.

18,000° F (10,000° C)

Core temperature

CONVENTIONAL PLANETARY SYMBOL FOR URANUS

ESSENTIAL DATA

Average distance from the Sun 1.78 billion miles (2.87 billion km)	
Solar orbit (Uranian year) 84 years 36 days	
Diameter at the equator 32,190 miles (51,800 km)	
Orbital speed 4.24 miles/sec (6.82 km/sec)	
Mass (Earth = 1) 14.5	
Gravity (Earth = 1) 0.89	
Density 1.32 g/cm³	
Average temperature –346° F (–210° C)	
Atmosphere Not dense	
Moons 27	

AXIAL TILT

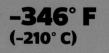

97.9°
One rotation takes 17 hours and 14 minutes

CORE
Comprising siliceous rocks and ice.

MANTLE 1
Comprising water, ice, methane gas, ammonia, and ions.

MANTLE 2
Around the mantle, there may be another layer of liquid molecular hydrogen and liquid helium with a small amount of methane.

ATMOSPHERE
Comprising hydrogen, methane, helium, and small amounts of acetylene and other hydrocarbons.

–346° F (–210° C)

Average temperature.

6,000 miles (10,000 km)

10,500 miles (17,000 km)

6,000 miles (10,000 km)

85 percent hydrogen

12 percent helium

3 percent methane

Nu and Mu
The planet's two outermost rings; their discovery was made public in 2005.

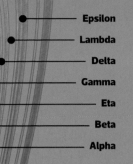

- Epsilon
- Lambda
- Delta
- Gamma
- Eta
- Beta
- Alpha

4
5
6
1986U2R

Rings

Just like all the Solar System's giant planets, Uranus has a planetary ring system similar to that which orbits Saturn, but much darker. As a result, its not possible to see the rings with any level of ease. The thirteen rings that orbit the planet's equator were discovered in 1977. In 1986, they were explored by *Voyager 2*.

Satellites

Twenty-seven orbit the planet. The first were discovered in 1787 and a further ten by the *Voyager 2* space probe in 1986. They were baptized in honor of the characters in the works of William Shakespeare and Alexander Pope, a feature that makes them unique. Only a handful can be considered large, with most measuring just a few miles across.

MOONS

Uranus has small moons that are as black as oil, discovered by *Voyager 2*, in addition to larger moons: Miranda, Ariel, Umbriel, Oberon, and Titania. The latter two measure over 900 miles (1,500 km) in diameter.

TITANIA
981 miles
(1,578 km)

UMBRIEL
727 miles
(1,170 km)

ARIEL
720 miles
(1,158 km)

MIRANDA
293 miles
(472 km)

OBERON
946 miles
(1,522 km)

Surface

For a long time, it was believed that Uranus's surface was smooth. However, the Hubble telescope showed that it is a dynamic planet with the brightest clouds in the Solar System, and with a weak planetary ring system that oscillates like an unbalanced wheel.

RAY REFRACTION

1 On Uranus, sunlight is reflected by a curtain of clouds that sits beneath a layer of methane gas.

2 When the light reflection penetrates this layer, the methane gas absorbs the beams of red light and enables blue light to pass, which is responsible for the planet's blue-green tone.

Atmosphere

Rays of sunlight

Uranus

Atmosphere

Rays of sunlight

Uranus

Neptune

The Solar System's outermost gas planet is 30 times farther from the Sun than Earth, and looks like an extraordinary blue ball. This effect is attributed to the presence of methane in the outermost part of its atmosphere. Its moons, rings, and incredible clouds all stand out, and its similarity to Uranus is also discernible. To scientists, Neptune is particularly special: its existence was proposed based on mathematical calculations and predictions.

Moons

Neptune has 14 natural satellites. Triton and Nereid, those farthest from the planet, were the first to be seen from Earth using a telescope. The remaining 11 were observed from space by U.S. spacecraft *Voyager 2*. All their names correspond to gods of the sea from Greek mythology.

89.8 percent hydrogen

10.2 percent helium

TRITON
Neptune's largest moon measures 1,681 miles (2,706 km) in diameter. At –391°F (–235°C) it is one of the Solar System's coldest bodies, and its surface is marked with dark grooves, formed by the dust precipitated following the eruptions of its geysers and volcanoes.

COMPOSITION
Neptune's rings are dark, although their composition is not known; it is also believed that they are not stable. For example, Liberty is the outermost part of the ring and it may completely vanish by the end of this century.

Rings

From Earth, they look like arcs. However, we now know that they are rings of dust that shine, reflecting rays of sunlight. Their names honor the first scientists to study the planet.

GALLE

URBAIN LE VERRIER

LASSELL

ARAGO

ADAMS
Located 39,000 miles (63,000 km) from the planet's core. It is a formation of three intertwining rings named Liberty, Fraternity, and Equality.

Equality

Fraternity

Liberty

DISCOVERY FACT™

Triton is the only large moon in the Solar System that orbits in the opposite direction to the rotation of its planet.

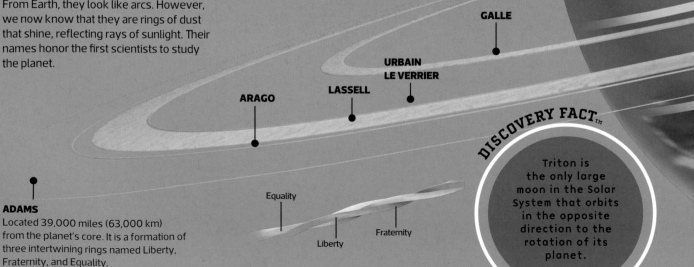

Surface

White methane clouds encompass the planet. The winds circulate from east to west, in the opposite direction to the planet's rotation, reaching speeds of 1,250 mph (2,000 km/h).

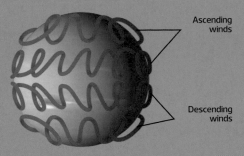

Ascending winds

Descending winds

GREAT DARK SPOT
A giant storm, the size of Earth, similar to the Great Red Spot on Jupiter, stood out against Neptune's surface. It was first seen in 1989 and broke up in 1994.

4,500 miles (7,200 km)

8,700 miles (14,000 km)

Structure

It has a rocky silicate core, covered by a layer of frozen water, ammonia, hydrogen, and methane, known as the "mantle." The core and mantle occupy two-thirds of Neptune's interior. The final third is the thick, dense atmosphere, which consists of a mix of hot gases, comprising hydrogen, helium, water, and methane.

CORE
The typical core of gas planets is repeated on Neptune—a rocky sphere that turns molten toward the surface.

3,750 miles (6,000 km)

CONVENTIONAL PLANETARY SYMBOL FOR NEPTUNE ♆

ESSENTIAL DATA

Average distance from the Sun 2.8 billion miles (4.5 billion km)	
Solar orbit (Neptunian year) 164 years 264 days	
Diameter at the equator 30,750 miles (49,500 km)	
Orbital speed 3.41 miles/sec (5.48 km/sec)	
Mass (Earth = 1) 17.2	
Gravity (Earth = 1) 1.12	
Density 1.64 g/cm³	
Average temperature –382° F (–200° C)	
Atmosphere Dense	
Moons 14	

MANTLE 1
The component materials of this layer convert from a solid to a gaseous state.

MANTLE 2
Containing a higher level of gaseous material than solid material.

ATMOSPHERE
The gases that make up the atmosphere are concentrated in similar bands as those found on other gas giants. They form a cloud system that is as active, or even more active, than the system on Jupiter.

AXIAL TILT

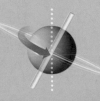

28.3°
One rotation takes 16 hours and 36 minutes

Pluto

Until 2006, Pluto was considered the ninth planet in the Solar System. That year however, the International Astronomical Union (IAU) decided to designate it a "dwarf planet." Little is known about this tiny body in the Solar System. However, some of its characteristics make it particularly special: its unique orbit, its axial tilt, and the fact that it is an object belonging to the Kuiper Belt.

Charon

Charon is Pluto's largest satellite. Incredibly, the diameter of Pluto's biggest moon is almost half that of the planet itself. Its surface appears to be covered in ice, unlike Pluto, the surface of which comprises frozen nitrogen, methane, and carbon dioxide. One theory is that Charon was formed from ice that was torn from Pluto following a collision with another object.

Rotating axis

Pluto

Charon

SYNCHRONIZED ORBITS

It is often considered that Pluto and Charon form a double planetary system. The rotation between the two bodies is unique: their sightline is never broken, and it appears as if they are united by an invisible bar. They are synchronized to such an extent that Charon can only, and permanently, be seen from one side of Pluto, while from the other side the moon is never seen.

CONVENTIONAL PLANETARY SYMBOL FOR PLUTO

P

ESSENTIAL DATA

Average distance from the Sun 3.7 billion miles (5.9 billion km)	
Solar orbit (Plutonian year) 247.9 years	
Diameter at the equator 1,396 miles (2,247 km)	
Orbital speed 2.95 miles/sec (4.75 km/sec)	
Mass (Earth = 1) 0.002	
Gravity (Earth = 1) 0.062	
Density 2.05 g/cm³	
Average temperature –382° F (–230° C)	
Atmosphere Very thin	
Moons 5	

AXIAL TILT

122°
One rotation takes 153 hours

728 miles
(1,172 km)

is the diameter of Charon, half that of Pluto.

Other moons

Besides Charon, discovered in 1978, Pluto has four other moons: Nix and Hydra, discovered in 2005 by the Hubble telescope, and two further moons (P4 and P5) that remain unnamed, discovered in 2011 and 2012.

DENSITY
The density of Charon is 0.98 oz/cu in (1.7 g/cm³); it is therefore assumed that rocks do not represent a large part of its composition.

Surface

Little is known about Pluto. However, the Hubble telescope has shown that its surface is covered by a combination of frozen nitrogen and methane. The presence of methane in its solid state would suggest that the surface temperature is less than -333° F (-203°C). However, this depends on the point at which this "dwarf planet" is in orbit, given its distance from the Sun can range between 30 and 50 astronomical units.

98 percent
nitrogen

2 percent
methane, with some traces of carbon monoxide

ATMOSPHERE
Pluto has a very fine atmosphere that is frozen and falls to the planet's surface as its orbit gets farther away from the Sun.

COMPOSITION
Based on different calculations, it has been deduced that 75 percent of Pluto consists of rocks mixed with ice. Large blocks of frozen nitrogen aside, it also features simple molecules containing hydrogen and oxygen—the indispensable sources of life.

CORE
Comprising a blend of iron, nickel, and rock, its exact diameter remains unknown.

MANTLE
The mantle, comprising a layer of frozen water, encompasses the planet's core.

CRUST
Made up of frozen methane and water at the surface; it has been calculated that it may be between 60 and 120 miles (100 and 200 km) thick.

A unique orbit

Pluto's orbit is considerably elliptical and inclined (17° with regard to other planets). It is located between 2.5 and 4.3 billion miles (4 and 7 billion km) from the Sun. For 20 years of the planet's 248-year long orbit, Pluto is closer to the Sun than Neptune. Although it would appear that Pluto's orbit crosses paths with Neptune, it would be impossible for the planets to collide.

Distant Worlds

Way beyond Neptune, there is a group of frozen bodies that are smaller in size than the Moon. There are more than 100,000 objects that form the Kuiper Belt. The belt is the main repository for "short periodic comets," those that appear with regular frequency. Other comets in turn originate in the huge sphere known as the Oort cloud, which encompasses the entire Solar System.

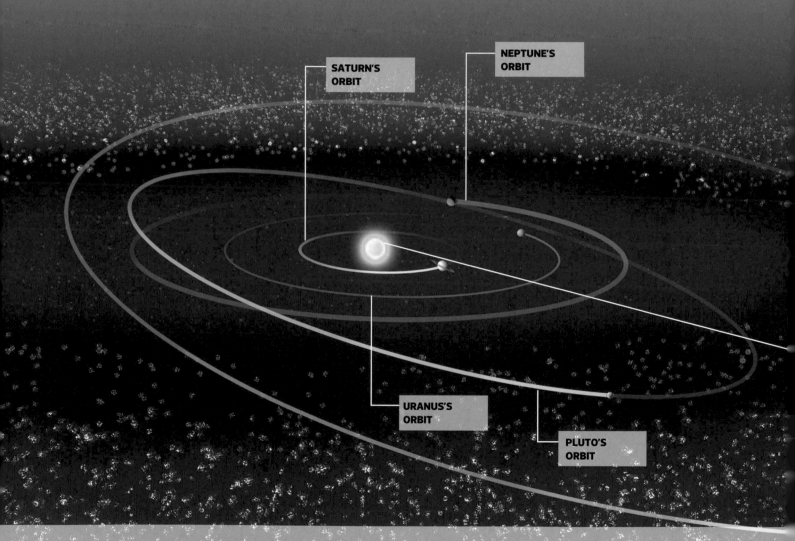

SATURN'S ORBIT

NEPTUNE'S ORBIT

URANUS'S ORBIT

PLUTO'S ORBIT

Comparative sizes

The discovery of Quaoar in 2002 offered scientists a much sought after link between the origin of the Solar System and the Kuiper Belt. Quaoar's orbit, which is almost circular, demonstrated that objects in the Kuiper Belt orbit around the Sun. Since 2006 and to date these objects have been considered by the International Astronomical Union as part of the "dwarf planet" category to which Pluto belongs.

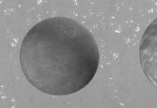

Quaoar
Diameter: around
800 miles (1,300 km).

Sedna
Diameter: around
1,000 miles (1,600 km).

Pluto
Diameter: 1,396
miles (2,247 km).

35,000

objects in the Kuiper Belt are estimated to measure over 60 miles (100 km) in diameter.

Kuiper Belt

Close to Neptune, in the Kuiper Belt, there are small frozen worlds that are similar to the Solar System's eighth planet, but which are much smaller in size. The belt comprises 100,000 chunks of ice and rock (including Pluto) spread out in the form of a ring, almost a thousand of which have been cataloged.

DISCOVERY FACT™

The Kuiper Belt gets its name from astronomer Gerard Kuiper, who predicted its existence in 1951, 40 years before it was seen for the first time.

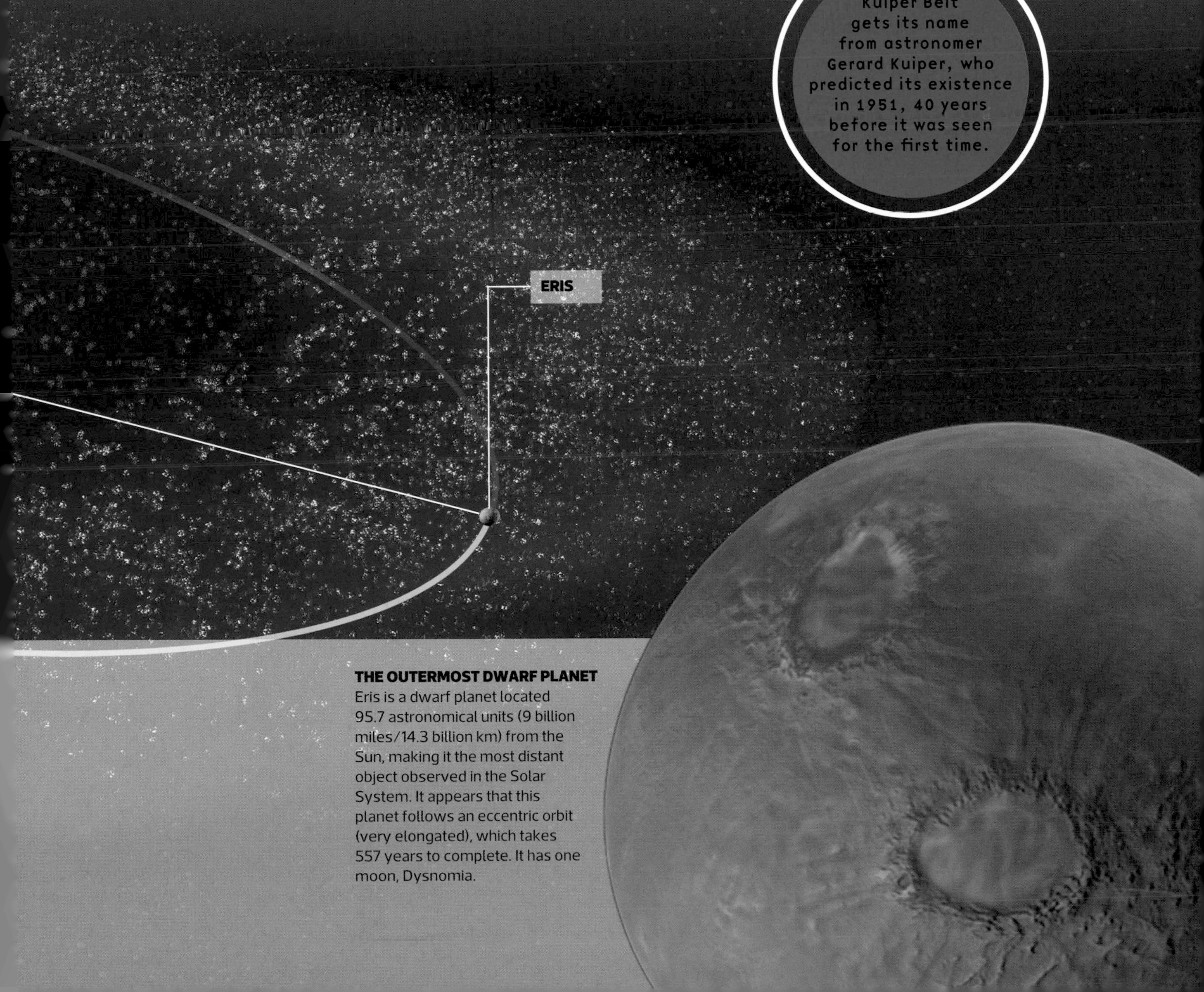

ERIS

THE OUTERMOST DWARF PLANET
Eris is a dwarf planet located 95.7 astronomical units (9 billion miles/14.3 billion km) from the Sun, making it the most distant object observed in the Solar System. It appears that this planet follows an eccentric orbit (very elongated), which takes 557 years to complete. It has one moon, Dysnomia.

Asteroids and Meteors

Since the time the Solar System began to form, the fusion, collision, and breakup of different materials has played an essential role in the formation of the planets. These "small" rocks are a remnant of this process. They are witnesses that provide data to help the understanding of the extraordinary phenomena that began 4.6 billion years ago. On Earth, these objects are associated with episodes that would later influence evolutionary processes.

The nature of meteorites

One of the main goals in the study of meteorites is to determine their makeup. They contain both extraterrestrial gases and solids. Scientific tests have made it possible to confirm that, in some cases, the objects came from the Moon or Mars. However, for the most part, meteorites are associated with asteroids.

HOW A METEORITE MAKES IMPACT
When penetrating Earth's atmosphere, they do not completely vaporize—on reaching the Earth's surface they leave a footprint called a "crater." Furthermore, they contribute exotic rock material to Earth's surface, such as large amounts of iridium, an element that is scarce on Earth but common in the composition of meteorites.

6–43 miles/sec
(10–70 km/sec)

is the impact speed of a meteorite on Earth.

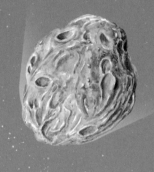

1 **EXPLOSION**
Friction with the air increases the temperature of the meteorite. Thus, it starts to ignite.

2 **DIVISION**
This fragmentation leads to a visual effect, known on Earth as a "shooting star."

3 **IMPACT**
On impact, it is compressed and carves out a hole in Earth's surface, creating a crater.

TYPES OF METEORITES

Aerolites
Notable for their olivine and pyroxene content. This category subdivides into chondrites and nonchondrites.

Iron meteorites
Abundant in iron-nickel compounds. Generated during the breakup of asteroids.

Siderolites
Objects comprising similar amounts of iron, nickel, and other silicates.

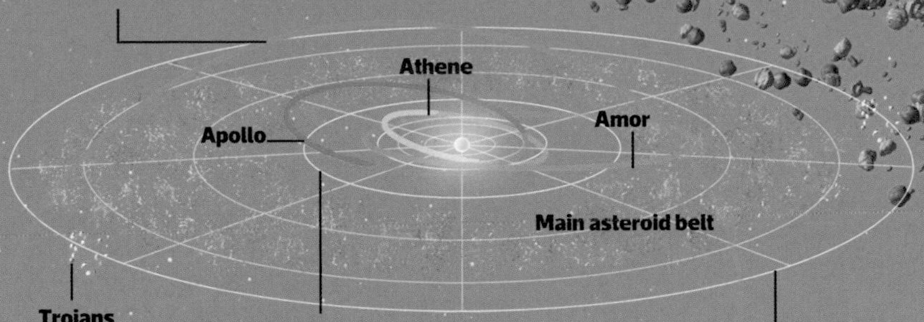

Hidalgo
Orbits the Sun once
every 14 years.

Athene

Apollo

Amor

Main asteroid belt

Trojans
They share their orbit
with Jupiter.

Mars's orbit

Jupiter's orbit

Asteroids

Fragments of rock and metal in a variety of shapes and sizes
that orbit the Sun. Most, over a million, are located in the main
asteroid belt between the orbits of Mars and Jupiter. Others circle
in orbits close to Earth (the Amor, Apollo, and Athene groups) or
share their orbit with Jupiter (the so-called Trojans). In reality, the
asteroid belt is not as densely packed as depicted.

TYPES OF ASTEROID
Despite the numerous
varieties of shapes and sizes,
three types of asteroid are
known. Depending on their
composition, they divide into
silicaceous, carbonaceous, or
metallic asteroids.

IDA
An asteroid measuring
35 miles (56 km) long,
the surface of which is
scarred as a result of
collisions with other
bodies.

DISCOVERY FACT™

A 55-ft
(17-m) wide
meteorite entered
Earth's atmosphere
on February 15, 2013,
and exploded over
Chelyabinsk, Russia,
in a 500 kiloton
fireball.

590 miles
(950 km)

is the diameter of
Ceres, the first asteroid
discovered and the
largest known to man.

Comets

Comets are small, irregularly shaped objects, measuring just a few miles in diameter, that are usually frozen and dark in color. They are made of dust, rock, gases, and organic molecules rich in carbon, and can be found orbiting in the Kuiper Belt or the so-called Oort cloud. However, many deviate toward the inner part of the Solar System, assuming new paths. When they warm up, their ice formations sublimate, forming their heads and long tails of gas and dust.

Deep Impact space mission

On January 12, 2005, as part of the Discovery Program, the U.S. Space Agency launched *Deep Impact*. This spacecraft was designed to launch a projectile that impacted against the comet 9P/Tempel to obtain samples to be studied on Earth.

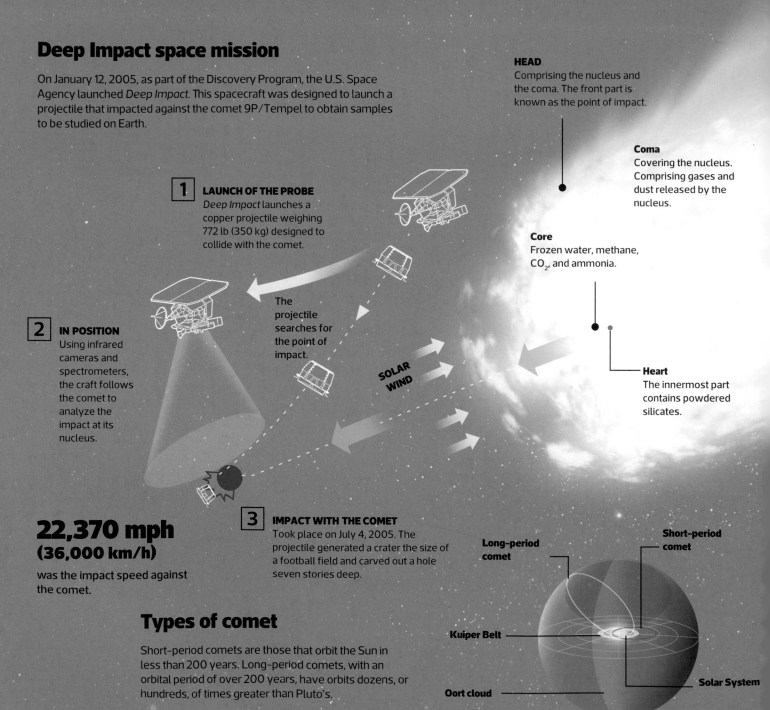

HEAD
Comprising the nucleus and the coma. The front part is known as the point of impact.

Coma
Covering the nucleus. Comprising gases and dust released by the nucleus.

Core
Frozen water, methane, CO_2, and ammonia.

Heart
The innermost part contains powdered silicates.

1 LAUNCH OF THE PROBE
Deep Impact launches a copper projectile weighing 772 lb (350 kg) designed to collide with the comet.

2 IN POSITION
Using infrared cameras and spectrometers, the craft follows the comet to analyze the impact at its nucleus.

The projectile searches for the point of impact.

SOLAR WIND

22,370 mph (36,000 km/h)

was the impact speed against the comet.

3 IMPACT WITH THE COMET
Took place on July 4, 2005. The projectile generated a crater the size of a football field and carved out a hole seven stories deep.

Types of comet

Short-period comets are those that orbit the Sun in less than 200 years. Long-period comets, with an orbital period of over 200 years, have orbits dozens, or hundreds, of times greater than Pluto's.

Long-period comet

Short-period comet

Kuiper Belt

Oort cloud

Solar System

DISCOVERY FACT™

Halley's Comet takes approximately 76 years to complete its orbit around the Sun, so it will next be visible from Earth in 2061.

TAIL

HEAD

TAIL OF DUST
Suspended dust particles form a wake that reflects sunlight, making the comet's luminous tail visible.

ENVELOPE
Layers of hydrogen that are capable of forming a third tail.

TAIL OF IONS
The tail of suspended gases generates a low intensity, luminous blue-colored area. Gas molecules lose an electron and acquire an electrical charge.

FORMATION OF THE TAIL AND HEAD
Due to the effects of solar winds, when the comet gets closer to the Sun, the gases released travel farther away. Meanwhile, the dust particles tend to form a wake that is curved, as it is less sensitive to the pressure of solar winds. As the comet travels farther away from the confines of the Solar System, the tails merge back together, disappearing when the nucleus cools down and stops releasing gas.

Close to the Sun, the tails get longer.

Moving away from the Sun, the tails disappear.

Sun

Earth

Mars

Jupiter

THE COMET'S ORBIT

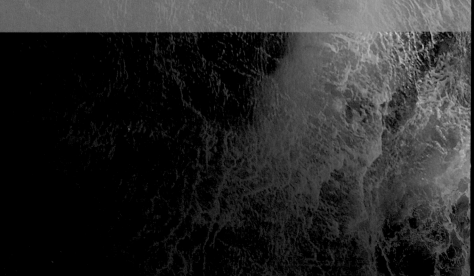

5

THE BLUE PLANET
The water that covers most of
the Earth's surface gives our
planet a blue color and the ability
to sustain life.

THE EARTH
AND
THE MOON

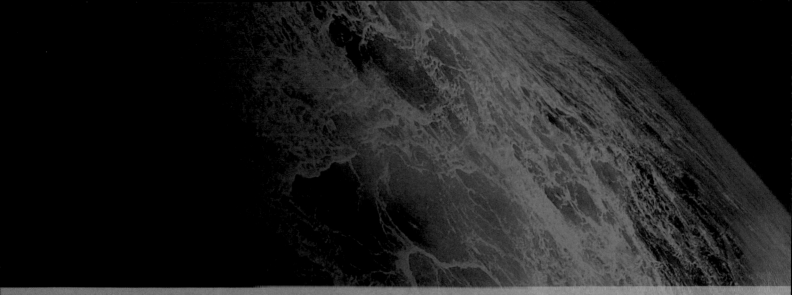

Initially, Earth was an incandescent mass that gradually started to cool down. This cooling made it possible for the continents to form and for the surface of Earth to take on its current form. Although the "blue planet" underwent significant and sudden changes in its early life, it has never stopped evolving. One very important point worth highlighting is that life would be impossible here without the presence of the atmosphere; this layer of invisible, odorless, and colorless gas surrounds us, provides air to breathe, and protects us from the Sun's harmful radiation. The atmosphere is approximately 435 miles (700 km) thick, although no defined limits have been established; as it reaches out into space, it becomes thinner until it completely disappears.

The Blue Planet

Slightly flattened toward the poles and wider around the equator, Earth is known as the blue planet, thanks to the color of the oceans that cover two-thirds of its surface. It is the only planet in our Solar System known to support life. It has abundant amounts of liquid water, a reasonable temperature, and a protective atmosphere.

The phenomenon of life

Water in liquid form. This is one of the main reasons that explains the existence of life on Earth, the only planet on which temperatures range from -85° F to 131° F (-65° C to 55° C). This makes it possible to have liquid water on its surface. Its suitable distance from the Sun, among other factors, also allowed life to develop 3.8 billion years ago.

1 EVAPORATION
As a result of solar energy, water evaporates into the atmosphere from the ocean and, to a much lower degree, from lakes, rivers, and different geographical features of the continents.

CONVENTIONAL PLANETARY SYMBOL FOR EARTH

2 CONDENSATION
Winds transport humidity-laden air until the climatic conditions cause this humidity to condense into clouds.

3 PRECIPITATION
It is gravity that causes rain, snow, and hail to fall to Earth, while the state of dew and frost changes directly on the surfaces that they cover.

ESSENTIAL DATA

Average distance from the Sun	93 million miles (149.6 million km)
Diameter at the equator	7,926 miles (12,756 km)
Orbital speed	17.27 miles/sec (27.79 km/sec)
Mass (Earth = 1)	1
Gravity (Earth = 1)	1
Density	5.52 g/cm³
Temperature	59° F (15° C)
Solar orbit (Earth year)	365.25 days

AXIAL TILT

23.5°

One rotation takes 23.56 hours

DISCOVERY FACT™

70.8 percent of the Earth's surface is covered with water. As a result, from space it is seen as a blue planet.

SOUTH POLE

AXIAL TILT

ROTATING AXIS

NORTH POLE

23.5º

is the axial tilt of Earth compared with the Sun; this is responsible for the different seasons experienced on the planet.

Gravity and magnetism

Earth possesses a powerful magnetic field produced by its outer core, where the turbulent currents of molten iron generate electric and magnetic fields. Magnetism changes direction as time passes, allowing the magnetic poles to flow.

The Earth's core works like a magnet.

Magnetic force

Solid core

Mantle

The Earth's magnetic field is created by convective currents in the outer core.

The outer core is in a constantly moving liquid state.

ITS CONSEQUENCES

The magnetic field protects the Earth from solar winds.

Certain particles are attracted toward the poles

Van Allen radiation belt

Solar wind

Magnetic field lines

Magnetosphere

The Van Allen radiation belt traps solar wind particles and causes phenomena like the aurora.

Axis

Earth

Magnetic field tail

24 lb
(11 kg)

On the Moon
Its mass is inferior to the Earth's mass; as a result, it has less gravity.

154 lb
(70 kg)

On Earth
Gravity pulls toward the center of Earth.

390 lb
(177 kg)

On Jupiter
Its mass is 300 times greater than Earth's mass; as a result, its gravitational pull is stronger.

GRAVITY AND WEIGHT
Weight is the gravitational pull exercised on an object.

Structure of the Earth

Earth is made up of different layers, which in turn are made up of different elements such as iron, nickel, and rock in solid and in liquid form, in addition to freshwater, saltwater, and air. A cloud of gases encompasses our planet: the atmosphere. One of these gases—oxygen—allows the planet to sustain the majority of life.

Inner layers

We live on a rocky surface comprising, for the most part, oxygen and silica. Underneath, there is the mantle; the rocks here are much heavier. Beneath the mantle are the outer and inner cores. The former consists of constantly boiling liquid metal. The latter, which is solid due to the effects of pressure, is the densest part of the planet.

HOW FAR HUMANKIND HAS REACHED

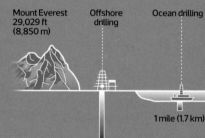

Mount Everest
29,029 ft
(8,850 m)

Offshore drilling

Ocean drilling

1 mile (1.7 km)

1.7 miles (2.8 km)

620 miles
(1,000 km)

3,965 miles
(6,380 km)

440 miles
(710 km)

1,360 miles
(2,200 km)

1,400 miles
(2,250 km)

1,500 miles
(2,400 km) diameter

INNER CORE
Comprising the same metals, iron and nickel, as the outer core. Unlike that layer, despite the extreme temperature, the center is solid due to the enormous pressures exerted on it, causing it to compress as a result.

OUTER CORE
Liquid and made up of molten iron and nickel. Its temperature is lower than the inner core and it withstands less pressure. The movement of the boiling liquid is responsible for the magnetic field.

INNER MANTLE
The intermediate layer between the core and the crust. It is solid and spreads high-temperature waves, as it is close to and in contact with the core.

THE ATMOSPHERE
It is over 435 miles
(700 km) thick, although no
defined limits have been
established.

EXOSPHERE

THERMOSPHERE

MESOSPHERE

STRATOSPHERE

TROPOSPHERE

Without the atmosphere
Direct solar radiation.
The temperature
difference between the
equator and the poles
would be more striking.

With the atmosphere
Solar rays are filtered.
Winds distribute heat,
cooling the equator and
heating the poles.

Hydrosphere and lithosphere

The hydrosphere, the liquid part of the Earth, includes
the oceans, lakes, rivers, underground waters, snow,
and ice. It covers 70.8 percent of the Earth's surface.
The lithosphere is the surface of the Earth and it is
elastic in nature. Beneath the ocean, it measures just
4–7 miles (6–11 km), whereas beneath the mountain
ranges, it can measure up to 43.5 miles (70 km) deep.

HYDROSPHERE AND LITHOSPHERE
The lithosphere includes the crust and the
upper part of the mantle; the hydrosphere
is the combined mass of water, distributed
among five oceans, lakes, and rivers.

OUTER MANTLE
Due to the high temperatures, the materials dilate
and generate a continuous rising movement that
creates convection currents and the force that
causes changes to the Earth's crust.

DISCOVERY FACT™

The distance from
the surface to the
center of the Earth
is 3,965 miles
(6,380 km)

WATER AND LAND

29.2 percent
land

70.8 percent
water

**TOTAL VOLUME
OF WATER**

94 percent
saltwater

6 percent
freshwater

FRESHWATER

4.3 percent
underground

0.03 percent
Surface and
atmosphere

1.7 percent
ice

The Atmosphere

Most life on Earth, and certainly human life, would be impossible if it were not for the atmosphere: it provides the air we breathe and the water we drink. Its makeup also allows the regulation of the amount and type of solar energy that reaches the Earth's crust; this protects us from the Sun's harmful radiation while maintaining a good temperature by retaining its heat.

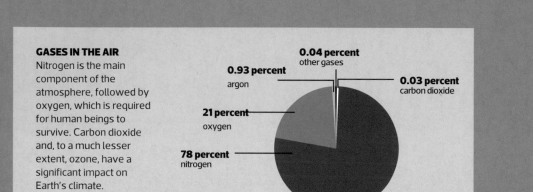

GASES IN THE AIR
Nitrogen is the main component of the atmosphere, followed by oxygen, which is required for human beings to survive. Carbon dioxide and, to a much lesser extent, ozone, have a significant impact on Earth's climate.

0.04 percent
other gases

0.93 percent
argon

0.03 percent
carbon dioxide

21 percent
oxygen

78 percent
nitrogen

Greenhouse effect

The Earth reflects the Sun's rays out into space. However, certain gases in the atmosphere are capable of retaining this heat. This is called the "greenhouse effect," and it allows the planet to maintain a stable temperature.

59° F
(15° C)

is the average temperature of the Earth's surface.

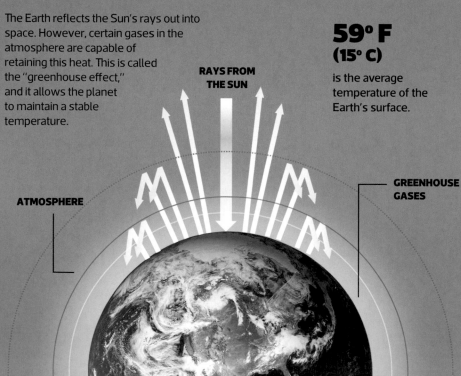

RAYS FROM THE SUN

ATMOSPHERE

GREENHOUSE GASES

5 **EXOSPHERE**
This layer starts at 300 miles (500 km) from the Earth's surface. It is the upper limit of the atmosphere, where material in a state of plasma escapes the confines of Earth and mixes with outer space.

4 **THERMOSPHERE**
Found between 55 and 300 miles (90 and 500 km) in altitude. Oxygen and nitrogen absorb UV rays and generate temperatures of over 1,800° F (1,000° C).

Sounding rockets
Used to scientifically study high regions of the atmosphere.

3 **MESOSPHERE**
Between 30 and 55 miles (50 and 90 km) in altitude. Temperatures decrease from 68° F to -130° F (20° C to -90° C) at its upper limit.

2 **STRATOSPHERE**
Ranges between 6 and 30 miles (10 km and 50 km) in altitude. The concentration of ozone, which absorbs ultraviolet light, is high here. From 12 miles (20 km) upward, there is a sudden increase in temperature.

1 **TROPOSPHERE**
Up to 6 miles (10 km) in altitude—75 percent of atmospheric gases can be found here, and it is responsible for the majority of climatic phenomena.

4 percent
of solar radiation is reflec by the oceans and land.

51 percent

of solar radiation reaches Earth. The rest is absorbed or reflected by the atmosphere.

SOLAR RADIATION

DISCOVERY FACT™

The solar energy absorbed by the atmosphere and the Earth's surface in one hour is more than all the energy used by humans in a year.

Auroras
Generated when solar winds excite electrically charged particles.

7 percent
of solar radiation is reflected by the atmosphere.

14 percent
of solar radiation is absorbed by the atmosphere.

24 percent
of solar radiation is reflected by clouds.

Distant orbits
Traced by meteorological satellites.

Military satellites
Their useful life decreases through wear from aerodynamic drag.

Meteorites
Due to friction, they overheat and gasify with gas molecules from the atmosphere. Shooting stars are incandescent particles that formed part of a meteor.

Cosmic rays
Generated by the Sun and other sources of radiation in outer space. When they collide with gases in the atmosphere, they cause particle showers.

Noctilucent cloud
The only clouds that exist above the troposphere, they are the subject of intense study.

Weather balloons
Used in the field of meteorology to make forecasts.

Commercial flights
The relative absence of meteorological changes in this zone makes it safer for commercial flights.

51 percent
of solar radiation is absorbed by the Earth's surface.

A Brief History of the Earth

Earth was most probably formed from small pieces of space debris left over from the creation of the Sun, which then joined together in an incandescent ball of rock and metal. The rocky crust was then shaped, and the surface cooled down sufficiently to allow the continents to form. Later, the oceans and plants arrived, supplying the atmosphere with oxygen. Over time, the levels of oxygen became sufficient to allow the development of primitive life forms.

Continental drift

We live on moving plates, called "tectonic plates," that gradually move the continents over the Earth's surface at the same speed at which our fingernails grow. This phenomenon, known as "continental drift," resulted in the separation of the continents, which were originally a single landmass.

CHRONOLOGY OF EVENTS
To standardize the study of Earth's geology, its life was divided into different eras, each lasting millions of years. These also serve to catalog evolutionary processes.

1 **290 MILLION YEARS AGO**
A single continent, Pangaea, was formed; it floated on a single, immense ocean known as Panthalassa.

2 **250 MILLION YEARS AGO**
Tethys Ocean slowly split Pangaea into two: Laurasia and Gondwanaland.

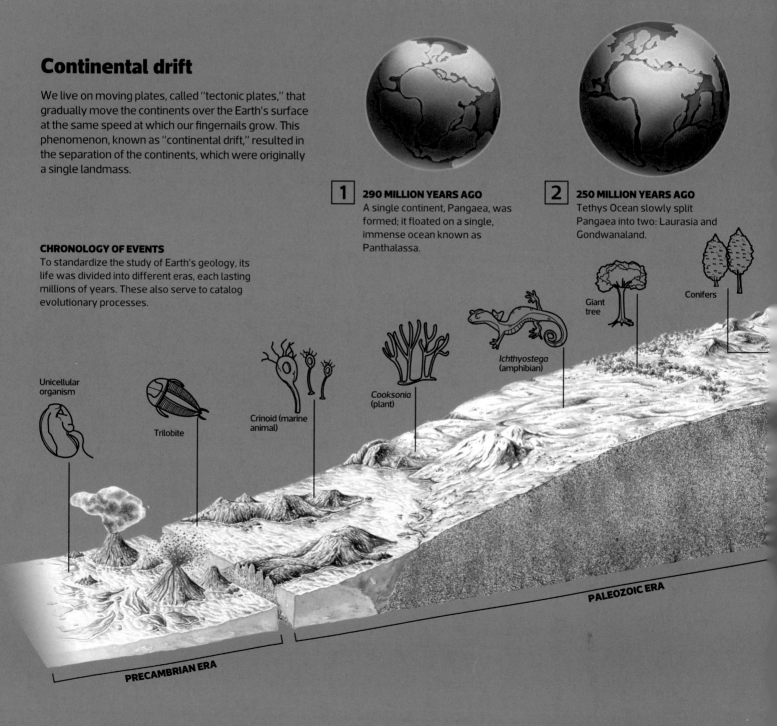

Unicellular organism

Trilobite

Crinoid (marine animal)

Cooksonia (plant)

Ichthyostega (amphibian)

Giant tree

Conifers

PALEOZOIC ERA

PRECAMBRIAN ERA

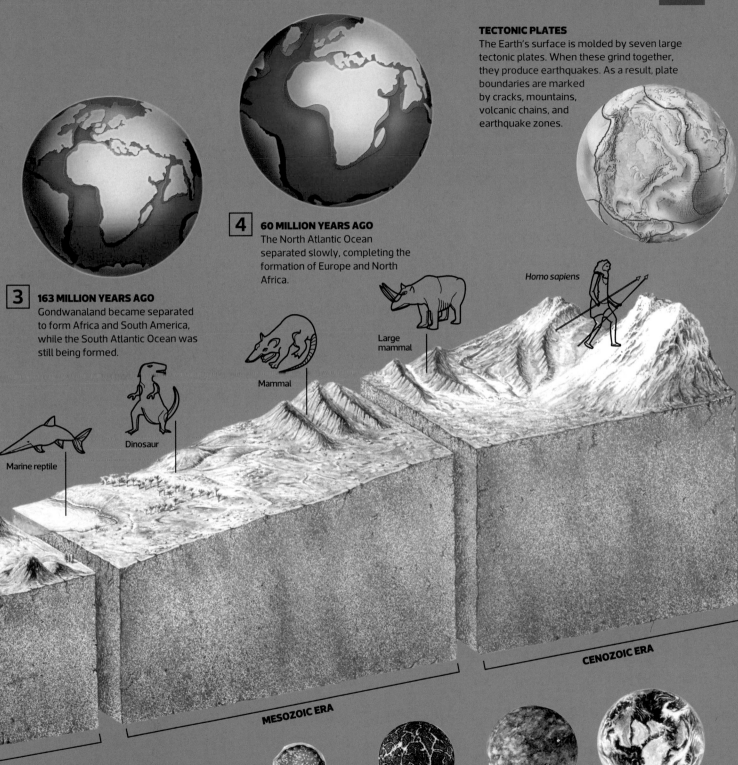

TECTONIC PLATES
The Earth's surface is molded by seven large tectonic plates. When these grind together, they produce earthquakes. As a result, plate boundaries are marked by cracks, mountains, volcanic chains, and earthquake zones.

4 **60 MILLION YEARS AGO**
The North Atlantic Ocean separated slowly, completing the formation of Europe and North Africa.

3 **163 MILLION YEARS AGO**
Gondwanaland became separated to form Africa and South America, while the South Atlantic Ocean was still being formed.

Homo sapiens

Large mammal

Mammal

Dinosaur

Marine reptile

MESOZOIC ERA

CENOZOIC ERA

The origin of Earth

Earth was formed 4.6 billion years ago from a cloud of dust and gas. Originally, it was a boiling mass. However, as time passed, Earth began to cool down and the atmosphere was created as rain fell and the oceans were formed.

1 **Fireball**
Earth was created from small planetesimals that careered around the Solar System.

2 **Crust**
Lava crossed the planet's surface; when cooled, it formed the crust.

3 **Atmosphere**
The atmosphere was created as the planet cooled, releasing gases and vapor.

4 **Water**
First appeared on the planet 3.9 billion years ago and made it possible for life to be sustained.

Planetary Movement

Earth rotates and orbits the Sun; both of these movements are responsible for phenomena such as day and night, summer and winter, and the passing of the years. To measure time, calendars, watches, and time zones were created; the latter were divided among the meridians, and each region was assigned a given time depending on its position in relation to the Sun.

Days and seasons

There are four movements that Earth carries out as it travels along its solar orbit. The most important are: rotations, which it performs on its own axis and are responsible for day and night; and revolutions around the Sun, following an elliptical path, which means that the distance between the Sun and Earth varies slightly throughout the year. This phenomenon is responsible for the different seasons.

23.5° N
S

1 ROTATION
1 day
Earth rotates in a movement that takes 23 hours and 56 minutes. This is what causes the transition from day to night and vice versa.

2 REVOLUTION
1 year
The movement of Earth around the Sun. One revolution lasts 365 days, 5 hours and 57 minutes.

3°

3 NUTATION
18.6 years
A rocking motion that Earth performs, which causes the geographical poles to move nine arc seconds.

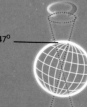

47°

4 PRECESSION
25,800 years
A slow swaying similar to the movement of a spinning top, attributable to the fact that Earth is not completely spherical and to the gravitational effects of the Sun and Moon.

MARCH 21
Spring equinox (northern hemisphere)
Fall equinox (southern hemisphere)
The equinoxes are two points at which the plane of the equator passes through the elliptical path of the Earth.

JUNE 21
Summer solstice (northern hemisphere)
Winter solstice (southern hemisphere)
The solstices are attributable to the axial tilt of the Earth. Hours of sunlight and the height of the Sun are lower in winter and higher in summer.

Aphelion
The point at which Earth, in its orbit, is farthest from the Sun (94 million miles/152 million km). This occurs at the beginning of July in the northern hemisphere.

SEPTEMBER 21
Fall equinox (northern hemisphere)
Spring equinox (southern hemisphere)
Twice a year, the Sun passes over the equator and night and day last exactly the same amount of time.

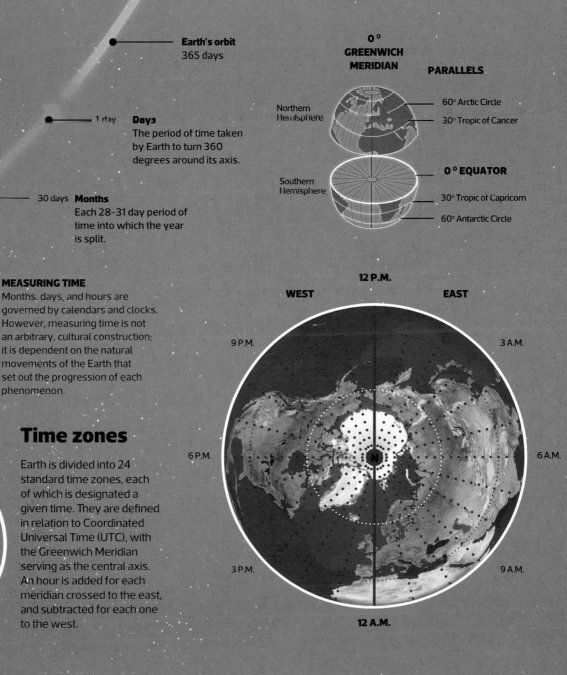

23.5°
Earth's axial tilt

91–94 MILLION MILES (147–152 million km)

SUN

Perihelion
The point at which Earth, in its orbit, is closest to the Sun (91 million miles/147 million km).

DISCOVERY FACT™

It wasn't until the eighteenth century, when very precise clocks were invented, that sailors could navigate accurately using longitude and latitude.

DECEMBER 21
Winter solstice (northern hemisphere)
Summer solstice (southern hemisphere)
In the southern hemisphere, the Sun rises to its zenith in summer over the Tropic of Cancer and, in winter, over the Tropic of Capricorn.

Coordinates

By combining two angles, latitude and longitude, it is possible to establish the position of any point on Earth ,with Greenwich, in London, at 0° longitude and the equator at 0° latitude.

0°
GREENWICH MERIDIAN
PARALLELS

Northern Hemisphere

60° Arctic Circle
30° Tropic of Cancer

Southern Hemisphere

0° EQUATOR
30° Tropic of Capricorn
60° Antarctic Circle

Earth's orbit
365 days

1 day
Days
The period of time taken by Earth to turn 360 degrees around its axis.

30 days
Months
Each 28–31 day period of time into which the year is split.

MEASURING TIME
Months, days, and hours are governed by calendars and clocks. However, measuring time is not an arbitrary, cultural construction; it is dependent on the natural movements of the Earth that set out the progression of each phenomenon.

Time zones

Earth is divided into 24 standard time zones, each of which is designated a given time. They are defined in relation to Coordinated Universal Time (UTC), with the Greenwich Meridian serving as the central axis. An hour is added for each meridian crossed to the east, and subtracted for each one to the west.

12 P.M. / WEST / EAST / 9 P.M. / 3 A.M. / 6 P.M. / 6 A.M. / 3 P.M. / 9 A.M. / 12 A.M.

The Moon and the Tides

It is believed that the Moon was created when a Mars-size body crashed into Earth while it was still in formation. The expelled material scattered around Earth and, over time, it joined together to form the Moon. It is our planet's only natural satellite, and its gravitational pull influences the tides. The Moon's gravitational pull over the Earth's bodies of water varies depending on its position.

Lunar movements

For each terrestrial orbit, the Moon spins on its own axis. As a result, the same side always faces Earth.

Lunar month
It takes 29.53 days to complete its phase.

Sidereal month
It takes 27.32 days to orbit Earth.

Hidden face
It was not until 1959, when the *Luna 3* probe photographed it, that the Moon's hidden face was seen for the first time.

Moon

Earth

Visible face

Lunar orbit

DISCOVERY FACT™
The far side of the Moon is covered in craters and has only a few small lava seas. It looks very different from the side we can see from Earth.

Aristarchus
Is the brightest point on the Moon.

Oceanus Procellarum
Is the biggest sea.

The tides

The body of water closest to the Moon feels its gravitational pull more strongly, while the opposite side of Earth is less affected. Nonetheless, the Sun's pull also influences the movement of the tides. When the tide rises, it is known as high tide; when it lowers, low tide.

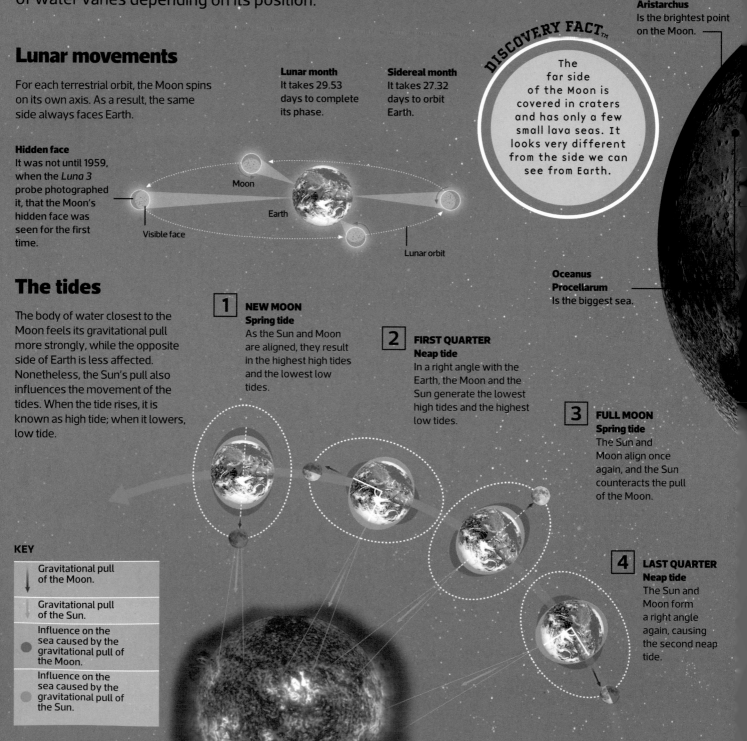

1 NEW MOON
Spring tide
As the Sun and Moon are aligned, they result in the highest high tides and the lowest low tides.

2 FIRST QUARTER
Neap tide
In a right angle with the Earth, the Moon and the Sun generate the lowest high tides and the highest low tides.

3 FULL MOON
Spring tide
The Sun and Moon align once again, and the Sun counteracts the pull of the Moon.

4 LAST QUARTER
Neap tide
The Sun and Moon form a right angle again, causing the second neap tide.

KEY

Gravitational pull of the Moon.

Gravitational pull of the Sun.

Influence on the sea caused by the gravitational pull of the Moon.

Influence on the sea caused by the gravitational pull of the Sun.

The surface of the Moon

Ancient astronomers deduced that the dark patches on the Moon that can be seen with the naked eye were *maria* (seas). These dark areas contrast with the light areas (highlands with a higher number of craters).

Mare Imbrium
3.85 billion years old.

ROCKY MANTLE
Less than half the depth of Earth.

OUTER CORE
Partially molten.

INNER STRUCTURE
Based on different seismic lunar analyses, it seems likely that the core of the Moon is solid or semisolid.

INNER CORE
Core temperature of 2,700°F (1,500°C).

Schickard

Tycho
100 million years old.

Maginius

Rupes Altai
Mountain range measuring 5,900 ft (1,800 m) in height.

Humboldt
Crater named after the German natural scientist.

MOUNTAIN RANGES
Formed from material expelled from the crater after a meteorite impacted against the surface of the Moon.

CRATERS
Different craters measure between 3 ft and 600 miles (1 m and 1,000 km) in diameter. They were formed as a result of cosmic collisions.

SEAS
They cover 16 percent of the Moon's surface and were formed by lava channels. Today, there is no volcanic activity on the Moon. However, this was not always the case.

Mare Crisium
Measuring 280 x 350 miles (450 x 563 km). It is scarred by large craters.

Mare Tranquillitatis

CRUST
Rocky, granitelike surface with 65 ft (20 m) of lunar dust known as "regolith."

Montes Apenninus
One of the most important mountain ranges on the Moon.

Copernicus
Crater measuring 58 miles (93 km) in diameter.

CONVENTIONAL PLANETARY SYMBOL FOR MOON

ESSENTIAL DATA

Distance from Earth	238,855 miles (384,400 km)
Orbit around Earth	27.3 days
Diameter at the equator	2,160 miles (3,476 km)
Orbital speed	0.63 miles/sec (1.02 km/sec)
Mass (Earth = 1)	0.01
Gravity (Earth = 1)	0.17
Density	3.34 g/cm³
Average temperature	302° F (150° C)—day / -148° F (-100° C)—night
Solar orbit (Earth year)	365.25 days

AXIAL TILT

5.14°

One rotation takes 27.32 days.

Eclipses

At least four times a year, the centers of the Moon, the Sun, and the Earth fully align, resulting in one of the most attractive astronomical events to the casual observer: an eclipse. Solar eclipses also provide astronomers with an amazing opportunity for scientific investigation.

Total lunar eclipse seen from Earth
The orange color is attributable to the refracted rays of sunlight, which are discolored by the Earth's atmosphere.

Annular solar eclipse seen from Earth

Solar eclipse

Is when the Moon passes between Earth and the Sun, projecting a shadow on a given part of Earth's surface, creating a shadow zone and a penumbra zone. Spectators in the shadow zone will see the Moon fully block the Sun; such events are known as total solar eclipses. Spectators in the penumbra zone will see a partial solar eclipse.

ALIGNMENT

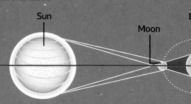

Sun

Moon

Earth

During solar eclipses, astronomers take advantage of the shadow cast over the stars to study their atmosphere using special equipment.

Watching a solar eclipse
A solar eclipse should never be viewed with the naked eye, as it can burn the retina. Special glasses must be used.

SOLAR ECLIPSE X3   SOLAR ECLIPSE X3

Black polymer filter with an optical density of 5.0. This prevents the retina suffering burn damage and offers a clear view of the Sun.

TYPES OF SOLAR ECLIPSES

Total
The Moon is positioned between the Sun and Earth, within the shadow zone.

Annular
The diameter of the Moon is smaller than that of the Sun, and part of the Sun can be seen.

Partial
The Moon does not fully cover the Sun, which appears as a crescent.

SOLAR LIGHT

7.5 minutes

is the maximum duration of a solar eclipse.

Lunar eclipse

When Earth passes between the Moon and the Sun, the resulting phenomenon is a lunar eclipse, which may be total, partial, or penumbral. A totally eclipsed Moon takes on a characteristic reddish color, as the light is refracted by the Earth's atmosphere. When part of the Moon is within the shadow zone, and the rest within the penumbral zone, the result is a partial eclipse.

107 minutes

is the maximum duration of a lunar eclipse.

ALIGNMENT

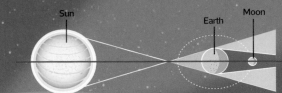

Sun   Earth   Moon

During an eclipse, the Moon is not completely black; it assumes an ocher color.

Shadow zone

FULL MOON TOTAL ECLIPSE

PARTIAL ECLIPSE

PENUMBRAL ECLIPSE

Penumbral zone

Lunar orbit

Shadow zone

Penumbral zone

EARTH

Earth's orbit

NEW MOON TOTAL ECLIPSE

TYPES OF LUNAR ECLIPSES

Total
The Moon is completely within the shadow zone.

Partial
The Moon is only partially within the shadow zone.

Penumbral
The Moon is within the penumbral zone.

CYCLE OF ECLIPSES
Eclipses are repeated every 223 lunar months, or every 18 years and 11 days. These periods are called "saros."

ECLIPSES IN A YEAR

2 MINIMUM

7 MAXIMUM

4 AVERAGE

ECLIPSES IN ONE SAROS

41 SOLAR ECLIPSES

29 LUNAR ECLIPSES

70 TOTAL

6

PLATEOSAURUS
This dinosaur inhabited Europe and
Greenland over 200 million years
ago. It measured approximately 23 ft
(7 m) long and was a herbivore.

LIFE
ON
EARTH

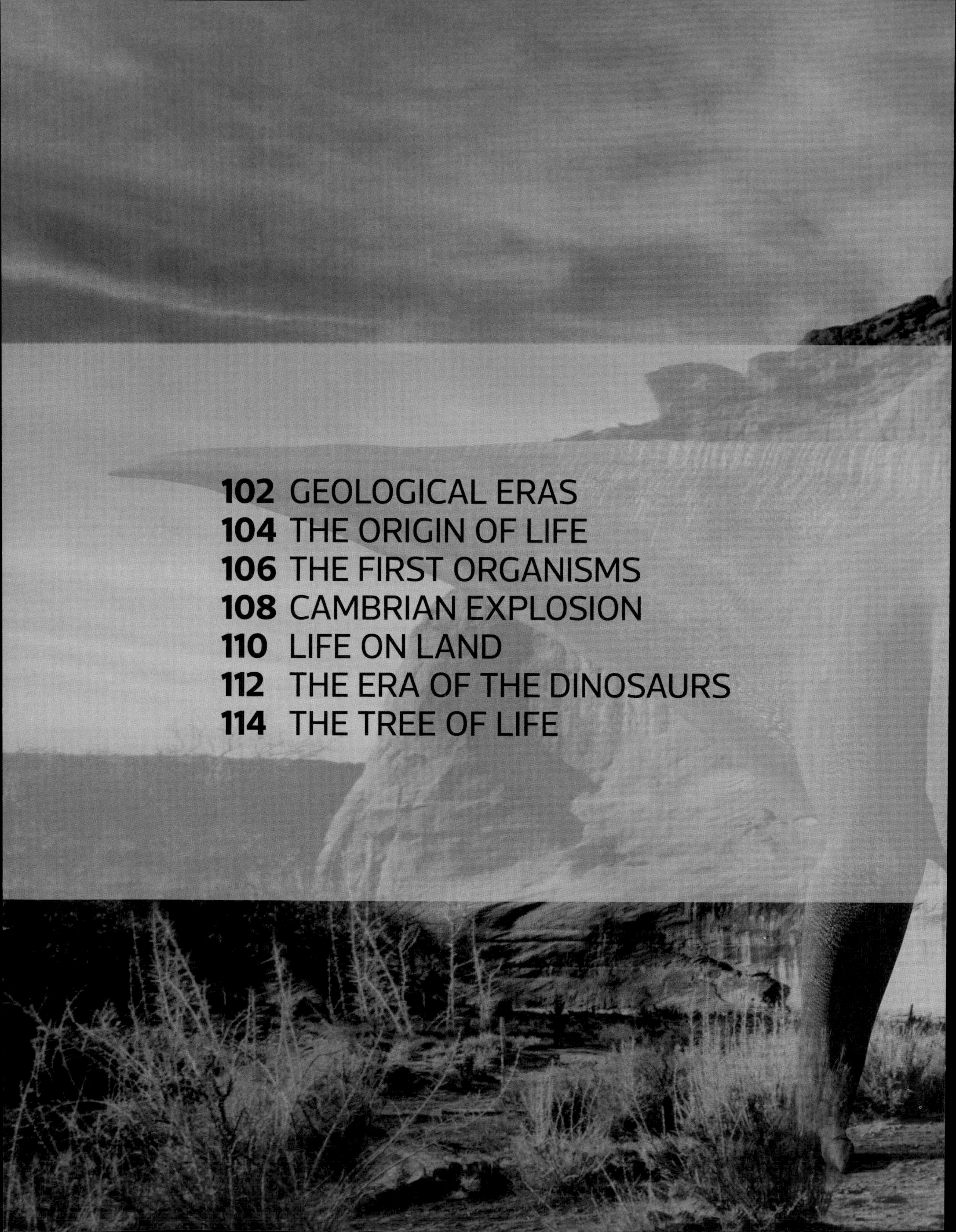

A significant amount of imagination is required to understand just how recently complex life-forms on Earth developed. For millions of years, development of life remained static. Then, during what is known as the Cambrian Explosion, many hard-shelled organisms developed, leaving behind fossils that we can discover today. Fossil records for the period demonstrate an impressive increase in the most varied of life-forms, with new species emerging in the seas. Gradually, plants and animals conquered the land, on which impressive creatures such as the dinosaurs emerged. They became extinct 65 million years ago; nevertheless, all beings that inhabit the Earth today share the same origin.

Geological Eras

Geological structures and fossil remains have allowed experts to reconstruct the history of life on Earth. Today, it is believed that Earth was created 4.8 billion years ago, and the first life-forms—bacteria—appeared one billion years later. To study the history of Earth, time is divided into "eras" in line with the geological and biological changes witnessed; these in turn are divided into "periods."

PRECAMBRIAN ERA		PALEOZOIC ERA						
ARCHAEAN	PROTEROZOIC	CAMBRIAN	ORDOVICIAN	SILURIAN	DEVONIAN	CARBONIFEROUS	PERMIAN
4,800–2,500 mya (million years ago)	2,500–543 mya	543–490 mya	490–443 mya	443–418 mya	418–354 mya	354–290 mya	290–252 mya

Mass extinctions

85% of species · 82% of species · 96% of species

FORMATION OF THE CRUST AND THE FIRST ORGANISMS

The oldest rocks found on Earth date back approximately 4 billion years. Before this, the planet had no solid surface. The first atmosphere had no oxygen; the first organisms (bacteria) used anaerobic respiration.

Lava turns into rock
The Earth's first surface was a thin layer littered with volcanoes that spewed lava. As it cooled down, this first crust solidified and grew thicker.

Presence of oxygen
Oxygen was introduced into the atmosphere around 2.1 billion years ago. With its arrival, the formation of compounds like water and carbon dioxide was possible.

Structure of carbon dioxide molecule.

First life-forms
Stromatolites, unicellular algae fossils, represent one of the first instances of evidence of life and date back around 3.5 billion years. The oldest multicellular animal fossils date back around 700 million years.

Mawsonite fossil (Australia), one of the oldest multicellular fossils.

THE CAMBRIAN EXPLOSION AND MASS EXTINCTIONS

During the Cambrian period, numerous multicellular species suddenly appeared; during the Silurian period, the first land species appeared. Significant climatic changes and other circumstances resulted in the first mass species extinctions.

First fish
The first fish, known as Agnathans, had no jaw. This *Pteraspis*, which lived in shallow waters, belonged to the Silurian period.

Crinoid fossil
Almost all modern-day sedimentary rocks are composed of the remnants of these ancient animals, characteristic of the Silurian period.

Scales
The image shows the scales of a *Lepidotus*, an ancient type of fish. They were also covered by a hard and shiny substance, similar to varnish. Today, almost all reptiles and fish have scales.

Ancient amphibians
This ancient amphibian, known as the *Acanthostega*, lived during the Devonian period.

TIMELINE

The vast majority of life-forms in the history of the planet were simple organisms, consisting of just one cell. This is particularly true of bacteria, the only life-form to have survived more than three billion years. The dominance of dinosaurs during the Mesozoic era is a comparatively recent event.

4,500 mya
Earth is created.

3,800 mya
The first bacterium appears.

2,100 mya
Oxygen appears in the atmosphere.

700 mya
The first multicellular animals appear.

PRECAMBRIAN

PALEOZOIC

MESOZOIC

CENOZOIC

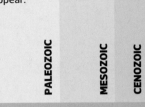

MESOZOIC ERA			CENOZOIC ERA	
TRIASSIC	JURASSIC	CRETACEOUS	TERTIARY	QUATERNARY
252–199 mya	199–142 mya	142–65 mya	65–1.6 mya	FROM 1.6 mya

76% of species

THE ERA OF REPTILES AND CLIMATIC CHANGE

Reptiles conquered land environments, although some also reigned over the seas and skies. The first mammals and birds appeared on Earth. There was a significant change in the climate toward the end of the Mesozoic era, with temperatures dropping drastically, giving way to an ice age.

BIRDS, MAMMALS AND HOMINIDAE

The first 20 million years of the period were relatively warm; however, the climate changed later and the ice caps were formed. Without the domination of the great dinosaurs, birds and mammals flourished. The spread of hominid species coincides with the expansion of grasslands as the dominant form of vegetation.

Fossilized vertebrae
This belonged to a *Barosaurus*, whose long neck was flexible thanks to the lightness of its vertebrae.

Birds
The *Titanis* was a carnivorous bird. Given its size (8 ft/2.5 m) and its short wings, it was unable to fly.

Great dinosaurs
The heaviest known dinosaur was the *Argentinosaurus*. It has been calculated that it may have weighed around 70 tons.

Homo neanderthalensis
This hominid, which shared a common ancestor with *Homo sapiens*, surfaced around 100,000 years ago.

Predators
The *Giganotosaurus carolinii* was the largest carnivorous dinosaur (40 ft/12.5 m).

Mammals
The *Thylacosmilus*, or "pouched saber," looked like a modern feline but was actually a marsupial. Its teeth never stopped growing. It lived during the Quaternary period.

The Origin of Life

Life began on Earth approximately 3.5 billion years ago in the form of microbes, which determined, and continue to determine, biological processes. Science tries to explain the source of life through a series of chemical reactions, which occurred by chance. Over millions of years, they would give rise to different living organisms.

DISCOVERY FACT™

DNA stands for Deoxyribonucleic acid, the molecule that encodes genetic information used in the development of all known living organisms.

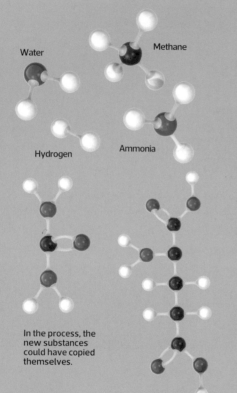

Water

Methane

Hydrogen

Ammonia

In the process, the new substances could have copied themselves.

Original cells

The first living organisms (prokaryotes) started to develop in groups, giving rise to a cooperative process known as "symbiosis." Thus, eukaryotes, more complex life-forms, were born containing a nucleus that housed genetic information (DNA). In large part, bacterial development was a chemical evolution that was the result of new methods of obtaining sunlight and extracting oxygen from water (photosynthesis).

Filaments

PROKARYOTES
The first life-forms, with no nucleus or cover membranes. The genetic code of these unicellular formations was stored between the walls of the cell.

The first reaction

The level of free oxygen and carbon dioxide in the atmosphere remained very low 4.5 billion years ago; however, it was rich in simple chemical substances such as water, hydrogen, ammonia, and methane. Electrical discharges and ultraviolet radiation triggered chemical reactions that formed complex organic compounds (carbohydrates, amino acids, nucleotides), thus creating the building blocks of life.

DNA free on the inside

Ribosomes

Plasma membrane

Cell wall

ARCHAEAN
4.8 billion years ago

4.5 billion years ago

4.2 billion years ago

The atmosphere distinguishes Earth from the other planets.

Volcanic eruptions and igneous rock dominate the Earth's landscape.

The Earth's surface cools and accumulates liquid water.

EUKARYOTES

Containing a central nucleus that holds nucleic acids (DNA) as well as other organelles. Different organelles have different functions: many are involved in producing energy in order for the organism itself to develop.

Smooth endoplasmic reticulum

Core
Contains genetic information and DNA filaments that give instructions to the cell in order to function, grow, and reproduce.

Rough endoplasmic reticulum

Nuclear pores

Mitochondria
Bodies that produce energy for different cellular functions.

Endoplasmic reticulum
Helps to transport substances through the cell and is involved in fat metabolism.

Inner membrane

Outer membrane

Ribosomes
Produce the proteins that form the cell.

Centriole
Key part of cell division, located at the heart of the cell.

Golgi apparatus
Flat pouches that receive proteins from the endoplasmic reticulum and release them through the cell membrane.

Microvilli

Lysosomes
Break down and eliminate harmful substances using powerful enzymes.

1 Animals
Certain aerobic bacteria with respiratory enzymes came from mitochondria and generated the ancestor cells of present-day animals.

2 Plants
Certain photosynthetic bacteria invaded eukaryotic cells and formed chloroplasts, creating the ancestral cells of plants.

Golgi apparatus

Core

Chloroplasts
Organelles specializing in obtaining energy by means of photosynthesis.

Tonoplast

Vacuole
Transports and houses substances ingested via water.

Mitochondria

4 billion years ago

3.8 billion years ago

Prebiological evolution, during which inert matter transforms into organic matter.

The first prokaryote appears, called Archaea.

The First Organisms

The oldest fossils found thus far date back to the end of the Proterozoic period, during the Precambrian era. Found in Ediacara (Australia), they represent the first evidence of multicellular organisms with different tissues. It is believed that these specimens were not animals, but prokaryote organisms formed by several cells with no internal cavities.

First species

It has been established that the Ediacara organisms were the first invertebrates on Earth. They appeared approximately 635 million years ago and were made up of several cells. Some had a soft, flat body while others were shaped like a disk, or a long strip. A single cell was no longer responsible for feeding itself, breathing, and reproducing; instead, several cells specialized in different functions.

CHARNIA
One of the largest fossils found in Ediacara. Its flattened, leaf-shaped body was attached to a structure similar to a disk that most likely anchored its body to the seabed.

STROMATOLITES
They provide the most ancient records of life on Earth. They were layered structures, primarily cyanobacteria and calcium carbonate, that stuck to the substrate. They grew in mass, helping the formation of reefs.

Calcium carbonate

Cynobacteria

3.5 billion years ago

Accumulation of iron oxide on the seabed.

2.5 billion years ago

Formation of stromatolite reefs.

635 million years ago

Traces of Ediacara fauna, among the oldest known.

CYCLOMEDUSA

Ancient circular fossil with a bump in the middle and up to five concentric ridges. Some radial segment lines extended across the outer disks.

3.5–4 in
(9–10 cm)
in diameter

MAWSONITES

This type of jellyfish moved slowly through the water, assisted by the currents. It contracted its umbrella, extended its tentacles, and shot its microscopic spears to capture its prey.

KIMBERELLA

The first known organism to contain a body cavity.

7.9 in
(20 cm)
in length

1.2 in
(3 cm)
in length

DISCOVERY FACT™

While the earliest organisms drifted on the ocean currents, jellyfish were the first to propel themselves through the water.

DICKINSONIA

Often considered a ringed worm given its similarity to an extinct species (*Spinther*). It may also have been a version of the soft-bodied fungus "banana coral."

TRIBRACHIDIUM

It is believed that this species, which developed in the shape of a disk with three symmetrical parts, is a distant relative of corals, anemones, and starfish.

2 in
(5 cm)
in diameter

543 million years ago

The Cambrian period begins. Significant development in multicellular life-forms.

540 million years ago

The period to which the first remnants of invertebrates date, found in Canada's Burgess Shale.

Cambrian Explosion

The great explosion of life that occurred during the Cambrian period, around 500 million years ago, gave rise to a wide variety of multicellular organisms protected by exoskeletons or shells. However, although these organisms represent the fauna typical of the Cambrian period, several species of soft animals lived side by side with them during the period.

The Burgess Shale field

Located in the Yoho National Park, in the Canadian province of British Columbia, the Burgess Shale is a famous fossil field discovered in 1909 by U.S. paleontologist Charles Walcott. The Burgess Shale is the world's greatest reservoir of soft animal fossils from the Cambrian period. It is home to thousands of extremely well-preserved fossilized invertebrates, such as arthropods, worms, and primitive chordates.

0.4 in (10 mm)

Equipped with a powerful exoskeleton, the *Anomalocaris* truly terrorized the Cambrian seas.

SPONGES
They often developed together with algae of different species, sizes, and shapes.

PRIAPULIDA
Benthic worms that lived in the sand and in the slush of deep or shallow waters.

0.8 in
(2 cm)
in length

CAMBRIAN
(543 to 490 million years ago)

Beginnings of the Cambrian period

The increased amount of oxygen helped in the formation of shells.

ANOMALOCARIS
The largest predator arthropod known at the time. It had a circular mouth, appendages that allowed it to firmly grasp its prey, and fins along both sides for swimming.

PIKAIA
One of the first chordata, similar to a swimming worm, with a tail in the shape of a fin. It is the oldest known ancestor of vertebrates.

Human scale comparison

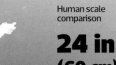

24 in
(60 cm)
in length

4 in
(10 cm)
in length, including its tail

MARRELLA
A tiny swimming arthropod, probably easy prey to the Burgess Shale predators.

HALLUCIGENIA
The defense system of this arthropod was its long spikes, which served as legs.

4 in
(10 cm)
in length, up to its extremities

4 in
(10 cm)
maximum length

Evolutionary explosion

The Cambrian period saw the formation of a wide range of body designs.

Coral reefs

Comprising countless soft-bodied animals.

Life on Land

The Paleozoic era was witness to a turning point in the evolutionary process: the conquest of land around 360 million years ago. Thus, adaptation mechanisms were required. The appearance of reptiles and their innovative amniotic eggs saw vertebrates definitively conquer land. Meanwhile, the pollen of plants made them completely independent from water.

26–30 in (65–75 cm)

was the approximate wingspan of the *Meganeura*.

JAW
Key to the evolution of vertebrates, allowing them to become predators.

New fish species

The period saw the development of armored, jawless fish, the first known vertebrates. Jawed and freshwater fish would appear later; their evolution coincided with the predominance of bony fish, from which amphibians evolved.

197 in (500 cm)

was the maximum length of the *Dunkleosteus*

Barracuda skull

Dorsal fin

Thin, lobed fin

Head and chest armor connected

Bony teeth with sharp edges

The Devonian period is known as the age of fish.

FIN
To move through the water, the *Acanthostega* moved its fin from side to side. It kept this fin during its transition on to land.

DUNKLEOSTEUS
Human scale comparison.

ORDOVICIAN
490 to 443 million years ago

The first organisms—lichens and bryophytes—appear.

SILURIAN
443 to 418 million years ago

Great coral reefs and certain types of small plants.

DEVONIAN
418 to 354 million years ago

Vascular plants and arthropods form a number of ecosystems on dry land.

From fins to extremities

Amphibian evolution facilitated the exploration of new food sources, such as insects and plants, and the adaptation to a new respiratory system. Aquatic vertebrates therefore had to modify their skeleton and develop muscle. Meanwhile, their fins evolved into legs, which allowed them to move over land.

35–47 in
(90–120 cm)

maximum length

ACANTHOSTEGA
Human scale comparison.

BACKBONE

With a system of projections, known as "zygapophyses," between the vertebrae, it was able to keep its backbone rigid.

PREDATOR

It developed a large mouth which allowed it to hunt other vertebrates.

BONE STRUCTURE

Just three bones (humerus, radius, and ulna) formed the bone composition of its leg. Unlike fish, it had a movable wrist and eight fingers that moved together like a spade.

AMNIOTIC EGG

The success of vertebrates' colonization of land is partly attributed to the evolution of the amniotic egg, enveloped by a leathery cover.

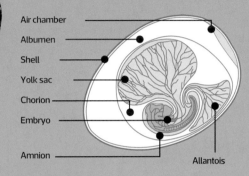

Air chamber

Albumen

Shell

Yolk sac

Chorion

Embryo

Amnion

Allantois

VASCULAR DEVELOPMENT OF PLANTS

The need to transport water from the root to the stalk, and the products of photosynthesis in the opposite direction, resulted in plants developing a system of internal tissues. Pollen-based reproduction allowed plants to definitively adapt on land.

DISCOVERY FACT™

During the Carboniferous period vast swamp forests dominated the land, and the oxygen the trees produced changed the Earth's atmosphere.

Pollen allows reproduction on land

Internal tissue elements

CARBONIFEROUS
354 to 290 million years ago

Land tetrapods and insects with wings appear.

PERMIAN
290 to 252 million years ago

A wide variety of insects and vertebrates appear on land.

The Era of the Dinosaurs

Dinosaurs were the dominant form of land animal life throughout the Mesozoic era, during which these great reptiles underwent constant species changes. Their feet, beneath their bodies rather than to the side like other reptiles, and their bone structure (articulated femur with a hollow pelvis) notably favored their ability to move. They became extinct toward the end of the Cretaceous period.

PLATEOSAURUS
23 ft (7 m)
approximately

Triassic period

Following the mass extinction and biological crisis at the end of the Permian period, a scarce number of animal and plant species managed to survive. Slowly, during the Triassic, a period of renovation began. In the seas, molluscs excelled, while on the continents, reptiles reigned supreme.

COMPARATIVE SIZE

Plateosaurus   *Stegosaurus*   *Giganotosaurus*

DISCOVERY FACT™

The biggest dinosaurs were the plant-eating sauropods, including Diplodocus and Brachiosaurus; they were the largest known land animals.

MAMMALS AND PLANTS

During the Middle to Late Triassic period, families of ferns, conifers, and bennettitales appeared. In turn, toward the end of the Triassic, there are records of mammals that evolved from reptiles to cynodonts.

Plateosaurus walked on four feet, but could reach higher foliage using its tail for balance.

Fern   Palm tree   Conifer   Ginkgo

TRIASSIC
252 to 199 million years ago

The equatorial supercontinent of Pangaea is formed.

Jurassic period

Increased sea levels flooded continental interiors, leading to warmer and more humid climates. Reptiles adapted to different environments and dinosaurs developed significantly. During this period, there are examples of herbivores living side by side with carnivores.

OTHER ANIMALS
Fresh water was the perfect environment for invertebrates, amphibians, turtles, and crocodiles to evolve. The first birds appeared.

Conifer   Horsetail

Cretaceous period

During this period, carnivorous dinosaurs appeared who developed sickle-shaped curved claws, designed to gut their prey. Toward the end of the period, 65 million years ago, land animals weighing more than 55 lb (25 kg) became extinct. The extinction is thought to have been caused by an asteroid or comet impact.

GIGANOTOSAURUS
41 ft
(12.5 m)

STEGOSAURUS
Up to 30 ft
(9 m)

POLLINATION AND MARINE FAUNA
During the Cretaceous period, the evolution of birds and insects continued, with flora developing as a result of pollination. New groups of predators appeared in the seas, such as teleosts and sharks.

Beech   Holly   Oak   Walnut

JURASSIC
199 to 142 million years ago

Pangaea fragments and the sea level rises.

CRETACEOUS
142 to 65 million years ago

Modern-day oceans and continental masses are defined.

The Tree of Life

This image, a phylogenetic tree, explains how all living beings are related. It is compiled using information from fossils and data obtained from a structural and molecular comparison of organisms. Phylogenetic trees are based on the theory that all organisms descend from a common ancestor: the protocell.

Eukaryote

Encompasses living species whose cellular makeup contains a genuine nucleus. Covers unicellular and multicellular organisms.

ANIMALS

Multicellular and heterotrophs. Characterized by their mobility and internal organ systems. They sexually reproduce and their metabolism is aerobic.

Archaea

These organisms are unicellular and microscopic. Most are anaerobic and live in extreme environments; half release methane as part of their metabolic process. There are 209 known species.

PLANTS

Multicellular autotrophic organisms containing cells with a nucleus. They perform photosynthesis using chloroplasts.

Cnidarians
Include species like jellyfish, polyps, and corals.

Bilaterality
Bilaterally symmetrical organisms.

Euryarchaeota
Halobacterium salinarum.

Korarchaeota
This group is among the most primitive.

Nonvascular plants
With no internal vascular system.

Vascular plants
With an internal vascular system.

Mollusks
Include octopuses, snails, and oysters.

Vertebrates
They have a backbone, a skull that protects the brain, and a skeleton.

Seed-bearing plants
Plants on which the seed is exposed and bear flowers or fruits.

Tetrapods
Having four limbs.

Crenarchaeota
Found at high temperatures.

Non-seed-bearing plants
Use spores to reproduce, rather than seeds.

Cartilaginous fish
Include rays, manta rays and sharks.

Origins

Available scientific evidence maintains that all species share a common ancestry. However, there is no conclusive data regarding their origin. It is known that the first expression of life must have been a prokaryote—unicellular beings whose genetic information was contained anywhere within the cell walls.

Gymnosperm
On which the seeds are naked.

Angiospermae
Flowering, fruit-bearing plants. Encompassing more than 250,000 species.

Amphibians
Require water in order to breed.

Bacteria

Unicellular organisms that live on surfaces in colonies. Generally, they have a cell wall made up of peptidoglycans and many have cilia. It is believed that they have existed for 3.5 billion years.

Cocci
Pneumococci are an example.

Bacillus
E. coli takes on this form.

Spirochetes
Helically or spirally shaped.

Vibrio
Found in salt water.

PROTISTS
Includes species that cannot be classified within other groups, such as algae and amoebas.

FUNGI
Heterotrophic cellular organisms with cellular walls thickened by chitin. Use external digestion.

Basidiomycetes
Include mushrooms.

Zygomycetes
They reproduce by means of zygosporangia.

DISCOVERY FACT™

Around 10 million species of animals are calculated to inhabit Earth in all its different environments.

Ascomycetes
The highest number of species fall into this group.

Chytridiomycetes
Some even have mobile cells.

Deuteromycetes
Not known to reproduce sexually.

Arthropods
They have an outer skeleton (exoskeleton). Their extremities are articulated appendages.

Insects
In evolutionary terms, the most successful.

Myriapoda
Millipedes and centipedes.

AMNIOTES
Species in this group protect their embryo in a sealed structure—the amniotic egg. Only a few mammals are still oviparous. However, in placental mammals (like humans), the placenta is a modified egg; its membranes have been transformed, but the embryo continues to be surrounded by an amnion full of amniotic fluid.

Bony fish
Equipped with bones and a jaw.

Crustaceans
Includes crabs and lobsters.

Arachnids
Spiders, scorpions, and mites.

Amniotes
Species born from an embryo within an amniotic egg.

MAN
Human beings form part of the order of Primates, one of the 19 orders into which placental or eutherian mammals are placed. We share characteristics with monkeys and apes and our closest relatives are great apes, like the chimpanzee or gorilla.

Placental mammals
Their young are born in a fully developed state.

Marsupials
The embryo completes its development outside the womb.

Mammals
Their young feed on their mother's milk.

Birds and reptiles
Oviparous species.

Monotremes
The only oviparous mammals. They are the most primitive form of mammals.

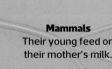

5,416

species of mammals are included in the three groups.

Tortoise
Reptile with the longest lifespan.

Crocodiles
Live in both fresh and saltwater.

Squamata
Includes lizards and snakes.

7

LAUNCH OF VOSTOK 1
The launch of the Soviet Spaceship
Vostok 1, on board which Yuri Gagarin
became the first cosmonaut to orbit
the Earth.

THE
CONQUEST
OF SPACE

Humankind's space adventure began with Yuri Gagarin, the first Russian cosmonaut, who managed to orbit the Earth at an altitude of 176 miles (327 km) on board *Vostok 1* on April 12, 1961. He had virtually no control over the craft, which was operated remotely by Soviet engineers. The next step gave the Americans the first man on the Moon: Neil Armstrong, followed by Edwin "Buzz" Aldrin. The success of the *Apollo 11* mission marked the culmination of a long and expensive space project that aimed to explore the only natural satellite of Earth. Today, thanks to ground- and space-based observatories, it is possible to gather information that some day will help uncover the unresolved mysteries of the Universe.

Space Exploration

The space age began in 1957 with the launch of the first artificial satellite. Today, advances in astronautics have helped develop the autonomous navigation system, by which a ship may orbit a planet by itself. An example is the *Mars Express*, launched in 2003 and powered exclusively by solar energy. It explored a number of objectives and took pictures of Mars.

Auto Navigation System

Unmanned spacecraft, such as satellites orbiting the planets, transmit their data back to Earth with radio equipment whose coverage depends on their type of orbit. Probes are used to land on the surface, as has been done on Venus, Mars, and the Moon. The real work begins when the unit reaches its target. The instruments are activated and collect data that are sent to Earth for analysis.

Solar panel
Provides energy for navigation.

Fuel tanks
Hold 71 gallons (267 liters) of propellant each.

Thrusters
Used to correct the orbit.

CONVENTIONAL NAVIGATION
During the rendezvous, optical navigation based on Earth is limited by the time the light takes to make the return trip to the ship.

Navigation systems based on Earth require radio tracking.

The pictures taken are transmitted to Earth and navigation commands are sent to the spacecraft.

2 The probe deployed its solar panels and began a life of its own, using solar energy. It sent signals to Earth to check the correct operation of the instruments.

LAUNCH

LAUNCH

The maneuvers are calculated in the ground station and the parameters are transmitted to the spacecraft.

1 On June 2, 2003 *Mars Express* took off with a *Soyuz* rocket from Kazakhstan. Once it had escaped Earth's orbit, the probe separated from its thrusters and began its path to Mars's orbit .

4 Data transmission to Earth occurs when the probe is at the maximum height of its orbit around Mars. At that time, it stops pointing toward the red planet and directs the high-gain antenna toward Earth. *Mars Express* began orbiting Mars in December 2003 and continues today.

High-gain antenna
To communicate with Earth when it is farther away.

3 *Mars Express* started its journey to Mars, which would last almost seven months. From Darmstadt, Germany, its activity was monitored in the Mission's Control Center, which established radio communication with the probe.

Space programs

Space probes are automatic vehicles. Some just pass by the planet they are studying at some distance, and others are placed in planetary orbit (orbiters), from where they can send smaller probes out to land. Manned spacecraft, on the other hand, demand design conditions related to survival, navigation, control, and transmission.

SPACEWALK
To collect more information, astronauts perform spacewalks outside the ship.

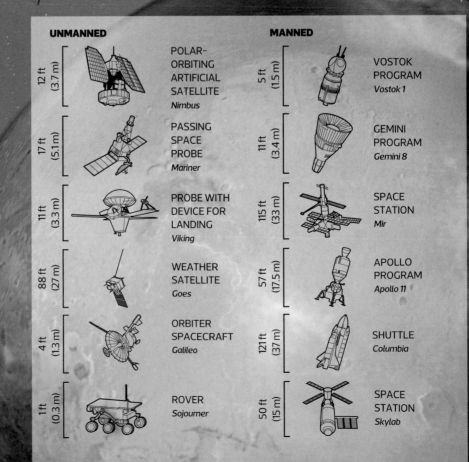

UNMANNED		MANNED	
12 ft (3.7 m)	POLAR-ORBITING ARTIFICIAL SATELLITE *Nimbus*	5 ft (1.5 m)	VOSTOK PROGRAM *Vostok 1*
17 ft (5.1 m)	PASSING SPACE PROBE *Mariner*	11 ft (3.4 m)	GEMINI PROGRAM *Gemini 8*
11 ft (3.3 m)	PROBE WITH DEVICE FOR LANDING *Viking*	115 ft (33 m)	SPACE STATION *Mir*
88 ft (27 m)	WEATHER SATELLITE *Goes*	57 ft (17.5 m)	APOLLO PROGRAM *Apollo 11*
4 ft (1.3 m)	ORBITER SPACECRAFT *Galileo*	121 ft (37 m)	SHUTTLE *Columbia*
1 ft (0.3 m)	ROVER *Sojourner*	50 ft (15 m)	SPACE STATION *Skylab*

The Space Race

Astronautics came about in the late nineteenth century, when the Russian Konstantin Tsiolkovsky (1857–1935) foresaw the ability of a rocket to overcome the force of gravity. But the space race, the rivalry between world powers to conquer space, officially began in 1957 with the launch of the first Soviet artificial satellite, *Sputnik I*.

Sputnik I

It consisted of an aluminum sphere of 2 ft (58 cm) in diameter, and for 21 days sent information on cosmic radiation, meteorites, and the density and temperature of the Earth's upper atmosphere. It was destroyed by aerodynamic drag upon entering the atmosphere 57 days later.

THE FIRST
In 1917 in Germany, Romanian Hermann Oberth (1894–1989) suggested a liquid-fueled rocket, which promoted the idea of spaceflight.

THE SECOND
American Robert Goddard (1882–1945) designed a rocket 10 ft (3 m) high. On ignition, it rose to 39 ft (12 m) and then crashed 184 ft (56 m) away.

THE THIRD
German physicist Wernher von Braun (1912–77), created the *Saturn V* rocket for NASA: the rocket that took men to the moon in 1969 and 1972.

TECHNICAL DATA SHEET

Launch	
October 1957	
Orbital altitude 373 miles (600 km)	
Orbital period 97 minutes	
Weight 184 lb (83.6 kg)	
Country U.S.S.R.	

Antennae
Sputnik I had four antennae of between 8 and 9.5 ft (2.4 and 2.9 m) in length.

1609
GALILEO
Built the first astronomical telescope and observed lunar craters.

1798
CAVENDISH
Showed that the law of gravity is true for any pair of bodies.

1806
ROCKETS
The British Navy used rockets as military weapons.

1838
DISTANCE
The distance to the star 61 Cygni, taking Earth's orbit as a reference, was measured.

1926
FIRST ROCKET
Robert Goddard launched the first liquid-fueled rocket.

Sputnik II

It was the second satellite launched into Earth orbit by the Russians and the first to carry a living being on board: the dog Laika. The dog was connected to a machine that recorded its vital signs, and an air-regeneration system provided it with oxygen.

TECHNICAL DATA SHEET

Launch	November 1957
Orbital altitude	1,030 miles (1,660 km)
Orbital period	103.7 minutes
Weight	1,120 lb (508 kg)
Country	U.S.S.R.

WEIGHT ON THE GROUND
1.120 lb
(508 kg)

13 ft (4 m)

6 ft 6 in (2 m)

- Aerodynamic nose cone
- Mechanism for expelling the nose cone
- Scientific instruments
- Radio transmitter
- Heat shield
- Ventilator
- Safety ring
- Retro boosters
- Telecommunications antenna
- Support structure
- Pressurized cabin

Laika the dog

Explorer I

The United States developed its first satellite, *Explorer I*, in 1958, launched from Cape Canaveral. It was a small cylindrical vessel 6 in (15 cm) in diameter that measured cosmic radiation and meteorites for 112 days, allowing the discovery of the Van Allen Belts.

WEIGHT ON THE GROUND
184 lb
(83.6 kg)

2 ft 7 in (0.58 m)

- Antenna with cable
- Micrometeorite detectors
- Nose cone
- Long-range transmitter
- Internal temperature indicator
- Fiberglass ring

TECHNICAL DATA SHEET

Launch	February 1958
Orbital altitude	1,585 miles (2,550 km)
Orbital period	114.8 minutes
Weight	31 lb (14 kg)
Organization	NASA

WEIGHT ON THE GROUND
31 lb
(14 kg)

2 ft (0.8 m)

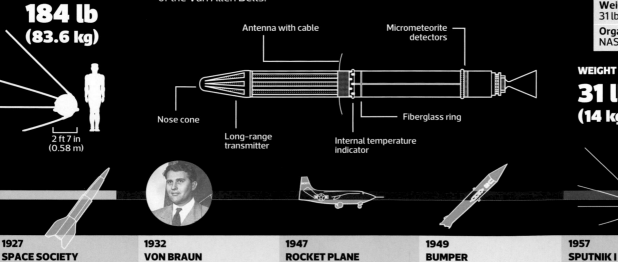

1927
SPACE SOCIETY
The Society for Space Travel was founded on July 5 in Germany.

1932
VON BRAUN
He began his research on rockets for the German army.

1947
ROCKET PLANE
Chuck Yeager broke the sound barrier aboard the X-1 rocket plane.

1949
BUMPER
First two-stage rocket, which reached an altitude of 244 miles (393 km).

1957
SPUTNIK I
On October 4, the Soviet Union launched the first satellite into space.

NASA

The National Aeronautics and Space Administration (NASA) is the U.S. space agency. It was created in 1958 as part of the "space race" being contested with the then Soviet Union, and it scheduled all national activities related to space exploration. NASA has a launch center (Kennedy Space Center) and several facilities throughout the country.

NASA bases

NASA has facilities throughout the United States, which develop research, flight simulation, and astronaut training. NASA headquarters are in Washington D.C., and the Flight Control Center is in Houston, which is one of the locations where the Deep Space Network operates. It is a communications system with three locations in the world: Houston, Madrid, and Canberra, which can capture signals in all directions and covers 100 percent of the Earth's surface.

AMES RESEARCH CENTER
Founded in 1939, it is the experimental base for many missions. It is equipped with simulators and advanced technology.

LYNDON B. JOHNSON CONTROL CENTER
The center at Houston selects and trains astronauts and controls the takeoff and landing of flights.

MARSHALL SPACE FLIGHT CENTER
Handles equipment transport, propulsion systems, and space shuttle launch operations.

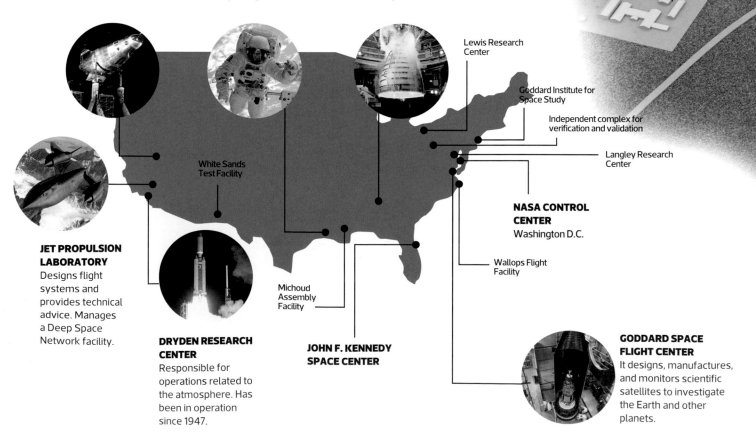

Indian River

SHUTTLE LANDING FACILITY

Visitor Complex

Lewis Research Center

Goddard Institute for Space Study

Independent complex for verification and validation

Langley Research Center

NASA CONTROL CENTER
Washington D.C.

Wallops Flight Facility

White Sands Test Facility

JET PROPULSION LABORATORY
Designs flight systems and provides technical advice. Manages a Deep Space Network facility.

DRYDEN RESEARCH CENTER
Responsible for operations related to the atmosphere. Has been in operation since 1947.

Michoud Assembly Facility

JOHN F. KENNEDY SPACE CENTER

GODDARD SPACE FLIGHT CENTER
It designs, manufactures, and monitors scientific satellites to investigate the Earth and other planets.

Kennedy Space Center

The KSC is located in Merritt Island, near Cape Canaveral, Florida. It measures 33 miles (54 km) long, covers an area of 136 sq miles (352 km²) and employs almost 17,000 people. It was established as the launch center on July 1, 1962. KSC launched the *Apollo 11* mission that led to man walking on the moon. It also hosted the takeoff and landing of the space shuttle.

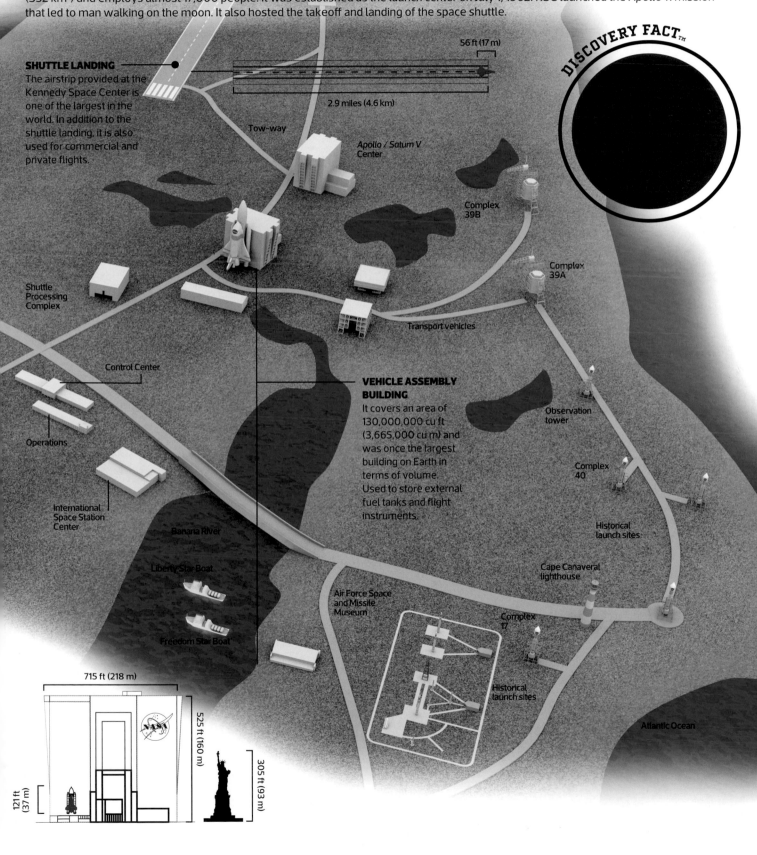

DISCOVERY FACT™

SHUTTLE LANDING
The airstrip provided at the Kennedy Space Center is one of the largest in the world. In addition to the shuttle landing, it is also used for commercial and private flights.

56 ft (17 m)

2.9 miles (4.6 km)

Tow-way

Apollo / Saturn V Center

Complex 39B

Complex 39A

Shuttle Processing Complex

Transport vehicles

Control Center

VEHICLE ASSEMBLY BUILDING
It covers an area of 130,000,000 cu ft (3,665,000 cu m) and was once the largest building on Earth in terms of volume. Used to store external fuel tanks and flight instruments.

Observation tower

Complex 40

Operations

International Space Station Center

Banana River

Historical launch sites

Cape Canaveral lighthouse

Liberty Star Boat

Air Force Space and Missile Museum

Complex 17

Freedom Star Boat

Historical launch sites

Atlantic Ocean

715 ft (218 m)

525 ft (160 m)

NASA

305 ft (93 m)

121 ft (37 m)

Other Space Agencies

Activity for exploration of the cosmos expanded in 1975, when the European Space Agency (ESA) was created. This intergovernmental organization has the largest investment budget after NASA. The *Mir* station, launched by the Russian Federal Space Agency (RKA), was 15 years in orbit and was a vital milestone for life in space. Other, younger agencies are Canada's CSA and Japan's JAXA.

Europe in space

The ESA was established as an organization in 1975, when the European Space Research Organization (ESRO) was merged with the European Launch Development Organization (ELDO). It has conducted missions of considerable importance, such as *Venus Express*, *Mars Express*, and the *Ulysses* probe, the latter in conjunction with NASA.

EUROPEAN SPACE AGENCY

Founded	1975
Members	20
Annual budget	4 billion euros
Employees	2,200

DISCOVERY FACT™

EUROPEAN LAUNCH BASE

Latitude : 5° North, 311 miles (500 km) north of the equator.
Being so near the equator makes it easier to launch rockets into high orbits. The area is almost uninhabited and free of earthquakes.

KOUROU, FRENCH GUIANA

Area	328 sq miles (850 km²)
Total cost	1.6 billion euros
First operation	1968 (as a French base)
Employees	600

THE ARIANE FAMILY

The development of the *Ariane* rocket has led the ESA to become market leader in launches. *Ariane* is chosen by Japanese, Canadian, and American manufacturers.

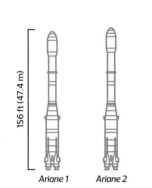

156 ft (47.4 m)

| Ariane 1 | Ariane 2 | Ariane 3 | Ariane 4 | Ariane 5 | Ariane 5 ECA |

Over 200

Ariane rocket launches have been made by the ESA so far.

Springboard
After covering 1.9 miles (3 km) at 2.2 mph (3.5 km/h), the *Ariane* is ready for takeoff.

Transportation route

Assembly building
Once assembly is completed, the rocket is transferred to the platform.

Toward the final design
The rocket is directed to the integration building to finalize details.

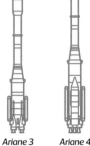

Canadian Space Agency

The CSA was established in 1990, although Canada had already developed some astronautical activities before that. The first Canadian launch was in 1962 with the satellite *Alouette I*. The most important project is the *Radarsat* CSA, launched in November 1995. It provides information on the environment and is used in cartography, hydrology, oceanography, and agriculture.

Russian Federal Space Agency

It was formed after the dissolution of the Soviet Union, and inherited the technology and launch sites. The new agency was responsible for the orbiting *Mir* Station, the forerunner to the International Space Station (ISS). The *Mir* was assembled in orbit by launching different modules separately, between 1986 and 1996. It was destroyed in a controlled manner on March 23, 2001.

РОСКОСМОС

Mir Station
Mir housed both cosmonauts (Russia) and astronauts (United States) in space.

Progress-M
Device for supplying food and fuel.

Solar panels
They provide power for the station.

Main module
For housing and overall control of the station.

Soyuz Rocket
Belonging to the Russian agency, it is used to launch a spacecraft into orbit.

Japanese Space Agency

Japan Aerospace Exploration Agency

On October 1, 2003, three independent organizations were merged to form JAXA: the Institute of Space and Aeronautical Science (ISSAS), the National Aerospace Laboratory (NAL) and the National Space Development Agency (NASDA). The highlight so far has been the *Hayabusa* mission, launched in May 2003. In November 2005, it became the first mission to land on an asteroid—the Itokawa.

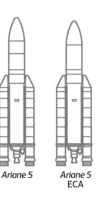

Russian Missions

After early successes with small animals aboard satellites, the former U.S.S.R. and the U.S.A. initiated the development of programs to launch humans into space. The first astronaut to orbit the Earth was Yuri Gagarin in 1961, the only crew member of the Russian spaceship *Vostok I*. Gagarin circled the Earth in the capsule, launched into orbit by a Vostok-K rocket, which allowed the cosmonaut to be ejected in an emergency.

Men in space

In *Vostok I*, the cosmonaut had virtually no control over the ship, which was operated remotely by Soviet engineers. The ship was made up of a spherical cockpit of 2.46 tons, 7 ft 6 in (2.3 m) in diameter. The one-man cockpit was mounted on the module containing the motor. Yuri Gagarin's reentry was made using a parachute.

VOSTOK I

Launch	April 1961
Orbital altitude	203 miles (327 km)
Orbital period	1 hour 48 min
Weight	11,000 lb (5,000 kg)
Organization	U.S.S.R.

11,000 lb (5,000 kg)
Weight on the ground

15 ft (4.5 m)

THE FIRST
On board *Vostok I*, Yuri Gagarin (1934–68) was the first person to go into space, which made him a national hero. He died on a routine flight aboard a MiG-15 aircraft.

THE FIRST WOMAN
The Russian Valentina Tereshkova (b. 1937) was the first woman cosmonaut. She traveled into space aboard the *Vostok VI* in 1963. The mission made 48 orbits around the Earth in 71 hours of flight.

SPACEWALK
Aleksei Leonov (b. 1934) was the first to perform a spacewalk, in March 1965. The ship that took him to outer space was the *Voskhod II*. In 1975, he was made commander of the *Apollo–Soyuz* mission.

Inflatable airlock

Nitrogen and oxygen tanks

Access gate

VHS antenna

Engine control

Retro boosters

1957
SPUTNIK II
Russian satellite launched November 3, with the dog Laika.

1958
EXPLORER I
First U.S. Earth orbiter satellite.

1958
NASA
Foundation of the U.S. space agency.

1959
LUNA I
Launched by the U.S.S.R., passed within 3,725 miles (6,000 km) of the Moon.

1959
LUNA III
Launched in October. Took pictures of the far side of the Moon.

1960
PUPPIES
Strelka and Belka came back alive from a one-day orbital voyage.

The Vostok program

Vostok (Russian for "east") was a Soviet space program that between April 1961 and June 1963 put six cosmonauts into orbit around the Earth. On June 16, 1963, *Vostok VI* took off carrying the world's first female cosmonaut, Valentina Tereshkova, on a joint flight with *Vostok V*, piloted by Valery Bykovsky.

VOSTOK MISSIONS PROGRAM

Vostok I	April 12, 1961
Vostok II	August 6, 1961
Vostok III	August 11, 1962
Vostok IV	August 12, 1962
Vostok V	June 14, 1963
Vostok VI	June 16, 1963

VOSTOK LAUNCH ROCKET

In order to leave Earth, the *Vostok* needed a launch rocket.

Nitrogen tanks

Cosmonaut

Cosmonaut ejection seat

Crew module

First stage

Second stage

Third stage

2 The separation is performed at 10:25 and the cosmonaut's reentry begins at 10:35.

3 The cosmonaut ejects from the rocket by parachute.

4 The cosmonaut is separated from the chair at an altitude of 13,100 ft (4,000 m).

1 The ship takes off from Baikonur cosmodrome in Tyuratam, at 9:07.

The route

After takeoff, it first crossed part of Siberia, then all of the Pacific, passed between Cape Horn and Antarctica and, after crossing the Atlantic, passed through the African sky over Congo. The capsule separated from the rocket carrier (which remained in orbit) while the capsule, with Gagarin inside, started landing. It came down in Saratov, about 460 miles (740 km) east of Moscow.

5 The cosmonaut lands in Saratov at 11:05.

1961
HAM
First chimpanzee sent into space on a suborbital trip.

1961
VOSTOK I
In a 108-minute flight, the Russian Yuri Gagarin orbited Earth.

1961
MERCURY
15-minute suborbital flight by Alan Shepard, from NASA.

1964
GEMINI I
Gemini I and *II* were launched unmanned in 1964 and 1965.

1964
VOSKHOD I
The first time that three crew traveled into space.

1965
VOSKHOD II
Aleksei Leonov took the first spacewalk.

United States Ships

Between 1959 and 1963, the United States developed the *Mercury* program. The ships were launched into space with two rockets: Redstone for suborbital flights, and Atlas for orbital flights. The Little Joe was used to test the escape tower and the controls to abort the mission. Before the first manned mission in May 1961, NASA sent three monkeys into space.

THRUSTERS

The Mercury experience

After the launch of *Sputnik I* in 1957, and in the context of the Cold War, the United States was quick to start its own astronaut program. The development of the *Mercury* spacecraft was the impetus for starting the *Apollo* project, announced as "Lunar Flyby" in 1961 and then modified, by the wishes of President Kennedy, to reach the moon.

HEAT SHIELD

DOUBLE WALL

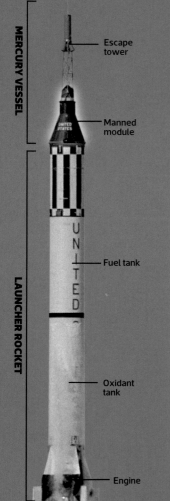

MERCURY VESSEL

Escape tower

Manned module

LAUNCHER ROCKET

Fuel tank

Oxidant tank

Engine

FIRST TESTS
The first space flights were made by animals. Ham was the first monkey to fly in space. Equipped with sensors and remote controlled, Ham survived life in space without problems.

THE FIRST
On May 5, 1961, Alan Shepard (1923–98) became the first American to fly aboard a *Mercury* spaceship. He then occupied important positions at NASA and in 1971 was part of the *Apollo 14* mission.

THE LAST
Gordon Cooper (1927–2004) was commander of the last *Mercury* mission, in May 1963, which lasted 22 orbits and closed the operational phase of the project. In 1965 he made a trip in the *Gemini* mission. He retired in 1970.

4,266 lb
(1,935 kg)
Weight on the ground

MERCURY

First tests 1959	
Maximum altitude 175 miles (282 km)	
Diameter 6 ft 6 in (2 m)	
Maximum duration 22 orbits (34 hours)	
Organization NASA	

1965
MARINER 4
Flew over Mars and took the first pictures of the planet.

1965
GEMINI 3
First manned flight of that program.

1965
DOCKING
Gemini 6 and *7* managed to find each other and join up in space.

1966
LUNA 9
First landing on February 3. Photographs were sent to Earth.

1966
SURVEYOR 1
First U.S. moon landing, on June 2. More than 10,000 photos taken.

1966
LUNA 10
In April, the U.S.S.R. sent another satellite, which sent radio signals.

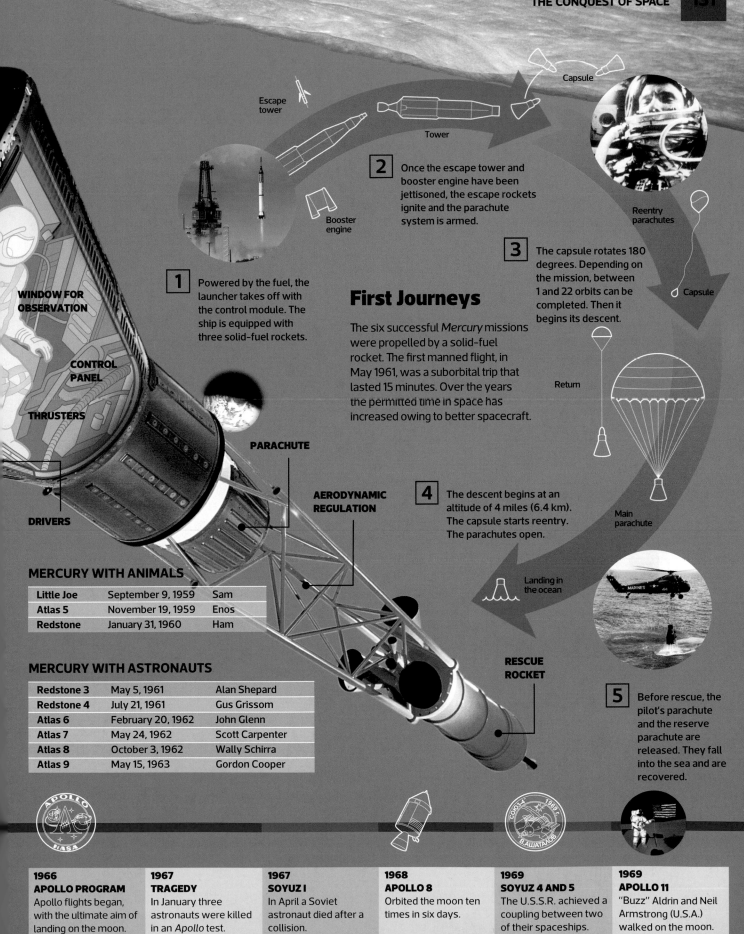

Escape tower

Tower

Capsule

2 Once the escape tower and booster engine have been jettisoned, the escape rockets ignite and the parachute system is armed.

Booster engine

Reentry parachutes

Capsule

3 The capsule rotates 180 degrees. Depending on the mission, between 1 and 22 orbits can be completed. Then it begins its descent.

1 Powered by the fuel, the launcher takes off with the control module. The ship is equipped with three solid-fuel rockets.

First Journeys

The six successful *Mercury* missions were propelled by a solid-fuel rocket. The first manned flight, in May 1961, was a suborbital trip that lasted 15 minutes. Over the years the permitted time in space has increased owing to better spacecraft.

Return

WINDOW FOR OBSERVATION

CONTROL PANEL

THRUSTERS

PARACHUTE

AERODYNAMIC REGULATION

4 The descent begins at an altitude of 4 miles (6.4 km). The capsule starts reentry. The parachutes open.

Main parachute

DRIVERS

MERCURY WITH ANIMALS

Little Joe	September 9, 1959	Sam
Atlas 5	November 19, 1959	Enos
Redstone	January 31, 1960	Ham

Landing in the ocean

MERCURY WITH ASTRONAUTS

Redstone 3	May 5, 1961	Alan Shepard
Redstone 4	July 21, 1961	Gus Grissom
Atlas 6	February 20, 1962	John Glenn
Atlas 7	May 24, 1962	Scott Carpenter
Atlas 8	October 3, 1962	Wally Schirra
Atlas 9	May 15, 1963	Gordon Cooper

RESCUE ROCKET

5 Before rescue, the pilot's parachute and the reserve parachute are released. They fall into the sea and are recovered.

| **1966** **APOLLO PROGRAM** Apollo flights began, with the ultimate aim of landing on the moon. | **1967** **TRAGEDY** In January three astronauts were killed in an *Apollo* test. | **1967** **SOYUZ I** In April a Soviet astronaut died after a collision. | **1968** **APOLLO 8** Orbited the moon ten times in six days. | **1969** **SOYUZ 4 AND 5** The U.S.S.R. achieved a coupling between two of their spaceships. | **1969** **APOLLO 11** "Buzz" Aldrin and Neil Armstrong (U.S.A.) walked on the moon. |

Man on the Moon

The space race culminated in Kennedy's words that pledged a lunar landing before the end of the 1960s and the subsequent successful arrival on the Moon. For the first time in history a man could walk on the Moon's surface, in a mission which, including both the journey and the landing, lasted one week. It was the first journey that used two propulsion systems: one for takeoff from Earth to the Moon and another to return from the Moon to Earth.

RADAR ANTENNA FOR COUPLING

CABIN

TAKEOFF

The module was powered by the *Saturn V* rocket, the heaviest ever built: almost 3,000 tons.

EAGLE LUNAR MODULE
It was divided into two parts, one for ascent and another for descent. It docked with the orbital module for the ascent and the descent.

DRIVE CONTROL ASSEMBLY

1 In 2 minutes 42 seconds the rocket reaches a speed of 6,090 mph (9,800 km/h) and enters Earth's orbit.

Launch platform

Stage 1

EXIT PLATFORM

The voyage

The overall mission lasted about 200 hours. Two modules were used for the trip: one orbital (Columbia) and the other, the lunar module (Eagle). Both were attached to the *Saturn V* rocket until just after the third stage. After reaching lunar orbit, the Eagle module separated, with two astronauts on board, and prepared the landing. The return took place on July 24. The stay on the moon lasted 21 hours 38 minutes.

OXYGENATOR TANK

Gyro

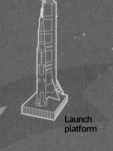

Stage 3

2 The second stage ignites and the ship reaches 14,290 mph (23,000 km/h).

360 ft (110 m)

Saturn V
The rocket was as high as a 20-story building.

EQUIPMENT FOR EXPERIMENTS

Linked modules

3 The orbital and lunar modules stay together until the trajectory correction.

4 After reaching lunar orbit, the Eagle module separates and prepares its landing.

LM–5 EAGLE

Moon landing	July 20, 1969
Height	21 ft (6.5 m)
Cabin volume	235 cu ft (6.65 m³)
Crew	2
Organization	NASA

Module

Correction

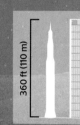

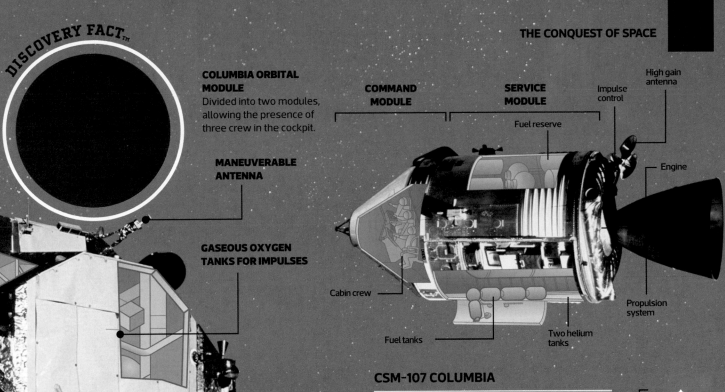

DISCOVERY FACT™

COLUMBIA ORBITAL MODULE
Divided into two modules, allowing the presence of three crew in the cockpit.

MANEUVERABLE ANTENNA

GASEOUS OXYGEN TANKS FOR IMPULSES

VERY HIGH FREQUENCY ANTENNA

FUEL TANK

UNDERCARRIAGE

COMMAND MODULE

SERVICE MODULE

Fuel reserve

Impulse control

High gain antenna

Engine

Cabin crew

Propulsion system

Fuel tanks

Two helium tanks

CSM-107 COLUMBIA

Launch	July 16, 1969
Height	36 ft (11 m)
Diameter	13 ft (3.9 m)
Cabin volume	219 cu ft (6.2 m³)
Crew	3
Organization	NASA

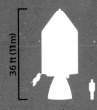

36 ft (11 m)

The crew

The three crew members had participated in the *Gemini* program, which was a very important preparation for the landing and moonwalks. Armstrong and Aldrin were the first humans to set foot on Earth's only satellite, while Collins orbited around the moon at 69 miles (111 km) away.

NEIL ARMSTRONG
(1930–2012)
In 1966, he made his first mission aboard the *Gemini VIII*. He was the first man on the Moon. He left NASA in 1971.

MICHAEL COLLINS
(b. 1930)
He was the third astronaut to perform a spacewalk, during the *Gemini X* mission. He was the command module pilot in *Columbia*.

EDWIN ALDRIN
(b. 1930)
He participated in the training tasks for the *Gemini XIII* mission, and was the second man to walk on the lunar surface.

The huge Eagle
The astronauts reached only a little more than halfway up one leg of the module.

21 ft (6.5 m)

The Apollo Program

Six *Apollo* missions successfully landed on the Moon. The exception was *Apollo 13*, which, after one of its oxygen tanks exploded, managed to return to Earth. Each trip, as well as providing data, drove the development of space science and increased the desire to carry out future expeditions to other parts of the Solar System.

The missions

The *Apollo* program began in July 1961. It was one of the greatest triumphs of modern technology. Six expeditions were able to land on the surface (*Apollo 11, 12, 14, 15, 16,* and *17*). Of the 24 astronauts who traveled there, 12 walked on the Moon. The *Apollo* Lunar Module was the first spacecraft without an aerodynamic design, designed to fly in a vacuum.

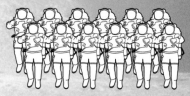

Twenty-four chosen ones
Apollo took six expeditions to the moon, with a total of 24 astronauts.

741 lb
(336 kg)

Lunar material
Moon rock samples turned out to be similar to the Earth's mantle.

16 miles
(25 km)

Route
This is the total distance traveled by the Lunar Rover on *Apollo 15, 16* and *17.*

301:51′:50″

Duration
The *Apollo 17* mission, the longest of all, lasted almost 302 hours.

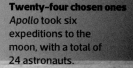

End of mission
The *Apollo–Soyuz* mission ended the lunar space race.

THE LUNAR ROVER
Electric vehicle used by the astronauts to explore the lunar surface.

High gain antenna

Low gain antenna

Television camera

Manual controller

Television camera

Communication transmission unit

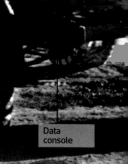

Data console

LUNAR ROVER

Launch	July 1971
Length	10 ft (3.1 m)
Width	3.74 ft (1.14 m)
Velocity	10 mph (16 km/h)
Organization	NASA

APOLLO MISSIONS

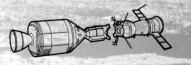

1970
APOLLO 13
The explosion in the liquid oxygen tank in the service module caused the early return of the crew, made up of James Lovell Jr., Fred Haise, and John Swigert.

1972
SAMPLES
In the last mission, the *Apollo 17* astronauts Eugene Cernan and Harrison Schmitt traveled around the Moon in the Lunar Rover and took rock samples from the surface.

1975
APOLLO-SOYUZ
The *Apollo* and Soviet *Soyuz* spacecraft performed a docking in space, in the first joint mission between NASA and the Soviet Space Agency. It was the last Apollo mission.

The Lunar orbiter

The *Lunar* Prospector was launched in 1998 and was in space for 19 months. It orbited the Moon at an altitude of 62 miles (100 km) traveling at a speed of 3,420 mph (5,500 km/h), and completed an orbit every two hours. Its purpose was to map the surface composition, possibly to recognize water deposits in the form of ice, and to measure the Moon's magnetic and gravitational fields.

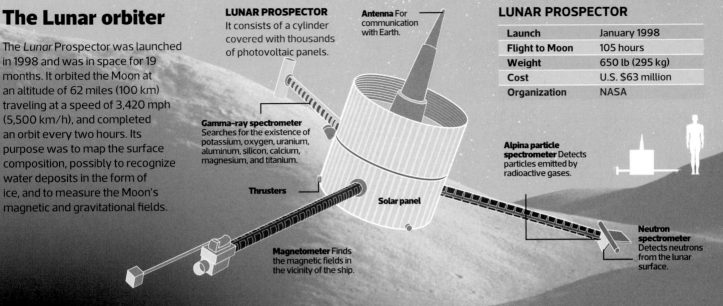

LUNAR PROSPECTOR
It consists of a cylinder covered with thousands of photovoltaic panels.

Antenna For communication with Earth.

Gamma-ray spectrometer Searches for the existence of potassium, oxygen, uranium, aluminum, silicon, calcium, magnesium, and titanium.

Thrusters

Solar panel

Magnetometer Finds the magnetic fields in the vicinity of the ship.

Alpina particle spectrometer Detects particles emitted by radioactive gases.

Neutron spectrometer Detects neutrons from the lunar surface.

LUNAR PROSPECTOR

Launch	January 1998
Flight to Moon	105 hours
Weight	650 lb (295 kg)
Cost	U.S. $63 million
Organization	NASA

End of the Apollo Program

After six lunar landings, the *Apollo* program was terminated. While *Apollo 18, 19* and *20* were canceled owing to budget issues, the program put the United States at the head of the space race.

WEIGHT ON EARTH
460 lb
(209 kg)

WEIGHT ON THE MOON
77 lb
(35 kg)

Collection bag for samples

James A. Lovell Jr. (b. 1928) Pilot of *Apollo 13*. The mission was aborted because of the explosion of a service module on board. Lovell was also an emergency pilot on *Gemini 4* and pilot on *Gemini 7* and *12*.

Harrison Schmitt (b. 1935) American geologist. He traveled aboard the spacecraft *Apollo 17*, the last *Apollo* mission, and was the first geologist and the only civilian to work on the Moon.

Aleksei Leonov (b. 1934) Russian cosmonaut. He was part of the test project for *Apollo* and *Soyuz* docking, which lasted seven days. Aboard the *Voskhod II*, he was the first person to walk in space.

LATER MISSIONS

1994 CLEMENTINE
The *Clementine* spacecraft orbited the Moon and mapped its surface. It also transmitted radio signals into the shadowed craters near its South Pole.

2003 SMART
ESA launched the *Smart 1*, its first unmanned spacecraft bound for the moon. Its aim was to analyze unexplored regions and test new technologies.

2009 LRO
NASA launched a rocket carrying the *Lunar Reconnaissance Orbiter* spacecraft in order to search for ice in the polar regions of the Moon.

The Paranal Observatory

The Very Large Telescope (VLT) is the most advanced astronomical observatory in the world. It has four telescopes that make it possible, for example, to see the flame of a candle on the surface of the moon. It is operated by a scientific consortium composed of fifteen countries, and one of its objectives is to find new worlds around other stars.

DOME
Protects and perceives any climate change through thermal sensors.

WEATHER CONDITIONS

The Cerro Paranal in northern Chile is located in the driest part of the Atacama Desert, where conditions for astronomical observation are extraordinary. It is a mountain 8,645 ft (2,635 m) high and offers nearly 350 cloudless nights per year, with an unusual atmospheric stability.

750 mbar
Air pressure

5–20%
Humidity

18/77º F
(–8/25º C)
Average temperature

0.96 kg/m³
Air density

DISCOVERY FACT™

Secondary mirror 4 ft (1.2 m) in diameter.

In history

Since ancient times men and women have observed the sky for answers. In all great civilizations we find examples of astronomical observatories that made it possible to gather knowledge of the Universe and gradually unravel its secrets.

2500-2000 BCE
STONEHENGE
Located in Wiltshire, U.K., it is an observatory temple from Neolithic times.

1000 BCE
EL CARACOL
Set in the Mayan city of Chichén Itzá, people worshipped the Sun, Moon, and Venus in it.

The complex

Finished in 2006, the very large telescope (VLT) has four reflecting telescopes, 27 ft (8.2 m) in diameter, that can observe objects 4 billion times weaker than can normally be seen with the naked eye. It also has four movable auxiliary telescopes of 6 ft (1.8 m) in diameter which, when combined with the large telescopes, produce what is called interferometry: a simulation of the power of a mirror 52 ft (16 m) in diameter and the resolution of a telescope of 650 ft (200 m), which could distinguish an astronaut on the moon.

215,000 sq ft (20,000 m²)
Total area

7,760 ft (2,365 m)
Altitude

OPTICAL ADAPTATION
To counteract the blurring effects of the Earth's atmosphere, the VLT has an active optical system featuring 150 pistons that move mirror segments to realign light into sharp images.

TELESCOPIC UNITS

Light tunnels for interferometry.

Auxiliary telescopic units (ATs)
There are four of these, each 6 ft (1.8 m) in diameter, and they are used for interferometry.

Melipal

Kueyen

Antu

Yepun

Rails to transport the ATs

THE TELESCOPE
The main feature of the VLT is its revolutionary optical design. Thanks to the active and adaptive optics, viewers get a resolution similar to being in space.

Mechanical structure

ACTIVE OPTICS

ADAPTIVE OPTICS

Light entering

Reflected light beam

Cell of 150 pistons

Curved mirror

Incorrect vision

Corrected vision

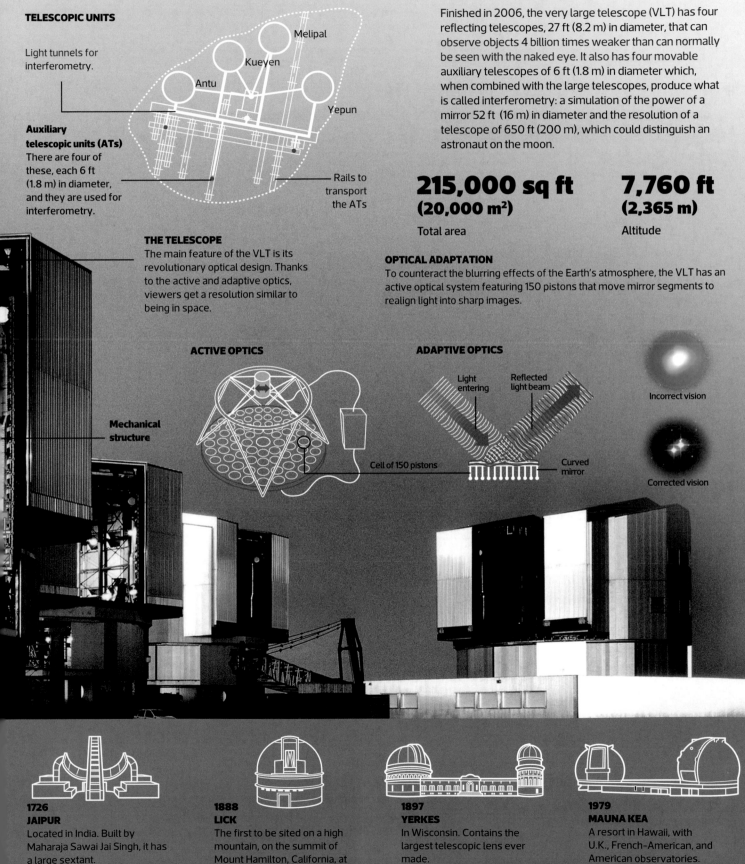

1726 JAIPUR
Located in India. Built by Maharaja Sawai Jai Singh, it has a large sextant.

1888 LICK
The first to be sited on a high mountain, on the summit of Mount Hamilton, California, at 4,265 ft (1,300 m).

1897 YERKES
In Wisconsin. Contains the largest telescopic lens ever made.

1979 MAUNA KEA
A resort in Hawaii, with U.K., French-American, and American observatories.

The WMAP Observatory

Thanks to the data sent in 2001 from the NASA observatory WMAP (Wilkinson Microwave Anisotropy Probe), scientists have managed to make the first detailed map of cosmic background radiation, something like the echo of the Big Bang. The experts' conclusion is that this map reveals clues about when the first generation of stars was formed.

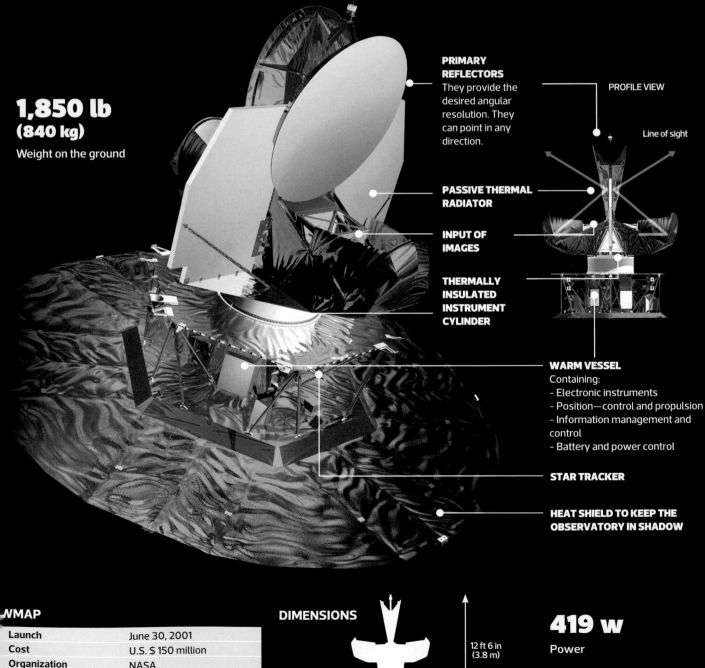

1,850 lb
(840 kg)

Weight on the ground

PRIMARY REFLECTORS
They provide the desired angular resolution. They can point in any direction.

PROFILE VIEW

Line of sight

PASSIVE THERMAL RADIATOR

INPUT OF IMAGES

THERMALLY INSULATED INSTRUMENT CYLINDER

WARM VESSEL
Containing:
- Electronic instruments
- Position—control and propulsion
- Information management and control
- Battery and power control

STAR TRACKER

HEAT SHIELD TO KEEP THE OBSERVATORY IN SHADOW

WMAP

Launch	June 30, 2001
Cost	U.S. $ 150 million
Organization	NASA
Working life	Nine years (until September 8, 2010)

DIMENSIONS

12 ft 6 in (3.8 m)

16 ft (5 m)

419 w

Power

Observation

In order to observe the whole sky, the probe is located at the so-called Lagrangian point L2, 900,000 miles (1.5 million km) from Earth. This provides a stable environment, away from the influence of the Sun. WMAP observes the sky at different stages and measures temperature differences between different cosmic regions. Every six months it completes a full sky coverage.

WMAP TRAJECTORY
Before heading to the L2 point, the probe performed a flyby of the moon, using its gravity to propel it toward L2.

PLAN VIEW
- Lunar orbit
- Rotational phase
- Sun
- Earth
- L2
- WMAP
- Encounter with the Moon

2 DAY 90 (3 MONTHS)
The probe has completed coverage of half the sky. Each hour it covers a sector of 22.5°.

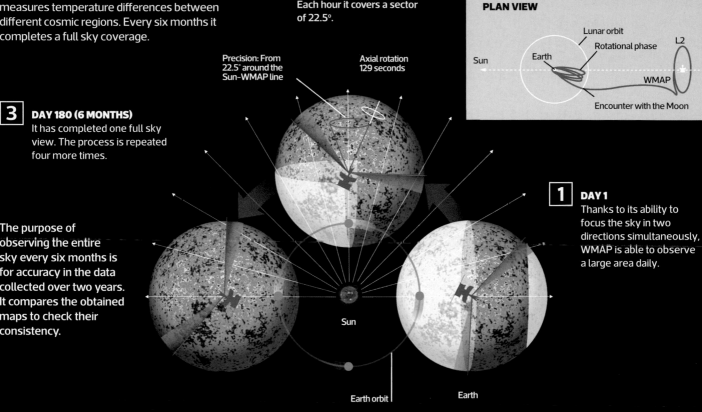

Precision: From 22.5° around the Sun-WMAP line

Axial rotation 129 seconds

3 DAY 180 (6 MONTHS)
It has completed one full sky view. The process is repeated four more times.

The purpose of observing the entire sky every six months is for accuracy in the data collected over two years. It compares the obtained maps to check their consistency.

1 DAY 1
Thanks to its ability to focus the sky in two directions simultaneously, WMAP is able to observe a large area daily.

Sun

Earth orbit

Earth

Map

The different colors of the regions detailed in the WMAP sky map are very slight temperature differences in the cosmic microwave background. This radiation, remnants of the Big Bang, was discovered 40 years ago, but can only now be described in detail.

Temperature difference between two points, measured by the WMAP

Regions with higher than the average temperature

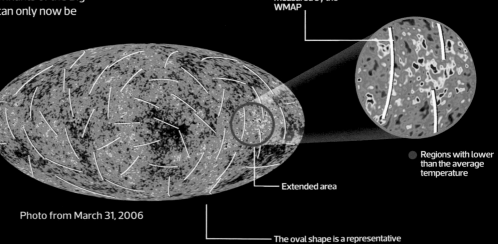

COBE, THE PREDECESSOR
COBE's results from 1989 provided the kick-start for the future. The resolution is much lower, so the spots are larger.

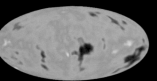

Regions with lower than the average temperature

Photo from March 31, 2006

Extended area

The oval shape is a representative projection to display the whole sky

8

SPACE SHUTTLE DISCOVERY
Space shuttle *Discovery* (partially visible by its heat shields, bottom left of image) is repaired at the International Space Station on its return from a mission in 2005.

SPACE
EXPLORATION

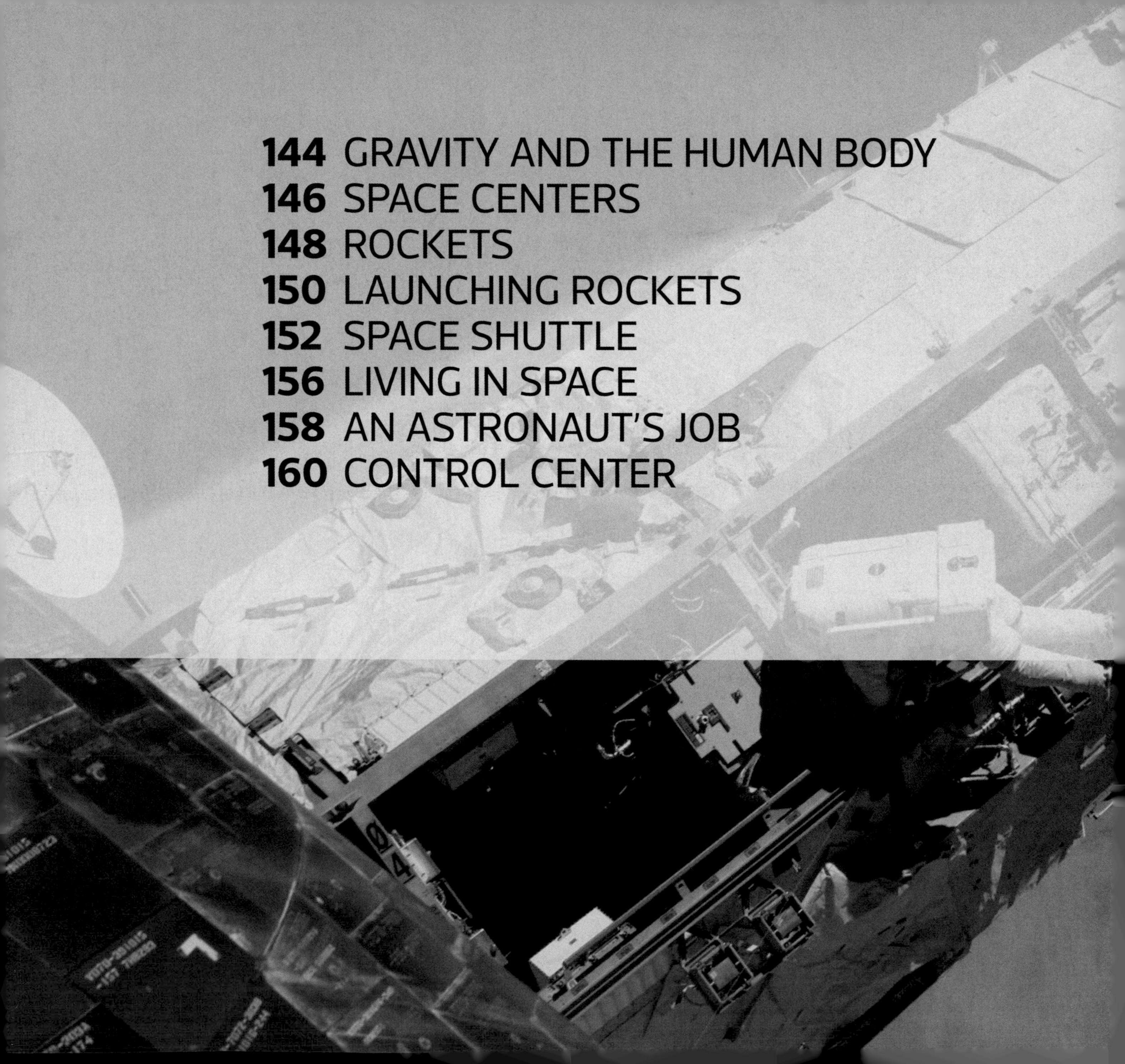

Equipped with vehicles that are increasingly smart and independent, human beings have exceeded many goals in their quest to explore the Universe, being able to discover new things about the origin and structure of other planets. On this journey, the space shuttle had become one of the key pieces of astronautics since 1981. There are still many problems to solve, but the future of the human species in the very long term is in space, and there is no other way but to keep trying. Like our ancestors, who emigrated to new regions of the planet to survive, our destiny is likely to be found outside Earth. When the Sun goes out, within six billion years, our only hope will be to find a new place to live.

Gravity and the Human Body

Astronauts must live for long periods of time in low gravity, which the human body is not accustomed to. Microgravity, among other things, lowers the astronauts' heartbeats, the muscles weaken and the bones lose calcium. Engineers and physicians collaborate with space agencies to investigate how to combat these effects.

Microgravity

Gravity is the universal force of attraction between two bodies, which depends on two main factors: mass and distance. The greater the mass, the greater the attraction, and second, at greater distances the attractive force decreases. This means that as we move away from our blue planet, this force decreases. Microgravity means an environment with "low gravity" ("micro" = "small"). Astronauts in orbit around the Earth do therefore experience less gravity, but typically only reduced by around 10 percent. Things seem to float because they are in a stable orbit, which is essentially a state of constant free fall.

DISCOVERY FACT™

Flying laboratories enable astronauts to experience "zero gravity" on Earth: NASA's low-gravity aircraft is unofficially nicknamed the "vomit comet."

ACTION AND REACTION
It is Newton's third law that says that when one body exerts a force on another, the latter exerts on the first a force that is equal and opposite.

ACTION
44 lb
(20 kg)

REACTION
44 lb
(20 kg)

LEGS
During weightlessness, legs lose mass through the lack of effort and muscle atrophy.

Parabolic flights

To investigate the effects of microgravity, parabolic flights are made with C-135 aircraft. The aircraft climbs at an angle of 47° until the pilot cuts the engines and the plane begins its "free fall," following a parabolic trajectory. During this phase, there is "zero gravity" on the aircraft.

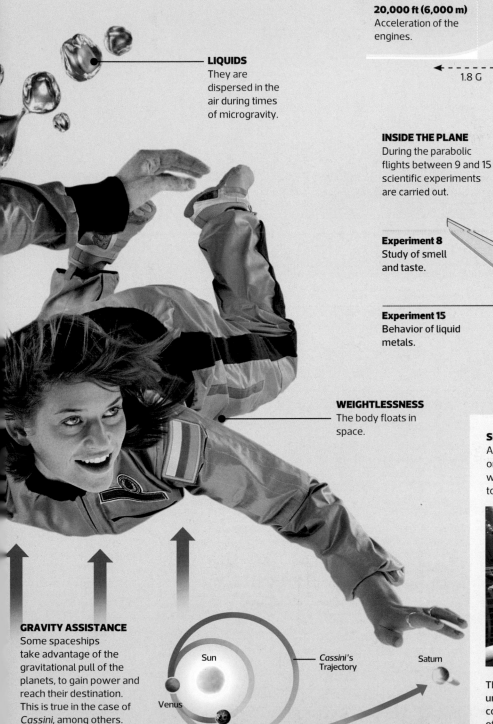

LIQUIDS
They are dispersed in the air during times of microgravity.

0 G

28,000 ft (8,500 m)
The engines stop.

The engines are started again.

25,000 ft (7,600 m)
Engine velocity is reduced.

31
flights per session

20,000 ft (6,000 m)
Acceleration of the engines.

1.8 G   1.8 G/ Microgravity   1.8 G
         1.5 G

INSIDE THE PLANE
During the parabolic flights between 9 and 15 scientific experiments are carried out.

15
in-flight experiments

Experiment 8
Study of smell and taste.

Experiment 7
Tests on a new shower system for astronauts.

Experiment 15
Behavior of liquid metals.

Free Flight Zone

WEIGHTLESSNESS
The body floats in space.

SIMULATIONS WITH WATER
Another method of training for astronauts is based on using a giant pool to create an environment where the weight is reduced by a similar proportion to the effects of space.

The Johnson Space Center has installed, completely under water, a simulator for testing the working conditions on the outside of the ship for members of the mission entrusted to repair the Hubble telescope.

GRAVITY ASSISTANCE
Some spaceships take advantage of the gravitational pull of the planets, to gain power and reach their destination. This is true in the case of *Cassini*, among others.

Sun

Cassini's Trajectory

Saturn

Venus

Earth

Space Centers

The launch bases for space rockets are often located in regions near the equator to facilitate launching of spacecraft. It is also better if it is a coastal site, to help the transport of materials, and it should have low population density to minimize damage in case of accidents during launch. One of these bases is the Kennedy Space Center at Cape Canaveral, Florida.

DISCOVERY FACT™

The Baikonur Cosmodrome in Kazakhstan was the world's first space center, built by the Soviet Union in the late 1950s, and it is still the largest.

Terrestrial platform

This steel giant is the point from which spacecraft take off. It is made up of fixed and rotating structures. The orbiter is transported from the assembly building to the terrestrial platform on a caterpillar carrier platform.

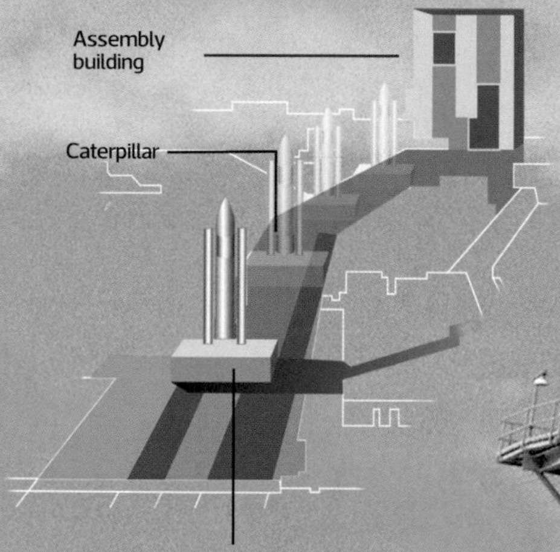

Assembly building

Caterpillar

Launch platform

ROTATING SERVICE STRUCTURE
It has a height of 189 ft (57.6 m) and moves in a semicircular path around the shuttle.

Assembly building

Spaceports have immense buildings where technicians prepare and assemble the rocket boosters and external tank with the shuttle. The dimensions of these hangars are amazing: they are 525 ft (160 m) high, 715 ft (218 m) long and 387 ft (118 m) wide.

ELEVATOR
Astronauts begin their isolation in the elevator. From here they go to the white room, and then into the shuttle.

LIGHTNING ROD
Protects people, the shuttle, and other elements of the platform against electrical shock. It is 348 ft (106 m) high.

FIXED SERVICE STRUCTURE
At 245 ft (75 m) high, it is spread over 12 floors. It has three arms that connect to the shuttle.

BOOSTER ROCKETS

WHITE ROOM
Exclusively for astronauts. From here they go on to the shuttle.

ORBITER ACCESS ARM

USA

NASA Endeavour

Floating platform

Some countries have developed projects for floating launch platforms, from which it is easier and safer to locate to the terrestrial equator. This is the place where the Earth's rotation speed is highest, which favors the launch of space missions into orbit.

Rocket

Platform

1 Assembly
A rocket is assembled in a mounting ship, 650 ft (200 m) long.

2 Transfer
The rocket is transferred to the launchpad.

3 Storage
The rocket is stored until the launch. The mounting ship floats away.

OTHER LAUNCH BASES
Spaceports are preferably located in close proximity to the equator because vehicles launched eastward from anywhere on this line travel with increased efficiency in terms of speed, cost, and payload capacity.

FIRST LAUNCHES FROM MAJOR BASES

Plesetsk (1966)

Kennedy (1967)

EQUATOR **Kourou** (1970) **San Marco** (1967)

REAR SERVICE MAST
These structures connect the platform with the ship. They provide oxygen and hydrogen to the external tank.

130 ft (40 m)

SHUTTLE CRAWLER
The orbiter moves to the platform on twin caterpillar tracks. A laser system guides it accurately at a speed of 2 mph (3.2 km/h).

Rockets

Developed in the first half of the twentieth century, rockets are needed to send any device into space. They have enough power to lift their load off the ground and soon acquire the speed needed to escape the effects of gravity and reach outer space.

ARIANE 5

First successful launch	October 21, 1998
Diameter	16 ft (5 m)
Total height	167 ft (51 m)
Weight of boosters	277 tons each (full)
Cost of the project	7 billion euros
Maximum load	13,670 lb (6,200 kg)
Organization	ESA

BOEING AIRCRAFT — 233 ft (71 m)

ARIANE 5 — 167 ft (51 m)

SPACE SHUTTLE — 121 ft (37 m)

25,054 mph (40,320 km/h)
Escape velocity of Earth

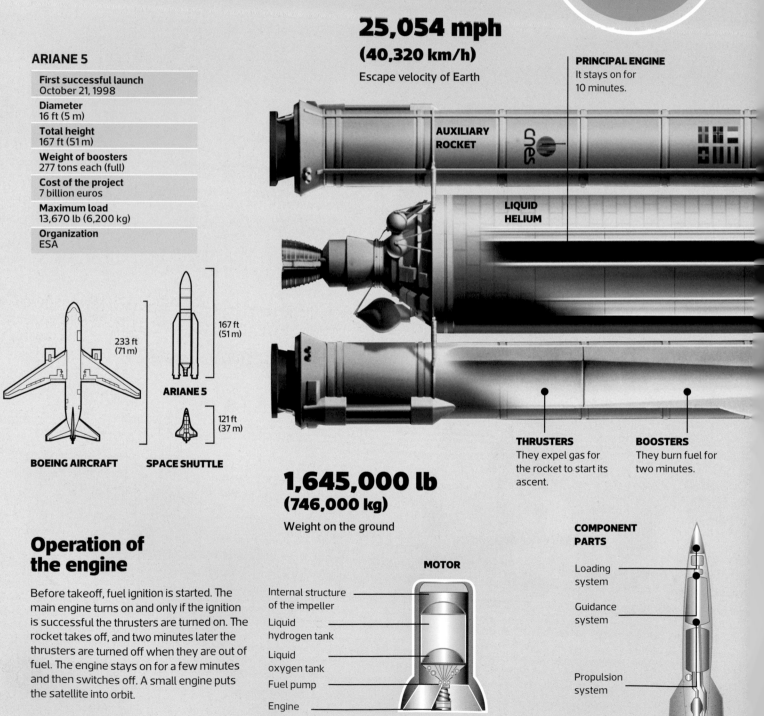

PRINCIPAL ENGINE
It stays on for 10 minutes.

AUXILIARY ROCKET

LIQUID HELIUM

THRUSTERS
They expel gas for the rocket to start its ascent.

BOOSTERS
They burn fuel for two minutes.

1,645,000 lb (746,000 kg)
Weight on the ground

Operation of the engine

Before takeoff, fuel ignition is started. The main engine turns on and only if the ignition is successful the thrusters are turned on. The rocket takes off, and two minutes later the thrusters are turned off when they are out of fuel. The engine stays on for a few minutes and then switches off. A small engine puts the satellite into orbit.

MOTOR

Internal structure of the impeller

Liquid hydrogen tank

Liquid oxygen tank

Fuel pump

Engine

COMPONENT PARTS

Loading system

Guidance system

Propulsion system

CHEMICAL ROCKETS ACCORDING TO FUEL

In liquid rockets, the hydrogen and oxygen are in separate containers. In solid rockets, they are mixed and placed in a single cylinder.

Gases removed
• • • • • • • • ➤

LIQUID **SOLID** **HYBRID**

THERMAL INSULATION

To protect the combustion chamber from the high temperatures of the fuel burned, the walls are covered by the used rocket propellant. This cools the engine.

COVER

PROPELLANT

INSULATION

LIQUID HYDROGEN TANK

The main engine weighs 225 tons.

LIQUID OXYGEN TANK

Contains 130 tons for combustion.

CONNECTOR TUBE

UPPER ENGINES

They release the satellite at exactly the right angle and speed.

LOWER LOAD

Up to two satellites.

UPPER LOAD

Up to two satellites.

NOSE CONE

Protects the load.

How it works

As it rises, the rocket burns fuel and reduces its mass. As the distance from the Earth's surface increases the atmosphere becomes thinner, greatly reducing the effect of air resistance. In addition, the force of gravity diminishes.

ACTION AND REACTION

The thrust of the rocket is the reaction to the action of the burning fuel against the surface.

Thrust of the rocket

Gravity of Earth

TYPE OF ROCKET ACCORDING TO PROPULSION

The chemical propulsion rocket is the most widely used. It is driven by combustion. The nuclear type is driven by fission or fusion. The ion motor provides the possibility of electrically charging atoms by stripping electrons.

Thrust
• • • • • • • ➤

Electrons

Water or liquid hydrogen

Nuclear reactor

Fuel

ION **NUCLEAR** **CHEMICAL**

Launching Rockets

Now that over 50 years have passed since the first space flights, access to space has become almost routine. The amazing thing about space rockets, those colossal machines that involve monstrous energy levels, is perhaps that the technology, despite advances in computers, engines, and guidance systems in the second half of the twentieth century, has hardly changed from its foundations.

Launch sequence

It lasts six hours in the case of *Ariane 5*. The launch, at the end of the countdown, starts with the ignition of the liquid fuel engines. Seven seconds later the solid fuel lights. Before ignition of these motors, the flight may be aborted.

– 06:00:00
Start of the sequence

– 04:30:00
The tank starts to be filled

– 01:00:00
Mechanical reinforcements

– 00:06:30
Start of the synchronized sequence

00:00:00
The liquid fuel engines on the main stage light.

1 **00:00:07**
The solid fuel rockets light. A split second later (0.3 sec) the rocket begins to rise.

HOW IT IS ORIENTATED

The rocket has a computer with navigation data, which works in coordination with laser gyroscopes to maintain the flight altitude and direction.

Laser gyro

Electronic signals

Computer

Cardan gimbal joints

Inclinations of the nozzles

2 **00:02:10**
At an altitude of 220,000 ft (60,000 m), the solid fuel rockets separate and fall into the sea in a safe area.

FAIRING
They separate as the atmosphere becomes sparse, and therefore poses no risk to the payload.

SOLID BOOSTERS

They provide 90 percent of the initial push to get the *Ariane 5* to escape Earth's gravity. They separate 130 seconds into the flight.

363 ft
(110.6 m)

was the height of *Saturn V*, the largest rocket ever launched, which took men to the Moon.

3 **00:10:00**

The main stage, ignited at the "zero" of the countdown and powered by liquid oxygen and hydrogen, is separated and falls away.

FINAL PHASE
The final stage commences, the only one that does not ignite on the launchpad and has the job of firing the payload into orbit. It can run for up to 19 minutes, and may switch on and off several times to save fuel.

SECOND PHASE
Separates at an altitude of about 75 miles (120 km) and falls to Earth.

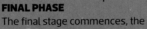

DISCOVERY FACT

A spacecraft needs a massive amount of heavy fuel to escape Earth's gravity, so to save weight it is built in stages that fall away as their job is done.

Stages of detachment

The *Ariane 5* rocket has three stages. On the launchpad the first two stages are ignited. In the ascent and as each section is consumed, they separate from the spacecraft through a series of explosive charges placed in the first and second stage. In the third stage the control elements and the cargo hold are housed.

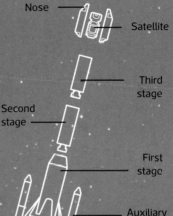

Nose

Satellite

Third stage

Second stage

First stage

Auxiliary rockets

Launch Window

The rockets are launched at specific times, depending on the objective of the mission. If it is a question of placing an object in orbit, the latitude at which the rocket is located must match the projection of the orbit sought. When it is also coupled with another object in space, the launch window may be only a few seconds.

STAGES OF THE ROCKET
It has two solid propellant motors. To get started it needs fuel storage and fuel elevators.

The final stage contains the payload and ignites once the rocket is already in space.

Second stage: this is the main stage.

First stage : these are the solid fuel rockets.

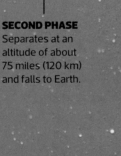

Rotation of the Earth

The latitude of the launch point

Launch window

Projection of the orbit

Planned orbit

Ideal trajectory

Space Shuttle

Unlike conventional rockets, the space shuttle could be used over and over again to put satellites into orbit. These vehicles were used to launch and repair satellites and as astronomical laboratories. The U.S. fleet has had five space shuttles over its history: *Challenger* and *Columbia* (exploded 1986 and 2003, respectively), *Discovery*, *Atlantis*, and *Endeavour* (retired 2011).

DISCOVERY

First launch	April 12–14, 1981
Orbital period	Between 5 and 20 days
Wingspan	79 ft (24 m)
Length	121 ft (37 m)
Organization	NASA

External fuel tank

Space orbiter

Auxiliary rockets

BOEING 747

STANDARD AIRCRAFT

121 ft (37 m)

SPACE SHUTTLE

SATELLITE
Stays in the cargo hold and is moved by the arm.

MECHANICAL ARM
Moves satellites in and out of the cargo module

25,575 lb
(11,600 kg)
Weight on the ground

SPACE ORBITER

COMMAND CABIN

Discovery

Cabin

Divided into two levels: an upper one for the pilot and copilot (and up to two astronauts), and a lower one where everyday work is done. The habitable volume of the cabin is 2,470 cu ft (70 m³).

CONTROLS
In the cockpit there are more than 2,000 separate controls.

Control keypad

Control cabin

Pilot's seat

Commander's seat

CERAMIC TILES
They are made up of layers that protect the spacecraft from heat.

Skin of orbiter

Adhesive felt

Silica fiber

Vitreous coating

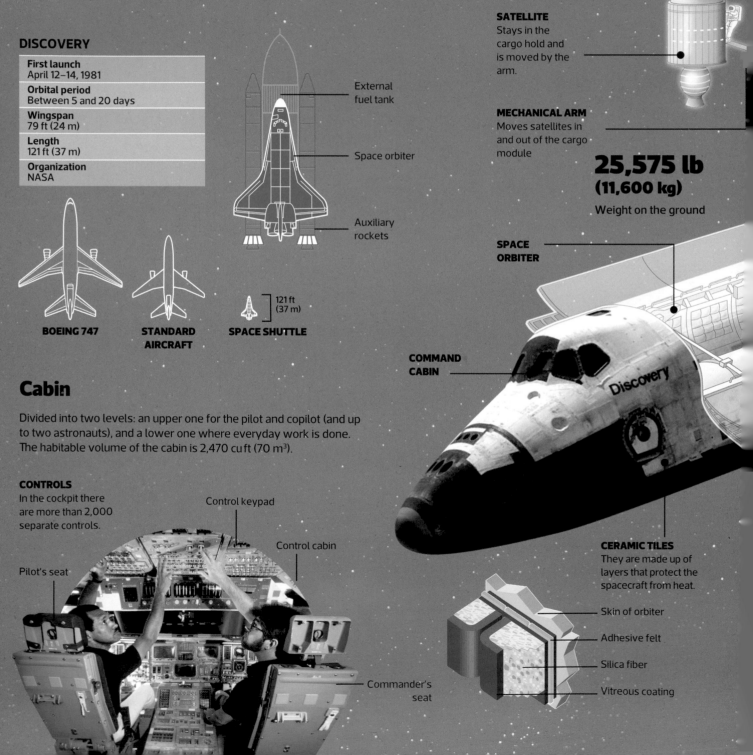

Liquid
oxygen

Liquid
hydrogen

The main engines

There are three of these, which feed liquid oxygen and hydrogen from the external tank. Each engine has a controller based on a digital computer, which makes adjustments for the thrust and correct fuel mixture.

MAIN ENGINES

Circulation of
liquid hydrogen

Heat
shield

EXTERNAL FUEL TANK
Connects the shuttle to the launcher rockets. Carries loads of liquid oxygen and hydrogen, which are combusted through a tube connecting each container with the next. The tank is lost on each trip.

ORBITAL MOTORS
Provide the thrust for orbit entry and orbital adjustments that may be needed. They are located on the outside of the fuselage.

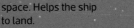

WING
Has no function in space. Helps the ship to land.

Thermal protection

When a shuttle reenters Earth's atmosphere, the friction heats the surface to temperatures of between 570 and 2,700°F (300–1,500°C). To avoid melting, the spaceship must have protective layers.

GATES
They open when the device reaches low Earth orbit. They are thermal panels that protect the spacecraft from overheating.

SOLID ROCKETS
They are designed to last about 20 flights. After each trip they are retrieved from the ocean and refurbished. They take the shuttle to an altitude of 27 miles (44 km) and on land can support the full weight of the shuttle.

Ignition
section

Solid fuel

Thruster
mouth

Felt. The heat is less than 700°F (370°C).

Metal or glass, no thermal protection.

Silicon ceramics. 700–1,200°F (370–648°C).

Carbon in areas above 2,300°F (1,260°C).

2,000–2,300°F (648–1260°C). Also silicon.

ORBITAL SPECIFICATIONS

Orbital altitude 193–329 miles (310–530 km)	
Orbital period 97 minutes	
Mean orbital velocity 17,275 mph (27,800 km/h)	

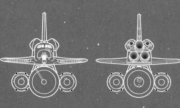

Front view   Rear view

ORBITAL MANEUVERING SYSTEM

00:02:00

27mile (44km) altitude is reached by solid rocket boost.

ROCKET BOOSTERS
They detach and begin their fall toward Earth. They are then reconditioned.

ASCENDING PHASE

The space shuttle rotates 120 degrees and rises inverted like that, with the crew upside down. It maintains this position until it reaches orbit.

00:00:00

1 TAKEOFF
The two solid fuel boosters and three main engines go into action. They burn 2,000,000 lb (900,000 kg) of propellant and the shuttle reaches an altitude of 27 miles (44 km). The solid fuel is completely consumed.

COMPARTMENT WITH THREE PARACHUTES
They are used for the detachment of the rockets.

CARGO BAY
Carries the device to be placed in orbit.

4.8 miles/sec
(7.8 km/sec)

Satellite launch speed

ROCKET BOOSTERS
Produce the essential first boost for takeoff.

EXTERNAL TANK
Holds the fuel to be used on takeoff.

SPACE SHUTTLE
Houses the astronauts and the cargo to be orbited.

00:08:00

The external tank detaches.

EXTERNAL TANK

Its fuel goes to the shuttle until just before reaching orbital altitude and speed. Then it detaches and is burned up by atmospheric friction.

CONTROL SYSTEM FOR ORBITAL MANEUVERING

Puts the shuttle into its proper orbit. Depending on the mission, it can reach an altitude of 685 miles (1,100 km).

Five to 30 days

2 **ORBIT IN SPACE**
After reaching the height needed for the mission, the shuttle remains in space for between 10 and 16 days, before positioning itself for return to Earth.

17,400 mph
(28,000 km/h)

Speed reached by the shuttle

3 **REENTRY TO THE ATMOSPHERE**
The shuttle suffers from a loss of communications as the temperature rises. They remain blocked until it begins its final descent.

Recovery system

Two minutes after liftoff, the booster rockets exhaust their fuel. They are ejected and deploy their parachutes to fall into the ocean. They are then picked up and transported by ship for refurbishment.

BOOSTER ROCKETS

4 **LANDING**
The space shuttle landing is fully automatic and comes into operation two minutes before returning to terra firma. On landing, it glides along a runway 3 miles (5 km) long.

2,700° F
(1,500° C)

Maximum temperature

20°

Landing angle

TURNS
Makes several S-shaped turns to reduce its speed.

DISCOVERY FACT™

At the end of a 30-year program, the final space shuttle mission ended when Atlantis landed at the Kennedy Space Center on July 21, 2011.

Living in Space

Leaving the Earth to live in a space station or make a shuttle journey implies adjusting to environments that man is not used to: no water, no air pressure, and an absence of oxygen. Everything must be provided on board: water is made electrically from oxygen and hydrogen, salt for food is liquid and waste is powdered.

Living area

The living module is located at the tip of the shuttle. On the upper level is the cockpit, and on lower levels, compartments for sleeping and living, and the hatch.

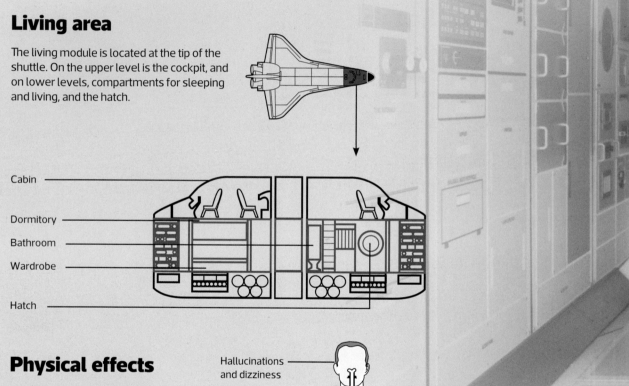

Cabin

Dormitory

Bathroom

Wardrobe

Hatch

Physical effects

Life in space can cause harmful effects on different body systems on returning to Earth. In many situations, living in confined spaces can cause psychological damage. In addition, the radiation emitted by the Sun can cause severe damage.

Diseased bone   Healthy bone

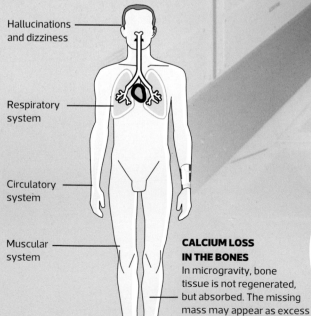

Hallucinations and dizziness

Respiratory system

Circulatory system

Muscular system

CALCIUM LOSS IN THE BONES
In microgravity, bone tissue is not regenerated, but absorbed. The missing mass may appear as excess calcium in other body parts (e.g. kidney stones).

HOME AWAY FROM HOME
Space stations serve as the astronauts' home for weeks or even months. This is a prototype of the space station's module.

DISCOVERY FACT™

Astronauts wash using special soap and shampoo that do not need water to rinse them off: they have to take care not to let the bubbles fly around.

90 minutes

Duration of the day in orbit

Sleeping bag

1 SLEEP
Once a day
In one space day the Sun rises and sets every hour and a half. Astronauts try to sleep eight hours a day, once at the end of each "Earth" day. They have to sleep tied up so they do not float away.

2 CLEANLINESS
They all wear the same clothes. After bathing, they change, because there is no way to do laundry in space. To go to the bathroom they use an air suction system, because it is impossible to use water.

3 FOOD
Three times a day
During the day, the astronauts have breakfast, lunch, and dinner. They have to be very careful putting the food in their mouths, and they have to drink plenty of water because they can suffer dehydration.

4 WORK
Eight hours a day
They work four hours on Saturdays, and Sundays are free days. During the week there is a normal workday. The most commonly performed tasks are maintenance and scientific experiments.

5 EXERCISE
Two hours a day
To maintain their health, astronauts must do physical exercise every day. As muscle is lost due to weightlessness, exercise helps maintain muscle tone.

Device to stop muscles degenerating.

Spacesuit for work in space

72
Variety of dishes

20
Variety of drinks

An Astronaut's Job

Before embarking on a mission in space, candidates must undergo rigorous tests, as the tasks they will have to perform are delicate and risky. They have to study mathematics, meteorology, astronomy, and physics intensively, and acquire familiarity with computers and space navigation. They also need to do physical exercise to help adjust to the low gravity in orbit and still be able to carry out repair work.

CAMERA
Color television equipment.

Unit for manned maneuvering

The training program is difficult and exhausting. Every day there are activities in flight simulators and simulations with specialized computers.

COMPUTER
Pocket communications equipment.

Visor

Digital camera

Image controller

FLIGHT SIMULATOR

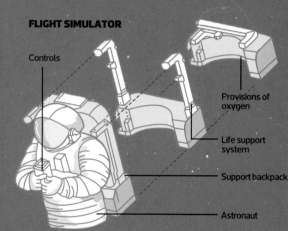

Controls

Provisions of oxygen

Life support system

Support backpack

Astronaut

OXYGEN
Enters through this part of the suit.

COOLANT
Provides a thermal layer and protection from meteorites.

1965
Astronaut Edward White used this spacesuit to make a spacewalk in the area near the *Gemini* rocket.

1969
Neil Armstrong wore this suit when he performed the historic first spacewalk on the surface of the Moon.

1984
Bruce McCandless conducted the first spacewalk without being attached to the shuttle in this suit.

1994
Space shuttle astronauts have suits that are much more modern as well as reusable.

THE HELMET
Contains a microphone for the communications equipment.

Plastic helmet treated to prevent fogging.

Snoopy cap.

Microphone

VISOR
For protection from the Sun.

ORIFICE
For entry and exit of water.

BELT
Holds the astronaut down to manage zero gravity.

GLOVES
To protect the astronaut's hands.

PARTS OF THE SUIT
The fabrics that compose the suit are specially designed to protect the astronaut's body.

FABRIC WITH WATER- CARRYING TUBES

NYLON

NEOPRENE

THERMAL COVER AGAINST MICROMETEORITES

RESCUE SPHERE
They serve to help crew with no suits. They are made of spacesuit materials and have a reserve of oxygen.

OXYGEN RESERVE

EXTERIOR

CARRYING HANDLE

Physical training

Represents the most difficult stage. To accustom the astronauts to conditions in space, they begin training in modified aircraft where they handle equipment, eat, and drink in a state of free fall to replicate weightlessness. The Manned Maneuvering Unit (MMU), with which the astronauts leave the ships to make repairs in space, has an underwater replica for prior training on Earth.

SIMULATOR OF SPACE OPERATIONS

GEARBOX
Used to move the unit backward and forward.

CONTROL PEDAL
Support for the astronaut.

Control Center

Astronautic activity is monitored in operation centers. In the United States, NASA manned missions are controlled from the Mission Control Center at Johnson Space Center in Houston, while unmanned missions are monitored from the Jet Propulsion Laboratory in Los Angeles. Flight controllers use telemetry technology to visualize real-time technical aspects.

Floor of Houston Space Center

It was first used in 1964 with the *Gemini 4* mission. The Operations Control Room has an auditorium, a screen with projections of the Earth with the locations of the stations and another with the passage of the satellites in orbit. Computers control each part of the ship.

ROW 3
Flight direction
Manage the countdown before liftoff and design the flight schedule.

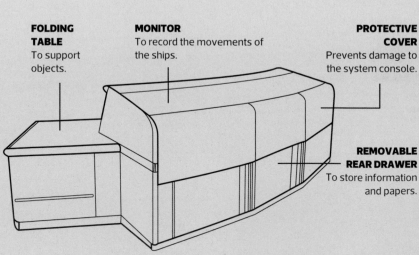

ROW 4
Directory
The highest authorities are located in the fourth row and they coordinate the flight operations of the crew.

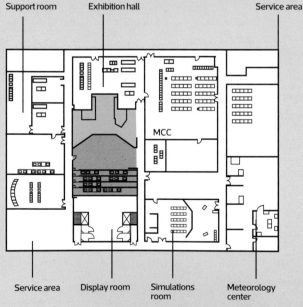

Support room

Exhibition hall

Service area

MCC

Service area

Display room

Simulations room

Meteorology center

The console

The controllers perform their tasks in consoles equipped with computers. There are around 100 consoles in the Operations Control Room. They are located in units containing two or more monitors. They also have drawers and tables to accommodate the workspace.

FOLDING TABLE
To support objects.

MONITOR
To record the movements of the ships.

PROTECTIVE COVER
Prevents damage to the system console.

REMOVABLE REAR DRAWER
To store information and papers.

365

days per year that
space controls are
performed.

The big screen

A huge screen is the focus of
the Operations Control Room.
It shows the locations of space
stations and performs orbital
tracking of ships in flight. It is vital
for operators, as it provides a quick
readout of the information to help
them act quickly and effectively, to
avoid any kind of accident.

SCREEN 1
Records the location of the
satellites and rockets that
are in space.

SCREEN 2
Shows the locations of
space stations as seen
from Earth.

ROW 1
Monitoring takeoff
It also controls
trajectory and makes
course changes to
ships.

ROW 2
Medical section
The second row
checks the health
of astronauts
and maintains
communication with
the crew.

Space Shuttle Control Center

It is smaller than the Houston center.
Every day 12 air traffic controllers work
there, increasing to 20 when a flight is
in progress. Each of the members has
a different job and they are organized
from back to front. The senior controllers
are in the fourth row.

Communicator
The controller
who stays in
contact with the
astronauts.

Flight Sergeant
The controller who
deals with all the
medical checks of
the crew.

Flight Director
Assists the mission
director in control.

Director of Missions
Has the ultimate
responsibility for flight
control.

VISITORS' ROOM
Contains 74 seats and is
located at the back of the
room.

24 hours

Operators work around-
the-clock shifts during
the mission.

CONTROL ROOM
With giant screen to
monitor flights.

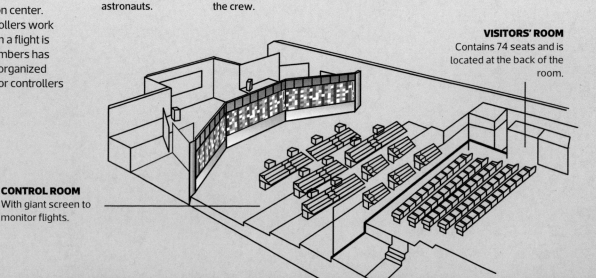

9

SPIRIT
Spirit, shown here with its panels extended, is one of the rovers charged with studying the surface of Mars.

SPACE
MISSIONS

Humans have managed to reach places in the Universe that were unthinkable barely half a century ago. Space probes have reached all the planets of the Solar System and have even moved to its extreme limits, sending images taken light years away back to Earth. Of all our neighbors, Mars is the most studied and visited. To investigate the surface of Mars, space agencies such as NASA and ESA have sent several robots, thanks to which large amounts of very interesting data have been collected, such as geological evidence of ancient environmental conditions where there was water, and life could have existed. Furthermore, space stations, observatories, and telescopes have been set up in space on a permanent basis, to help gather information.

Interest in the Planets

Ancient astronomers just saw points of light that appeared to move among the stars. These objects were called planets, and were given the names of Roman deities. In the sixteenth and seventeenth centuries, leading physicists were able to explain the behavior of the Universe. But it was only in the twentieth century that technological advances allowed detailed study.

Over 50 missions

have traveled to Mars, of which 16 have been successful.

MARS
The most visited planet and the priority of space agencies.

The Moon

The obsession to reach the Moon began with Russian programs in the late 1950s. In 1962, President John F. Kennedy announced that the primary objective of the United States would be to put a man on the Moon before the end of the decade, and in 1969 *Apollo 11* landed on the Moon, beginning a series of successful manned missions.

EARTH
Space telescopes like Hubble and the ISS (International Space Station, with astronauts on board) orbit Earth.

Earth's Moon

Extended area

Face of the Moon visible from Earth

Sea of Showers

Sea of Serenity

15   17

Ocean of Storms

Sea of Tranquillity

6

1   3

11   Sea of Nectar

12   14   16

Sea of Clouds

7

REFERENCES
In chronological order, the landings of the key missions to the Moon.

- Apollo
- Luna
- Surveyor

Mariner 10 took pictures of 57 percent of Mercury's surface.

MERCURY
Visited by *Mariner 10* and *Messenger*.

VENUS
Key missions: *Venera* (Russian program), *Venus Express* (ESA), and *Magellan* (NASA).

Martian surface

Chryse Planitia   *Viking 2*

Viking 1   Utopia Planitia

Olympus Mons   *Pathfinder*   Isidis Planitia

Valles Marineris   *Opportunity*   Gusev

Spirit

Sites of most important Mars landings.

JUPITER
Some probes passed by the planet and took pictures. *Galileo* spent seven years orbiting it and made the most thorough study of its largest moons.

Eight missions
have traveled successfully to Jupiter.

The Planets

From Galileo's observations to the construction of space stations capable of harboring life, interest in unraveling the mysteries of the planets has never stopped. The detailed study of Saturn's rings, patches of ice on the Martian poles, the exploration of comets and asteroids, and flying over the larger moons of the major planets are some of the latest milestones of space exploration.

Titan, Saturn's moon

TITAN
The *Huygens* probe descended to the surface of Titan, Saturn's largest moon.

Extended area

It is believed that this image is of a cinder-cone volcano.

Extended area

The atmosphere looks red

The surface is green and blue

350 photographs
were obtained by ESA from the atmosphere and surface of Titan.

SATURN
The *Voyager* and *Cassini-Huygens* missions studied its rings in detail.

URANUS
Voyager 2 took pictures of Uranus in 1986.

NEPTUNE
Only visited by *Voyager 2*, which took photographs in 1989.

12 missions
have landed on Venus.

PLUTO
Since 2006 this no longer officially considered a planet. *New Horizons*, launched in 2006, will pass by it in 2015.

The Sun

The Skylab space station collected more than 150,000 images of the Sun between 1974 and 1979. The *Ulysses* spacecraft, still active, has studied the Sun's poles and the effects of its magnetic field. For its part, the SOHO observatory studies the internal structure of the Sun and the origin of the particles of solar wind.

21 missions
successfully landed on the Moon.

DISCOVERY FACT™
Several spacecraft have successfully landed on Venus and transmitted data, but were quickly destroyed by its intense heat and atmospheric pressure.

Satellite Orbits

The space available for broadcast satellites is finite and could become saturated. Errors of 1 or 2 degrees in terms of location may cause interference between neighboring satellites. Therefore, their positions are regulated by the International Telecommunication Union (ITU). Geostationary satellites (GEO) maintain a fixed position relative to Earth. In contrast, those in low (LEO) and medium (MEO) Earth orbit require monitoring from ground stations.

Different types

The satellites transmit information of a given quality according to their position in relation to Earth. GEO orbits can cover the entire Earth with only four satellites, when lower orbits like the LEO need constellations of satellites to have full coverage. Both LEO and MEO satellites follow elliptical orbits.

ORBITS	LEO	MEO	GEO
Distance from Earth	125–1,865 miles (200–3,000 km)	1,865–22,400 miles (3,000–36,000 km)	22,400 miles (36,000 km)
Cost of satellites	Low	Medium	High
Type of network	Complex	Medium	Simple
Life of satellite	3–7 years	10–15 years	10–15 years
Coverage	Short	Medium	Continuous

INTELSAT

Polar Orbit

22,400 miles (36,000 km) altitude

GEO Orbit ▶

The geostationary orbit is circular. The period of the orbit is 23 hours 56 minutes, the same as that of the Earth. Its most frequent use is for television.

Equatorial orbit

LEO orbit ▶

Low altitude, between 125 and 1,865 miles (200 and 3,000 km). Was first used in cellular telephony after the saturation of GEO orbits. The orbits are circular and consume less power, although they do require terrestrial centers to track the satellites.

ELLIPTICAL ORBIT

Apogee
Farthest point from Earth.

Perigee
Closest point relative to Earth.

CIRCULAR ORBIT

Same distance

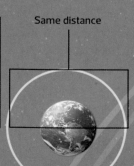

DISCOVERY FACT™

22,400 miles (36,000 km) is the required distance of a satellite's orbit so that it remains fixed with respect to Earth.

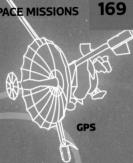

GPS

FREQUENCY BANDS
The satellites transmit information at different frequencies depending on their role.

L Band
For GPS systems, mobile phones and digital radio. It is the band with the lowest data transmission capacity.

K Band
Used for television and radio broadcasts.

LEO orbit

MEO Orbit

GEO Orbit

Ka Band
Used by space instruments for multipoint local transmission. It is the band with the greatest capacity for data transmission.

Orbital inclination 55°

GLONASS

SPOT

387 miles
(623 km)

MEO Orbit
Satellites in this orbit are in a range from 1,865 miles (3,000 km) up to the height of geostationary satellites. They follow an elliptical orbit and consume more energy than satellites in LEO orbit.

Earth axis 23°

11,800 miles (19,000 km)

64.8° orbital inclination

IRIDIUM

GALILEO

60° orbital inclination

HUBBLE TELESCOPE

A **First Van Allen Belt**
Between 620 and 3,100 miles (1,000 and 5,000 km) above the surface.

B **Second Van Allen Belt**
Between 9,320 and 18,640 miles (15,000 and 30,000 km) above the surface.

VAN ALLEN BELTS
These are areas of the Earth's magnetosphere where charged particles are concentrated. They are divided into two: an inner and an outer belt, with protons and electrons in spiral motion.

The Chandra Observatory

In July 1999, the *Chandra* Observatory was put into orbit. This telescope can view the heavens using X-rays with an angular resolution of 0.5 arc seconds, one thousand times more powerful than the first orbital X-ray telescope, *Einstein*. This feature allows it to detect X-ray sources that are 20 times more diffuse. The group tasked with constructing the X-ray telescope was responsible for developing technologies and processes that had never been applied before.

Five years
was the life expectancy of the mission, although this has already been surpassed.

Cutting-edge technology

The satellite system provides the structure and equipment required for the telescope and scientific instruments to work as an observatory. To control the critical temperatures of its components, Chandra has a special system comprising radiators and thermostats. The satellite's electricity is supplied by solar panels, and is stored in three batteries.

HOW THE IMAGE IS CREATED
The information gathered by Chandra is extracted into tables and images with coordinates on the x- and y-axes.

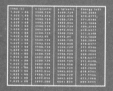

1 Table
Contains the time, position, and energy collected on Chandra's travels.

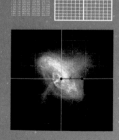

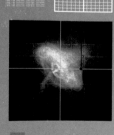

2 X-axis
The data extends horizontally through the grid.

3 Y-axis
The data extends vertically through the grid.

1 OBSERVATION
The telescope's camera takes an X-ray image and sends it to the Deep Space Network for processing.

Photographic camera

High-resolution mirror

Solar panel

4 hierarchical hyperboloids

X-rays

4 CHANDRA X-RAY CONTROL CENTER
Tasked with ensuring the observatory's functionality and receiving images. The operators are also responsible for preparing commands, determining the altitude, and monitoring the condition and safety of the satellite.

3 JET PROPULSION LABORATORY
Information is received from the Deep Space Network and processed.

CHANDRA X-RAY OBSERVATORY

Launch	July 23, 1999
Orbit height	65,438 miles (105,312 km)
Energy range	0.1-10 KeV
Cost	U.S. $1.5 billion
Organization	NASA

33 ft
(10 m)

10,560 lb
(4,800 kg)
Weight on Earth.

Spacecraft module

Solar panel

Deep Space Network

NASA's international network of antennae supports interplanetary missions orbiting Earth and radio-astronomy missions. It has three complexes, each of which have at least four Deep Space stations, equipped with ultrasensitive receiver systems and large-scale parabolic antennae.

Transmission grids

Optical array

Scientific instrument module

High-resolution camera

Goldstone complex in California, U.S.A.

Madrid, Spain

Canberra, Australia

Low gain antenna

Every eight hours

Chandra contacts the Deep Space Network.

THE ANTENNAE

Each complex has a system comprising at least four antennae.

- Antenna measuring 85 ft (26 m) in diameter.

– High gain antenna measuring 79 ft (24 m) in diameter.

- Low gain antenna measuring 112 ft (34 m) in diameter.

- Antenna measuring 230 ft (70 m) in diameter.

2 **DEEP SPACE NETWORK**
This network is used to communicate with the spacecraft and to receive information.

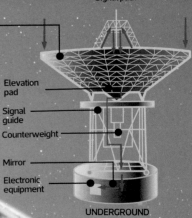

Signal path

Elevation pad

Signal guide

Counterweight

Mirror

Electronic equipment

UNDERGROUND

Space Probes

Since the first spacecraft, such as *Mariner* in the 1960s, the contribution to science made by space probes has been considerable. Mostly solar powered, these unmanned machines are equipped with sophisticated instruments that make it possible to study planets, moons, comets, asteroids, and the Sun in detail. One particularly renowned probe is the *Mars Reconnaissance Orbiter* (MRO), launched to study Mars from close up in 2005.

Mars Reconnaissance Orbiter

The main objective of this orbiting probe is to seek out traces of water on the surface of Mars. The probe was launched in summer 2005 by NASA and reached Mars on March 10, 2006. It traveled 72 million miles (116 million km) in seven months. The mission has been extended until October 2014.

72 million miles
(116 million km)

were traveled by the probe on its journey to Mars.

APPROACH TO MARS

It made 500 orbits

C Final orbit
It traveled along an almost circular orbit, suitable for obtaining data.

Orbit

Mars

B Braking
To get closer to the planet, the spacecraft slowed down over a six-month period.

A Start
The probe's first orbit traveled along an enormous elliptical path.

Mars's orbit

Sun

Earth's orbit

Mars

Earth

1 Launch
Took place on August 12, 2005 from Cape Canaveral, U.S.A.

2 Cruising
The probe traveled for seven and a half months before reaching Mars.

3 Path correction
Four maneuvers were made to ensure the correct orbit was reached.

4 Arrival on Mars
In March 2006, MRO passed into the southern hemisphere of Mars. The probe slowed down considerably.

5 Scientific phase
The probe began its analysis phase on the surface of Mars. It found evidence of water.

2,273 lb
(1,031 kg)

Weight on Earth

TECHNICAL DATA

Weight with fuel	4,806 lb (2,180 kg)
Panel resistance	Up to –328° F (–200° C)
Launch rocket	Atlas V–401
Duration of the mission	Five years (extended to nine)
Cost	U.S. $720 million

MRO   MGS   Odyssey

DISCOVERY FACT™

Mars is often described as the "red planet" because much of its surface is covered in fine iron oxide dust, which gives it a rusty appearance.

On Mars

The main objective of the *MRO* was to find evidence of water on the surface of Mars. In doing so, the evolution of the planet could be explained. The probe's devices facilitate high-resolution imagery of the surface and analysis of minerals. It also created daily climatic maps of Mars.

3,744

cells on each panel convert solar energy into electricity.

SOLAR PANELS
The probe's main power source is the Sun. The craft has two solar panels with a total surface area of 430 sq ft (40 m²).

Opening the panels
The panels are opened while in orbit.

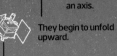

They also move from left to right.

Once unfolded, they use an axis.

They begin to unfold upward.

The panels are almost closed.

SHARAD RADAR

SOLAR PANEL

HIGH GAIN PARABOLIC ANTENNA
Its data transfer capacity is ten times greater than the capacity of previous orbiters.

SOLAR PANEL

INSTRUMENTS
Used at the same time, HiRISE, CTX, and CRISM offer very high quality information of a given area.

MGS
Observes Mars's atmosphere.

CRISM Spectrometer
Divides visible and infrared light in the images into various colors that identify different minerals.

HiRISE high-resolution camera
Provides details on geological structures and has considerably improved resolution when compared to previous missions.

MARCI
Provides the images with color.

CTX Context Camera
Offers panoramic views that help to provide context to the images captured by HiRISE and CRISM.

HiRISE
Mars Reconnaissance Orbiter (2005)

MGS
Mars Global Surveyor (1996)

12 in (30 cm)/pixel

60 in (150 cm)/pixel

HiRISE   **CRISM**   **CTX**

The type of image taken by the CTX that helps to provide context to an image taken by HiRISE.

Detailed image taken by HiRISE.

Robots on Mars

Spirit and *Opportunity*, the twin robots launched in June 2003 from Earth, arrived on Mars in January 2004. Both form part of NASA's Mars Exploration Rovers mission and are equipped with tools to drill rocks and collect samples from the ground for analysis.

Water and life on Mars

The main objective of the mission was to find evidence of past water activity on Mars. Although the robots have found evidence of this, they have been unable to find living microorganisms, given that the ultraviolet radiation and oxidizing nature of the soil make life on Mars unlikely. The question that remains unanswered is whether life may have existed on Mars at some stage in the past. And what's more, whether life currently exists in the subsoil on Mars, where conditions may be more favorable.

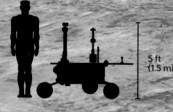

5 ft
(1.5 m)

342 lb
(155 kg)

Weight on Earth

TECHNICAL DATA

Landing date	*Spirit*: January 3, 2004 *Opportunity*: January 24, 2004
Cost of the mission	U.S. $820 million
Progress per day	330 ft (100 m)
Plutonium load	Each spacecraft carries a 0.1 oz (2.8 g) load
Duration of the mission	Spirit: communication lost in 2010 Opportunity: operational

HOW TO REACH MARS
The journey to Mars took seven months. Once inside Mars's atmosphere, a parachute was deployed to slow down the descent.

Aeroshell

Parachute

1 Deceleration
80 miles (130 km) from the surface, the aeroshell slows down from 10,000 to 1,000 mph (16,000 to 1,600 km/h).

2 Parachute
6 miles (10 km) from the surface, the parachute opens to slow down the descent.

Input module

3 Descent
The shield that offered the rover heat protection separates from the input module.

4 Rockets
30–50 ft (10–15 m) from the surface, two rockets are ignited to slow down the descent. Two airbags are inflated to surround and protect the landing gear.

5 Airbags
The landing gear and airbags detach from the parachute and fall to Mars's surface.

Descent rockets

6 Landing
The airbags deflate. The "petals" that protect the spacecraft open. The vehicle emerges.

Vectran airbags

7 Instruments
The robot opens its solar panels, the mast camera, and its antennae.

Photograph of the surface taken by *Spirit*.

70,000
images were obtained by *Spirit* during its first two years.

Rover footprint in photo taken by *Opportunity*.

80,000
images were obtained by *Opportunity* during its first two years.

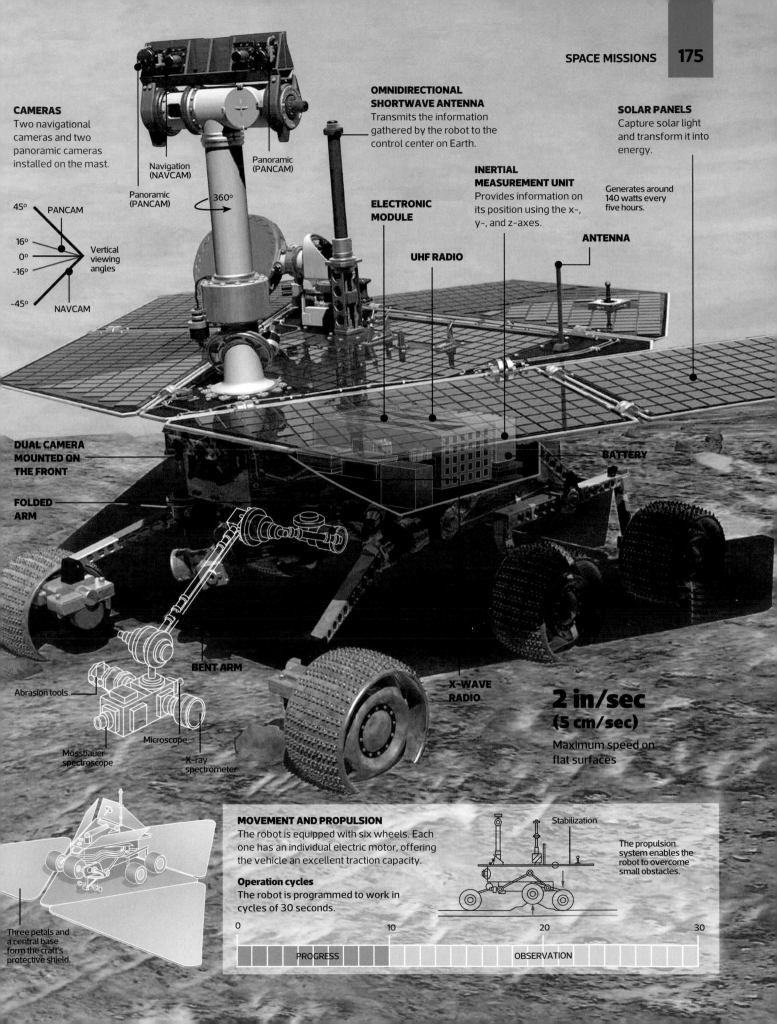

CAMERAS
Two navigational cameras and two panoramic cameras installed on the mast.

Navigation (NAVCAM)

Panoramic (PANCAM)

Panoramic (PANCAM)

360°

45° PANCAM
16°
0°
-16°
-45° NAVCAM

Vertical viewing angles

OMNIDIRECTIONAL SHORTWAVE ANTENNA
Transmits the information gathered by the robot to the control center on Earth.

INERTIAL MEASUREMENT UNIT
Provides information on its position using the x-, y-, and z-axes.

ELECTRONIC MODULE

UHF RADIO

SOLAR PANELS
Capture solar light and transform it into energy.

Generates around 140 watts every five hours.

ANTENNA

DUAL CAMERA MOUNTED ON THE FRONT

BATTERY

FOLDED ARM

BENT ARM

Abrasion tools

Microscope

Mössbauer spectroscope

X-ray spectrometer

X-WAVE RADIO

2 in/sec
(5 cm/sec)
Maximum speed on flat surfaces

Three petals and a central base form the craft's protective shield.

MOVEMENT AND PROPULSION
The robot is equipped with six wheels. Each one has an individual electric motor, offering the vehicle an excellent traction capacity.

Operation cycles
The robot is programmed to work in cycles of 30 seconds.

Stabilization

The propulsion system enables the robot to overcome small obstacles.

0   10   20   30

PROGRESS   OBSERVATION

Space Stations

Life on space stations makes it possible to study the effects of remaining in outer space for long periods of time, while providing an environment for carrying out scientific experiments in laboratories. These stations are equipped with systems that provide the crew with oxygen and that filter exhaled carbon dioxide.

Orbit
The ISS performs around 16 complete orbits of the Earth each day, at a height of between 208 and 286 miles (335 and 460 km).

The ISS

The International Space Station (ISS) is the result of the merger of NASA's *Freedom* project with *Mir-2*, run by the Russian Federal Space Agency (RKA). Construction started in 1998 and to this day it continues to expand, using modules provided by countries across the globe. Its inhabitable surface area is equal to that of a Boeing 747.

PROVISION AND WASTE
The Russian spacecraft ATV connects to the ISS, to provide supplies and remove waste.

ISS

ATV

TECHNICAL INFORMATION

Inhabitable space	29,560 cu ft (837 m³)
Speed	17,200 mph (27,700 km/h)
Measurements	360 x 330 x 100 ft (110 x 100 x 30 m)
Surface area of the panels	43,000 sq ft (4,000 m²)
Laboratories	6
Production	U.S.A., Russia, Japan, EU, Canada

ZVEZDA module

ISS

SKYLAB

MIR

ZVEZDA MODULE
The main Russian contribution to the station, the first living space. It houses three to seven astronauts.

Beds

Shower

Storage and kitchen

Control and communications area

Wardrobe

Connecting node between modules

The floor and roof are different colors, to facilitate orientation

Unfolding solar panels

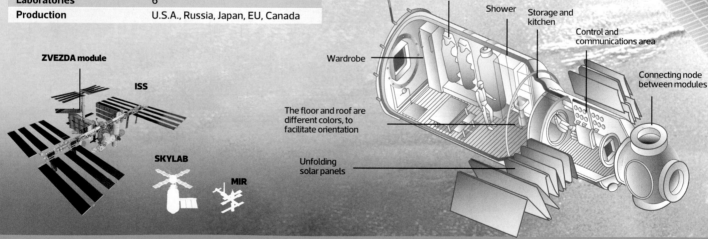

PHASES OF CONSTRUCTION

NOVEMBER 1998
Zarya module
First sector put into orbit. It powered the first construction stages of the ISS.

DECEMBER 1998
Unity module
Connection finger between the living and working area modules. Provided by the EU.

JULY 2000
Zvezda module
The structural and functional heart of the ISS. Fully built and put into orbit by Russia.

OCTOBER 2000
Z1 Truss and Ku–Band antenna
Neutralizes the static electricity generated in the ISS and facilitates communication with Earth.

NOVEMBER 2000
P6 Truss
Structural module that features radiators to disperse the heat generated in the station.

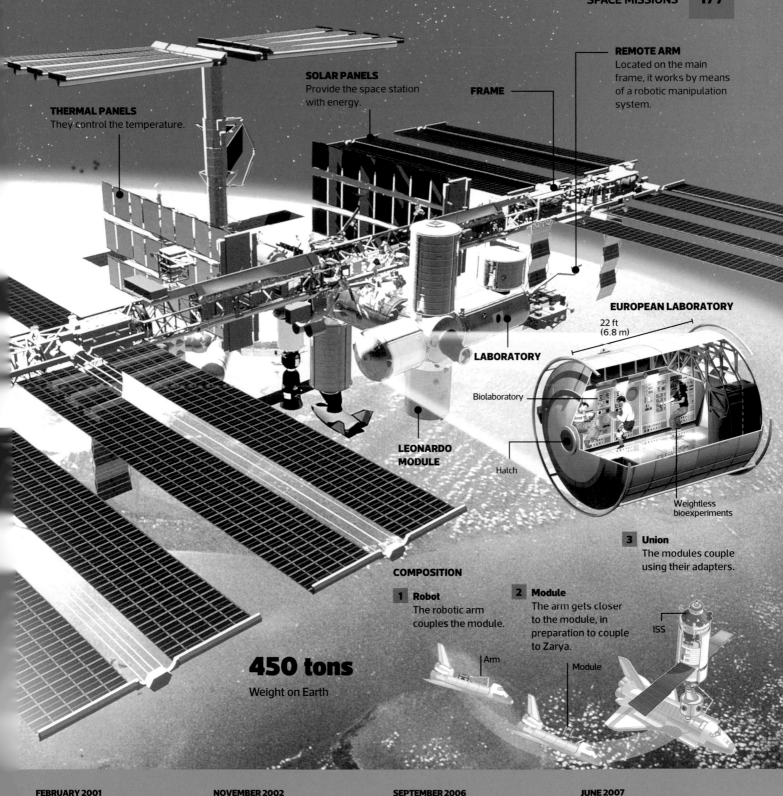

THERMAL PANELS
They control the temperature.

SOLAR PANELS
Provide the space station
with energy.

FRAME

REMOTE ARM
Located on the main
frame, it works by means
of a robotic manipulation
system.

EUROPEAN LABORATORY

22 ft
(6.8 m)

LABORATORY

Biolaboratory

Hatch

Weightless
bioexperiments

**LEONARDO
MODULE**

450 tons

Weight on Earth

COMPOSITION

1 **Robot**
The robotic arm
couples the module.

2 **Module**
The arm gets closer
to the module, in
preparation to couple
to Zarya.

3 **Union**
The modules couple
using their adapters.

Arm

Module

ISS

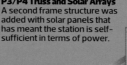

FEBRUARY 2001
Destiny laboratory
Central section. Different
scientific experiments
are performed in a zero-
gravity environment.

NOVEMBER 2002
P1 Truss
The P1 structural module
was added opposite S1,
as part of the integrated
framework.

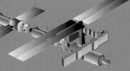

SEPTEMBER 2006
P3/P4 Truss and Solar Arrays
A second frame structure was
added with solar panels that
has meant the station is self-
sufficient in terms of power.

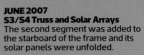

JUNE 2007
S3/S4 Truss and Solar Arrays
The second segment was added to
the starboard of the frame and its
solar panels were unfolded.

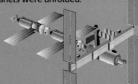

The Hubble Telescope

Space telescopes are artificial satellites sent into orbit to explore different areas of the Universe, avoiding the effects of atmospheric turbulence that affect the quality of images. Hubble, put into orbit on April 25, 1990 by NASA and ESA, is managed by remote control, operated by astronomers in several countries.

Accurate cameras

On the Hubble telescope, the place of human observers is occupied by sensitive light detectors and cameras that photograph views of the cosmos. In 1993, after the discovery of a fault with its main mirror, corrective lenses (COSTAR) were installed to correct its focus.

ENTRANCE
Opened during observations to allow light to enter.

24,250 lb
(11,000 kg)
Weight on Earth

TECHNICAL DATA

Launch date	April 25, 1990
Orbital height	373 miles (600 km)
Orbital period	97 minutes
Type of telescope	Ritchey – Chrétien Reflector
Organization	NASA and ESA
Launch cost	U.S. $2 billion
Diameter of the primary mirror	8 ft (2.4 m)

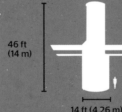

46 ft (14 m)

14 ft (4.26 m)

OUTER COVER
Protects the telescope from the effects of outer space.

HOW IMAGES ARE CAPTURED

Hubble uses a system of mirrors that capture light and converge it until it becomes focused.

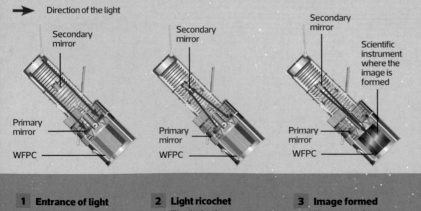

Direction of the light

Secondary mirror

Secondary mirror

Secondary mirror

Scientific instrument where the image is formed

Primary mirror

Primary mirror

Primary mirror

WFPC

WFPC

WFPC

SECONDARY MIRROR
After being reflected here, light reaches the camera.

WIDE FIELD PLANETARY CAMERA (WFPC)
Main electronic camera.

1 **Entrance of light**
Light enters through the opening and reflects against the primary mirror.

2 **Light ricochet**
The light then converges toward the secondary mirror, which returns it to the primary mirror.

3 **Image formed**
The rays of light concentrate on the focal plane, where the image is formed.

HOW IMAGES ARE TRANSMITTED

1 Hubble
It selects the target and processes it to obtain data.

2 TDRS satellite
Information is collected from Hubble here and at the antenna station at White Sands, New Mexico.

3 Earth
From New Mexico, the information is transmitted to Goddard Space Flight Center in Greenbelt, Maryland, where it is analyzed.

IMAGES
As they are taken outside the Earth's atmosphere, the clarity of images produced by Hubble is much better than those taken from telescopes on Earth.

ETA CARINAE STAR   **SUPERNOVA**   **CAT'S EYE NEBULA**

HIGH GAIN ANTENNA
It receives orders from Earth and returns photographs as TV signals.

SOLAR PANEL
Power is provided by means of directional solar antennae.

PRIMARY, OR MAIN, MIRROR
Measuring 8 ft (2.4 m) in diameter, it captures and focuses light.

COSTAR
Optics device that corrected the original defective mirror fitted on Hubble.

CAMERA FOR BLURRY OBJECTS

OTHER TELESCOPES

CHANDRA
Launched in 1999, it is NASA's main X-ray observatory.

SOHO
Developed jointly by NASA and ESA, it allows scientists to view interactions between the Sun and Earth in detail. Placed into orbit in 1995.

SPITZER
Launched in August 2003, it observes the Universe in infrared light.

Voyager Probes

The *Voyager 1* and *2* space probes were launched by NASA to study the outer Solar System. Launched in 1977, they reached Saturn in 1980 and Neptune in 1989, and they are currently continuing on their journey beyond the Solar System. Both probes have become the farthest reaching artificial instruments launched by humankind into space.

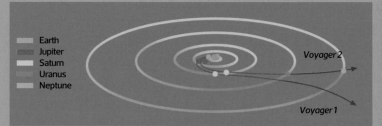

PIONEER 10 AND 11
Pioneer 10 was the first spacecraft to perform a flyby of Jupiter, in 1973, and to study Saturn, in 1979. It was followed by *Pioneer 11* in 1974, which lost communication in 1995.

Voyager Interstellar Mission

When *Voyager 1* and *2* left the Solar System, the project was renamed the Voyager Interstellar Mission. Both probes continue studying the fields that they detect.

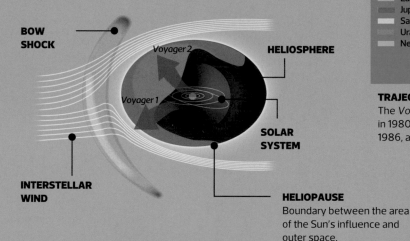

BOW SHOCK

Voyager 2

HELIOSPHERE

Voyager 1

INTERSTELLAR WIND

SOLAR SYSTEM

HELIOPAUSE
Boundary between the area of the Sun's influence and outer space.

Earth
Jupiter
Saturn
Uranus
Neptune

Voyager 2

Voyager 1

TRAJECTORY
The *Voyager 1* probe passed by Jupiter in 1979 and by Saturn in 1980. *Voyager 2* did the same and arrived at Uranus in 1986, and Neptune in 1989. Both are still active.

BEYOND THE SOLAR SYSTEM
Once outside the heliopause, *Voyager* can measure waves that escape the Sun's magnetic field, from the so-called bow shock, an area where solar winds suddenly decrease due to the disappearance of the Sun's magnetic field.

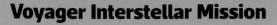

DISCOVERY FACT™

New Horizons was launched by NASA in 2006 to study Pluto and the Kuiper Belt, and is expected to become the fifth interstellar probe.

LANDMARKS

1977
Launches
The *Voyager 1* and *2* probes were launched by NASA from Cape Canaveral in Florida. This marked the beginning of a long, successful mission that is still ongoing.

1977
Photo of the Earth and the Moon
On September 5, *Voyager 1* sent photographs of the Earth and the Moon, demonstrating that it is fully functional.

1986
Uranus encounter
On January 24, *Voyager 2* reached Uranus. It sent photographs of the planet and measurements of its satellites, rings, and magnetic fields back to Earth.

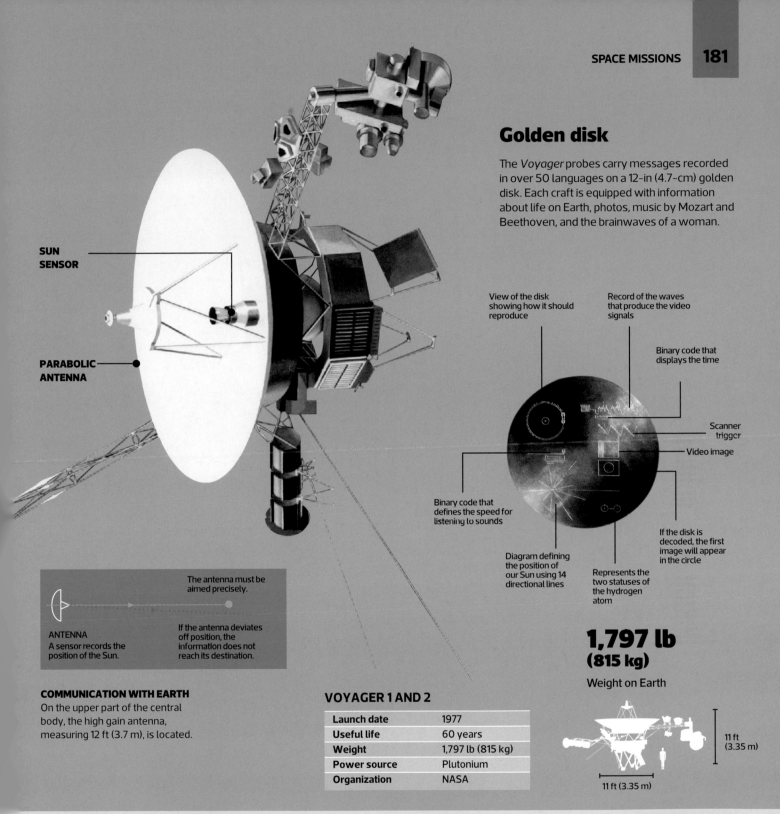

SUN SENSOR

PARABOLIC ANTENNA

Golden disk

The *Voyager* probes carry messages recorded in over 50 languages on a 12-in (4.7-cm) golden disk. Each craft is equipped with information about life on Earth, photos, music by Mozart and Beethoven, and the brainwaves of a woman.

View of the disk showing how it should reproduce

Record of the waves that produce the video signals

Binary code that displays the time

Scanner trigger

Video image

Binary code that defines the speed for listening to sounds

Diagram defining the position of our Sun using 14 directional lines

Represents the two statuses of the hydrogen atom

If the disk is decoded, the first image will appear in the circle

The antenna must be aimed precisely.

ANTENNA
A sensor records the position of the Sun.

If the antenna deviates off position, the information does not reach its destination.

COMMUNICATION WITH EARTH
On the upper part of the central body, the high gain antenna, measuring 12 ft (3.7 m), is located.

VOYAGER 1 AND 2

Launch date	1977
Useful life	60 years
Weight	1,797 lb (815 kg)
Power source	Plutonium
Organization	NASA

1,797 lb
(815 kg)
Weight on Earth

11 ft (3.35 m)

11 ft (3.35 m)

1987
Observation of a supernova
Supernova 1987A appeared in the Large Magellanic Cloud. A high quality photograph was taken by *Voyager 2*.

1989
Color photo of Neptune
Voyager 2 was the first spacecraft to observe Neptune. It also photographed its largest moon, Triton, from close up.

1998
Beating the record set by Pioneer 10
Pioneer 10 flew past Jupiter in 1973. On February 17, *Voyager 1* passed the planet and became the farthest reaching spacecraft in history.

Space Debris

Since the launch of the first satellite in 1957, the space around Earth has become littered by a huge amount of debris. Spent satellite batteries, parts of rockets, and spacecraft orbit around Earth. The danger of these objects' presence is the possibility of a collision: they travel at speeds ranging from 18,640 to 43,500 mph (30,000 to 70,000 km/h).

DISCOVERY FACT™

Australian scientists are working on a project to blast items of space debris with giant lasers fired from Earth.

Cosmic rubbish

Any useless, artificial object that orbits Earth is considered space debris. Rockets used just once continue orbiting the planet, just like bits of spacecraft or devices intentionally destroyed so that they do not move into incorrect orbits.

THE SIZE OF SPACE DEBRIS
More than 11,000 cataloged objects have been accumulated, in addition to millions of tiny particles.

Measure less than 0.4 in (1 cm)
Very small particles cause limited surface damage.

+30,000,000

Measure between 0.4 in and 4 in (1 cm and 10 cm)
Particles that can create holes in satellites.

+100,000

Measure more than 4 in (10 cm)
Capable of causing irreparable damage. They have been cataloged and are monitored from Earth.

+11,000

OBJECTS IN SPACE BY COUNTRY
Since 1957, 25,000 objects have been launched into low orbit. Most come from Russia and the United States.

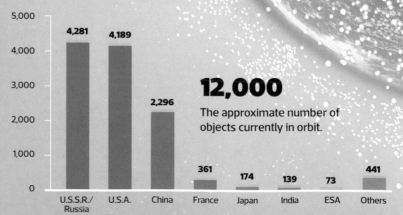

	U.S.S.R./Russia	U.S.A.	China	France	Japan	India	ESA	Others
	4,281	4,189	2,296	361	174	139	73	441

12,000
The approximate number of objects currently in orbit.

What can we do?

One solution could be to return all debris to Earth, rather than leaving it orbiting around the planet. However, what has been achieved is to work on satellite debris to remove it from Earth's orbit.

Sail
Just like on a boat, the sail is released when the satellite stops working and the solar winds divert it.

Space probe
It impacts against the satellite, which is diverted from its orbit and driven in a pre-established direction.

Cable
A cable drags the satellite to lower orbits. It disintegrates when entering the atmosphere.

SOURCE AND LOCATION

95 percent of objects in space around Earth are considered "space waste." NASA is studying a way of using rockets that do not reach orbit and that will return to Earth, preventing the creation of more waste.

21 percent inactive satellite

31 percent rockets and rocket boosters

5 percent active satellites

43 percent fragments of satellites

2,000 tons

of rubbish are orbiting at less than 1,245 miles (2,000 km).

**HIGH ORBIT
62,000 MILES
(100,000 KM)**
Astronomic satellites operate at the highest orbit.

**POLAR ORBIT
250 MILES (400 KM)**
The ISS and the Hubble telescope orbit here.

**LOW ORBIT
125-1,865 MILES
(200-2,000 KM)**
Telecommunication and environmental satellites.

**GEOSTATIONARY ORBIT
22,400 MILES (36,000 KM)**
Spy satellites, which generate a significant amount of waste.

Waste

Functional

Nuclear spills

10

ANCIENT ASTRONOMY
Lithograph dating from 1881 depicting
renowned Greek astronomer
Hipparchus of Nicaea (190–125 BCE), who
is credited with cataloging the stars for
the first time.

THE UNIVERSE
AND
MANKIND

Astronomy was born of man's need to orient himself, to measure time and the seasons, and to know when it was best to sow crops. Since ancient times, mankind has referred to the stars for the keys to life on Earth, and has proposed theories about the objects found in space. Some have been demonstrated as inaccurate over the centuries, whereas others have proved surprisingly accurate. It was Nicolaus Copernicus and his heliocentric theory that resulted in a genuine scientific revolution, built upon by other great astronomers such as Galileo Galilei and Isaac Newton. During the twentieth century, Einstein's theory of relativity represented another large step forward in our understanding of the Universe, the keys to which are still being sought by today's cosmologists.

Astronomical Theories

For a long time, it was believed that the Earth did not move, that it was static and that the Sun, the Moon, and the planets orbited around it. With the invention of the telescope, our way of looking at the Universe changed. The center was no longer occupied by the blue planet, and the concept that all planets orbited the Sun was established.

Geocentric model

The great promoter of the geocentric model (according to which the Earth was the center of the Universe) was Egyptian astronomer Claudius Ptolemy; in the second century CE, he collated the astronomical ideas of the ancient Greeks, Aristotle in particular. Although other ancient astronomers, such as Aristarchus of Samos, asserted that the Earth was round and that it orbited the Sun, Aristotle's proposals were adopted, preserved, and defended by the Catholic Church as the commonly accepted beliefs for 16 centuries.

MEASUREMENTS

Having observed that the Sun, the Moon, and the stars moved cyclically, ancient civilizations discovered that they could use the heavens as a clock and a calendar. However, they found it difficult to simplify complex calculations when forecasting the position of the stars. A tool that would serve them to this end was the astrolabe.

Astrolabe
The different engraved plates reproduce the celestial spheres in two dimensions, so that the height of the Sun and the stars can be measured.

Great astronomers

2ND CENTURY
Claudius Ptolemy
(90–168)
He collated the work of renowned Greek astronomers. He became the unopposed leader of the field.

16TH CENTURY
Nicolaus Copernicus
(1473–1543)
He proposed that the Sun was the center of the Universe, not the Earth.

17TH CENTURY
Johannes Kepler
(1571–1630)
German astronomer who formulated three renowned laws of planetary motion.

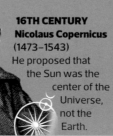

Heliocentric model

In 1543, just a few months before his death, Nicolaus Copernicus published his book, *De revolutionibus orbium coelestium*, the result of which would become what is now known as the "Copernican Revolution." The Polish astronomer developed the heliocentric theory, which opposed the geocentric theory. Heliocentrism established the Sun as the center of the Universe and the Earth as just another satellite. This theory contrasted with the teachings of the Church, with both the Catholic and Protestant churches banning all documents that promoted these beliefs. Galileo Galilei himself was prosecuted for sustaining this undeniable truth.

GALILEO'S TELESCOPE
It would appear that the telescope was invented in 1608 by Dutch lens maker Hans Lippershey. However, it served no scientific purpose until Galileo Galilei developed it for use in observing the heavens.

10 times

The magnification of objects using the first telescope built by Galileo.

Functionality
Galileo's first telescope was a leather tube with a lens at each end facing each other—one was convex and the other was concave.

17TH CENTURY
Galileo Galilei
(1564–1642)
He discovered sunspots, the four brightest moons of Jupiter, the phases of Venus, and the Moon's craters.

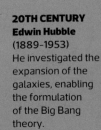

17TH CENTURY
Isaac Newton
(1643–1727)
He developed the theory of gravitation: all the heavenly bodies are governed by the same laws.

20TH CENTURY
Edwin Hubble
(1889–1953)
He investigated the expansion of the galaxies, enabling the formulation of the Big Bang theory.

The First Astronomers

Since the dawn of humanity, civilizations have developed their own ideas about the stars. They sought gods, divine messages, signs of their prophecies, and points of reference for their calendars in the heavens. It can be asserted that the origins of astronomy can be found in the careful and systematic observation of the stars undertaken by these ancient peoples to satisfy their own social needs, such as measuring time or planning their agriculture.

DISCOVERY FACT™

The Goseck Circle in Germany is a Neolithic circular enclosure nearly 7,000 years old that was used for observation of the solar year.

Calendars and forecasts

In short, astronomy was born from necessity. Over 5,000 years ago, the Egyptians developed a calendar based on the solar cycle (very similar to the one we use today), which helped them to identify dates for sowing, cultivation, harvesting, and the flooding of the Nile Delta, where they lived. Mesopotamian populations (Sumerians and Babylonians) depended on climate variations for their subsistence, inventing astrology as a way of "forecasting" and controlling their environment.

Mayan astronomy

The astronomical knowledge of Mesoamerican civilizations was surprisingly advanced. Among them, the Mayans are particularly noteworthy; their priests understood the movement of the stars and could predict eclipses and the path of Venus. Their calendar was also extremely accurate.

SUMERIAN ASTROLOGY
In ancient Mesopotamia, astronomy (a natural science) and astrology (divination using the stars) formed part of the same set of knowledge. In Western societies, these fields were separated after the Renaissance.

SCRIBES
Scribes, or *sangha*, preserved religious, literary, and scientific knowledge. Centuries later, the first Sumerian pictograms traced wedge-shaped lines.

SLATS
Clay fragments used to record the position in which the Sun rose and set, the stellar groups, and the phases of the Moon.

MAYAN WISDOM
Mayan constructions reflected their astronomical knowledge. The temple at Chichén Itzá, for example, has 365 steps, the same number as the days of the year.

Mesopotamian astronomy

Mesopotamian astronomers analyzed the movement of the Sun, planetary conjunctions, and the position and appearance of the stars, among other observations. They developed a calendar and were able to identify the frequency of solar eclipses and forecast lunar eclipses.

CONNECTIONS
They sought to relate heavenly activities with events on Earth.

RECORDS
Their calculations and measurements were considered important by the state.

ASTROLABE
The Sumerians invented a rudimentary version of this instrument, which enabled them to establish the position and movement of the stars.

BARU PRIESTS
With an understanding of mathematics, astronomy and religion, the *baru* was a fortune-teller or religious agent who interpreted heavenly signs, such as meteors and lunar eclipses, as premonitions.

The Constellations

The constellations take the names of different animals, mythical characters, or other figures assigned to them by civilizations to use them as points of reference or to guide them on their travels. They are groups of stars that appear aligned, whereas in reality there are significant distances between them. Depending on the hemisphere from which they are observed, the hour and time of the year, different constellations are visible.

Chi1 Orionis

Xi Orionis

Mu Orionis

Betelgeuse

ORIGINS

The origin of the constellations in Western culture can be traced to the first astronomical observations of the Mesopotamian peoples: the Greco-Latin culture preserved them and as a result, most have Classical mythical names. Later, as other constellations were discovered, they were most commonly named after phenomena related to science.

DISCOVERY FACT™

Eighty-eight constellations are recognized by the International Astronomical Union; they are used to create a map of the sky.

The changing skies

As the Earth follows its orbit, the sky changes, with different areas of space coming into view. Therefore, the constellations that can be seen depend on the time of year and the latitude from which they are observed. It is only from the equator that all constellations can be seen in a single night.

Blanket of stars

Earth

Sun

Orbit

LEO
The brightest star is Regulus, which is the the lion's heart.

CANCER
The least spectacular of the 13.

GEMINI
The stars Castor and Pollux appear as the heads of the twins.

TAURUS
The brightest star, Aldebaran, is red.

ARIES
It has just one very bright star: Hamal ("sheep" in Arabic).

PISCES
It doesn't have any bright stars.

The Zodiac

The 13 constellations positioned within the elliptical path of Earth, where the Sun appears to travel as seen from Earth, are called the "zodiac constellations." However, Ophiuchus, the 13th, is not considered by astrologers.

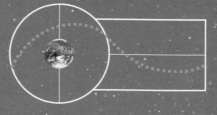

NORTH AND SOUTH
The zodiac constellations can be seen from both hemispheres. However, it is difficult to see Scorpius from the north; whereas it is difficult to see constellations such as Gemini from the south.

▼ Orion

Its name alludes to the mythical Greek character: a handsome giant and hunter. It is one of the most widely known constellations, and depending on the season it can be seen throughout the night.

Heka

Bellatrix

Omicron Orionis

Pi1 Orionis

Pi2 Orionis

Pi3 Orionis

Pi4 Orionis

Pi5 Orionis

Pi6 Orionis

THE MYSTERY OF GIZA
The three stars in Orion's belt appear closely related to the alignment of the three pyramids in Egypt.

Mintaka

Alnilam

Alnitak

Saiph

Rigel

Cultures

In ancient times, each culture developed constellations that were very different to one another. For example, the Chinese used smaller, more detailed patterns, making it possible to obtain more accurate information about positions. Thus, different names may be given to the same constellations.

SCORPIUS
Known to Mesopotamian peoples, Greece, Rome, Mesoamerica, and Oceania.

URSA MAJOR
The bear used to depict this constellation is strange, as it has a large tail.

CENTAURUS
A half-man, half-horse creature from Greek mythology. He accompanied Orion in the quest to recover his sight.

Babylonia

The Babylonians were responsible for giving roots to the concept of the zodiac 2000 years BCE as a way of measuring time. As such, it served as a symbolic calendar.

OPHIUCHUS
It is not recognized within the zodiac, because when astrology was born around 3,000 years ago, it was too far from the elliptical path of the Earth.

LIBRA
It was once part of Scorpius.

SAGITTARIUS
Points toward the center of the Milky Way, full of nebulae and stars.

VIRGO
The constellation rich in galaxies.

AQUARIUS
Contains globular clusters and nebulae.

CAPRICORNUS
One of the least impressive.

SCORPIUS
It points toward the Milky Way. Its brightest star is Antares.

The Astronomical Clock of Su Song

Between the fourth century BCE and the thirteenth century CE, China experienced extraordinary scientific and technical advances, the results of which would remain unknown to the West for a long time. Among them was the sensational, giant astronomical clock created by Su Song. Invented in 1088, it was the first highly accurate clock and it demonstrates the advanced knowledge of astronomy held by the Chinese civilization in the Middle Ages.

DISCOVERY FACT™

A full-size replica of the clock was built in Taiwan in the 1990s and stands in the National Museum of Natural Science.

Precision in the form of a clock

Although scarce evidence of his ingenuity remains, Su Song's treatise about the clock tower, *Xinyi Xiangfayao*, was published in 1092. Construction of the clock was completed in 1090, after confirming the functionality of a prototype. Powered using water, its inaccuracy was less than 100 seconds per day and showed the stellar constellations independently of weather conditions.

WORKERS
Given its size, the tower was capable of housing several operators.

MAIN WHEEL
It measured 10 ft (3 m) in diameter and contained 36 vanes. Its system of cogs transferred the power required to activate the time and the armillary sphere mechanisms.

ARMILLARY SPHERE
Invented in 978 and comprising a series of rings, it was the first instrument to determine the position of the stars, preceding the invention of the telescope in the seventeenth century.

MATERIAL
The tower was made from wood. Its most important components were cast in bronze.

Su Song's contributions

Su Song (1020–1101) had many occupations, including civil servant, engineer, botanist, poet, antiquarian, and ambassador of the Song Dynasty. Although his most famous work was the Great Clock Tower, he made numerous contributions to other scientific fields. In addition to treatises on mineralogy, botany, and pharmacology, he produced maps of the Earth with time zones, and an atlas with several maps of the stars.

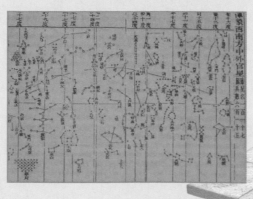

MAP OF THE STARS
Published by Su Song in a treatise in 1092, it is one of the oldest printed star charts in the world.

DESTRUCTION
The clock was destroyed by the Tartars in the twelfth century, during the invasion of China.

COMPOSITION

1 Armillary sphere
Toward the top, the inside of the bronze sphere automatically turned a ringed globe, which served to establish the position of the stars.

2 Water tanks
A channel provided running water: from a tank, a trickle of water flowed onto the vanes of a wheel, which started turning.

3 Telling the time
The mechanism displayed small figures that showed the time, the lunar cycles, and the movement of the skies.

4 Drainage
The construction also featured a container for the continuous runoff.

POWER
The mechanism required a constant flow of water in order to work.

20 ft
(6 m)
The height of the tower that housed the clock.

Copernicus and Galileo

In just 150 years, our view of the Universe was changed dramatically. Toward the end of the fifteenth century, Nicolaus Copernicus turned astronomy on its head with the philosophical assertion that Earth was not the center of the Universe, as upheld by the Church. Despite being outlawed, astronomers such as Tycho Brahe, Johannes Kepler, and Galileo Galilei perfected Copernicus's theory.

The Copernican Revolution

Prior to the publication of Nicolaus Copernicus's theories in 1543, the geocentric theory of the Universe, developed by Ptolemy in the second century, was the commonly accepted belief. Copernicus, who discovered anomalies in Ptolemy's system, mathematically reached the conclusion that Earth moved, turning on its own axis in addition to orbiting the Sun (heliocentrism). He also revealed that the Earth's axis was tilted. His ideas gave rise to a new period: they marked the beginning of the scientific revolution and served as the basis for modern astronomy.

TELESCOPE
This instrument was developed a year earlier in Holland, but Galileo was the first to use it to view the sky, in 1609. At the time, it was known as a spyglass.

SPHERICAL ASTROLABE
Also known as an armillary sphere, it fixed the position of the stars in space.

THE LEGACY OF COPERNICUS
Many of Copernicus's followers worked in the royal courts. Among them were Tycho Brahe from Denmark, Johannes Kepler from Germany, and Galileo Galilei of Italy.

DE REVOLUTIONIBUS ORBIUM COELESTIUM
Copernicus never considered publishing his work, *On the Revolutions of the Heavenly Spheres*, but his pupil, Rheticus, was convinced. It was a decision that would change history.

GALILEO GALILEI
The astronomer was forced to retract his ideas, but immediately afterward stated: "And yet it moves."

The ecclesiastical powers in Rome did not accept Galileo's ideas and he was convicted of heresy in 1633.

What Galileo saw

Florentine astronomer and physicist Galileo Galilei (1564–1642) was one of the fiercest defenders of heliocentrism. He tried to convince ecclesiastical sceptics that there were mountains on the Moon and that Jupiter had several of its own moons.

DOGE OF VENICE
When Galileo presented his telescope to the Doge of Venice, the latter became interested in its military uses.

SENATORS
Galileo gave the senators of Venice the rights to manufacture the telescope (although strictly it was not his invention).

SCIENTIFIC METHOD
Galileo was one of the creators of modern scientific thinking, when he combined inductive reasoning and mathematical deduction. Ever since this has been the method used in physics.

Isaac Newton

Famed for his theory of universal gravitation, Englishman Isaac Newton (1643–1727) is considered one of the greatest scientists of all time. His field of research and his contributions to science exceed the boundaries of astronomy. Physicist, philosopher, inventor, and mathematician, he is also famed for his works on light and optics, and the development of mathematical calculus.

Universal gravitation

In his work, *Philosophiae Naturalis Principia Mathematica*, published in 1687, Newton described one of the theories that has most influenced modern astronomy: the law of universal gravitation. This asserts that bodies exert a mutual force of attraction, depending on their mass and the distance between them. Furthermore, he suggested that all bodies are governed by the same physical laws of the Universe. Using his law of gravitation, Newton explained the movement traced by the planets in the Solar System, and demonstrated that the gravitational pull of the Sun and the Moon on the Earth's oceans were responsible for the tides.

NEWTON AND THE APPLE
Legend has it that Newton started to develop his theory of universal gravitation when studying how an apple fell from the tree, asking himself why objects fall to the ground.

EXPERIMENT
With small holes in the screen, Newton was able to isolate each color.

3

The laws of motion

Newton put forward a series of laws of motion that were named after him, which explain the movement of bodies, their effects, and their causes. These principles are: the law of inertia; the law of interaction and force; and the law of action–reaction.

DISCOVERY FACT™

Newton worked out his key theories about light and planetary motion at home on his farm while Cambridge University was closed because of the plague.

Spectral light

Around 1666, Newton was able to demonstrate that light, considered white, was actually made up of colored light whose paths diverted at different angles (due to refraction) when passing through a glass prism. In 1671, Newton baptized the image created as the "spectrum of light."

1 Light source
Through a small hole in the window, natural light enters Newton's laboratory.

2 Prism
Purchased from a fair, the triangular glass prism breaks up the white light into the color spectrum.

3 White screen
Against a surface prepared in front of the window, the spectrum of seven colors is formed, containing: red, orange, yellow, green, blue, indigo, and violet.

TELESCOPE
As part of his studies on the nature of light, Newton created a kind of reflecting telescope.

DETAILS
Newton personally illustrated all the details of his experiment in a diagram.

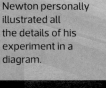

Einstein and Relativity

Over the course of the first decades of the twentieth century, physicist Albert Einstein shook the world with his (special and general) theory of relativity, implying significant changes to the concepts of space, time, and gravity that had been considered as well established since the times of Newton and Galileo. Similarly, our perception of the origin, evolution, and structure of the Universe was to change just as dramatically.

The theory of relativity

In 1905, Albert Einstein proposed the special theory of relativity that time and space are not absolute and independent of one another, but that they "merge" in a constant four-dimensional dynamic known as "space-time," which can bend itself as if it were an elastic band. A decade later, in 1916, Einstein incorporated gravity into his theory (general relativity) and concluded that gravity is the result of the space-time curvature. Einstein's ideas would go on to suggest the concept of the Big Bang, in addition to the existence of black holes.

SOLAR MASS
At the heart of the scene, the Sun curves the surrounding space-time and "diverts" the light of the stars, which are seen in an inaccurate position.

LUNAR SHADOW
When positioned between the Sun and Earth, the shadow of the Moon blocks out solar light, and the resulting eclipse allows stars to be seen during the day.

CURVED LINE
The path of stellar light is curved or "deflected" by the Sun.

1 **EXPEDITIONS**
In 1919, two scientific missions used a solar eclipse to test Einstein's theory: if it were correct, the light of the stars should move at a certain angle when passing close to the Sun.

1919 ECLIPSE
Just a few minutes were enough. On May 29, 1919, two British expeditions confirmed Einstein's theoretical prediction. One viewed the total eclipse of the Sun from northern Brazil, and another from western Africa.

Apparent position of star 1 from Earth.

Star 1

Star 2

Apparent position of star 2 from Earth.

3 **PRESENTATION**
The announcement in London transformed Einstein into a world famous celebrity overnight.

TRADITIONAL NOTION
According to classical physics, the Sun would prevent both stars from being seen.

The issue of position

From stars in a given location, their light reaches Earth directly during the night whereas, during the day, the Sun intervenes. The presence of this huge mass causes a deviation in our perception of their location.

2 **EVIDENCE**
The Sun's gravitational field diverted the light of the stars at the angle predicted by Einstein.

Time

Future light cone

Space

Observer

Hypersurface of the present

Space

Past light cone

LIGHT CONE
German mathematician Hermann Minkowski (1864–1909) illustrated Einstein's concept of space-time with a light cone. It represents the evolution of a beam of light over time (past, present, and future)—the image shows two of the three dimensions of space: space-time and the observer at the origin of the coordinates.

DISCOVERY FACT™

Although Einstein's theory of general relativity led to the proposition of black holes, he himself did not believe that they existed.

COSMOLOGY ACCOMPLISHMENTS

1916
THEORETICAL BASE
Albert Einstein's general theory of relativity became the most precise theoretical framework to describe the Universe.

1922
SIGNIFICANT EXPANSION
Russian mathematician Alexander Friedmann suggested that the Universe expands: laying the groundwork for the Big Bang theory.

1929
EDWIN HUBBLE
Proposed that the Universe comprised numerous separate galaxies and that the Milky Way is just one of them.

1974
DARK MATTER
Soviet scientists demonstrated that the majority of the Universe is made up of dark matter, a fact that had been suspected for decades.

Hadron Collider

The Large Hadron Collider (LHC) is the largest scientific instrument ever made by humankind, and offers a great insight into understanding how the Universe works. Its purpose is to smash high-speed, energized particles into one another, in order to obtain data about the basic forces of the Universe and to discover new elementary particles.

The LHC complex

Located on the border between Switzerland and France, the LHC consists of several elements: several ring-shaped tunnels measuring 5.6 miles (9 km) in diameter, which raise the energy of particles to levels never before induced artificially, and superconducting magnets to direct and shoot them. Six experiments have been carried out to analyze the results of the collisions.

CMS detector

This instrument weighs around 12,500 tons and is designed to analyze, during collisions between highly energized protons, the particles generated (such as photons, muons, and other elementary particles) and aspects such as their mass, energy, and speed.

DISCOVERY FACT™

CERN scientists announced in 2013 that they had found the Higgs boson, the subatomic particle that confirms the Standard Model of physics.

1 PARTICLE ACCELERATOR
Here, the nuclei of atoms are separated from the electrons, converting them into ions. Hydrogen ions contain just one proton whereas others, such as lead, have more than one. These ions are directed toward the underground complex.

2 SPEED
The ions are energized and accelerated until they reach speeds close to the speed of light.

3 RAISING THE ENERGY
Powerful radiowave blasts increase the energy of the ions to four billion electron volts (small-scale units, equivalent to 1.6×10^{-19} joule).

4 COLLISION
The two ions are introduced in clusters of billions of units into the accelerator, in opposite directions. There, propelled by the superconducting magnets, their high energy levels are multiplied by 10, making them collide.

SUPERCONDUCTING MAGNETS
Chilled to almost absolute zero (-459° F / -273° C) using liquid nitrogen, they provide the particles with their high levels of energy and guide them.

MUON IDENTIFIER
This facilitates the detection of any fundamental element and the measurement of its mass and speed.

INPUT
Entrance of particles that will collide.

HADRON CALORIMETER
It records the energy of the hadrons (elementary particles smaller than atoms that last just fractions of seconds) and analyzes their interactions with atomic nuclei.

ELECTROMAGNETIC CALORIMETER
It measures the energy of light particles, such as electrons and photons, with precision.

49 ft (15 m)

71 ft (21.5 m)

Atlas detector

An instrument designed to explore the fundamental nature of matter and the basic forces that govern the Universe as a result of particle collisions. It weighs 7,000 tons (the same as 60 diesel locomotives).

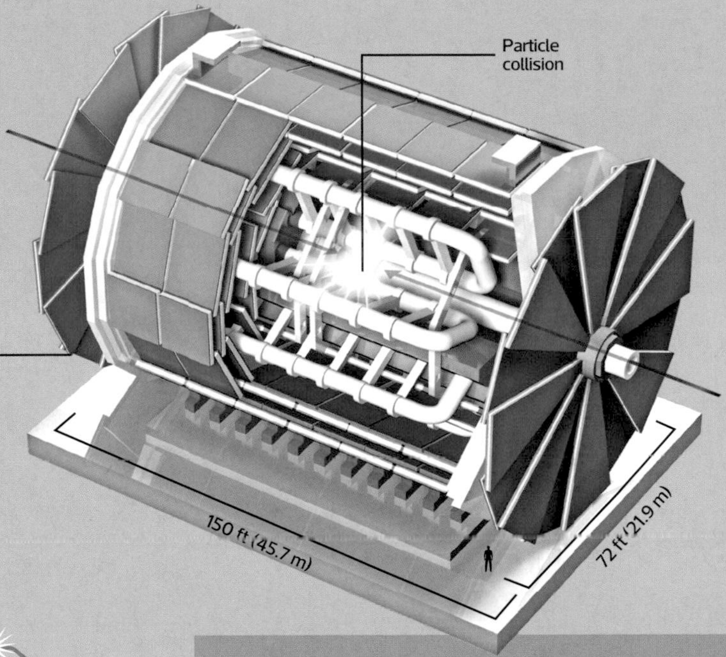
Particle collision
150 ft (45.7 m)
72 ft (21.9 m)

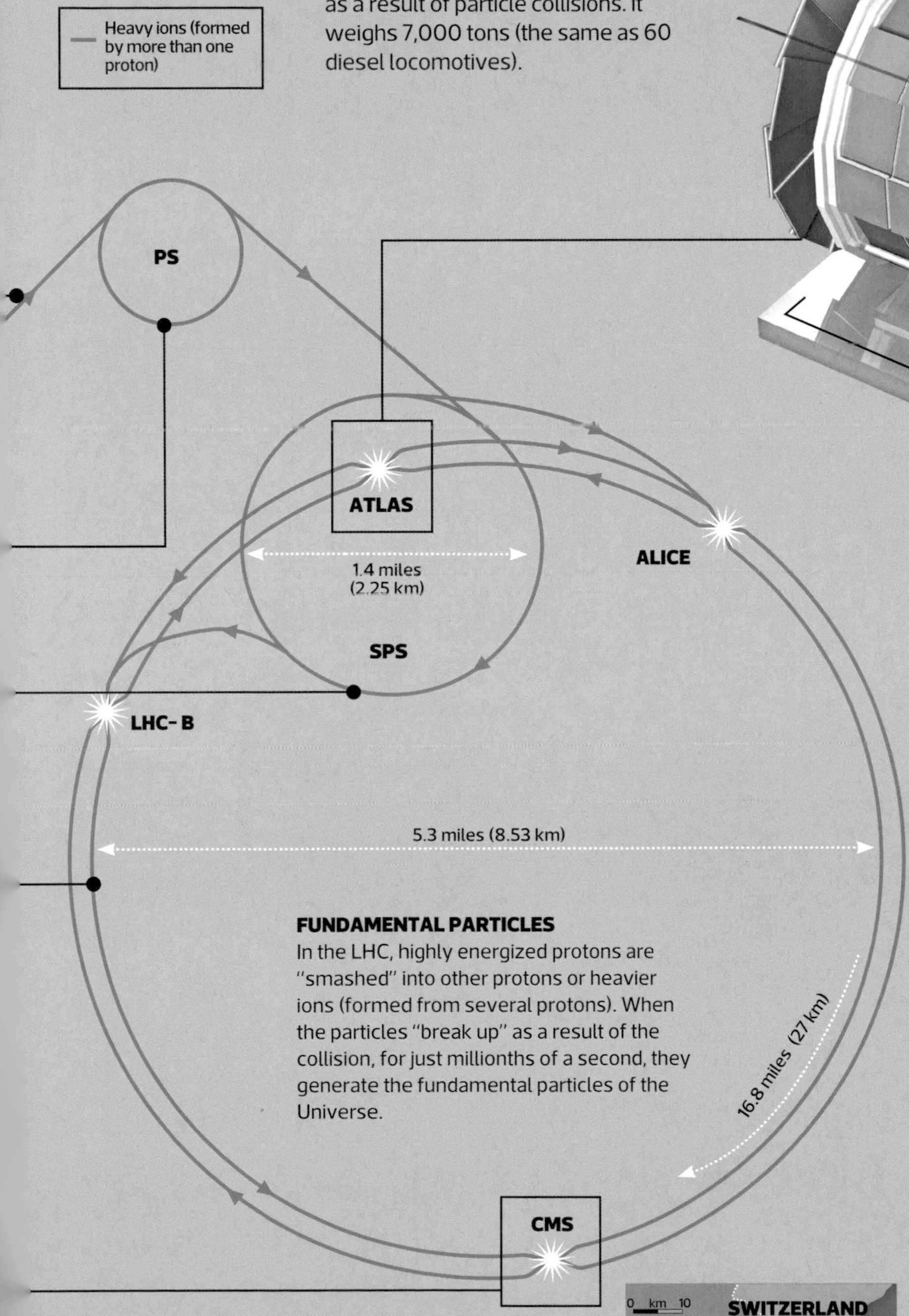
Heavy ions (formed by more than one proton)
PS
ATLAS
ALICE
1.4 miles (2.25 km)
SPS
LHC- B
5.3 miles (8.53 km)
16.8 miles (27 km)
CMS

FUNDAMENTAL PARTICLES
In the LHC, highly energized protons are "smashed" into other protons or heavier ions (formed from several protons). When the particles "break up" as a result of the collision, for just millionths of a second, they generate the fundamental particles of the Universe.

INPUT
Entrance of the particles that will collide.

SILICON TRACKER
This device makes it possible to track charged particles and measure their speed and mass.

THE RINGS
These circular tunnels are buried at depths of between 330 and 575 ft (100 and 175 m) underground.

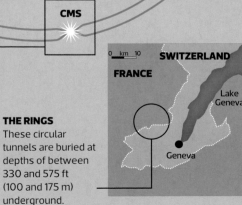

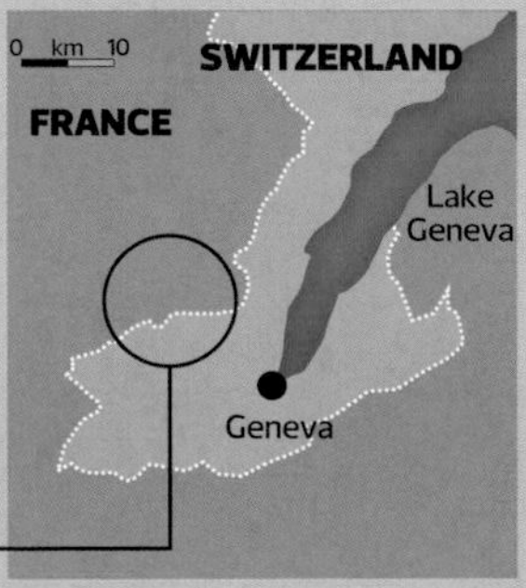
0 km 10
SWITZERLAND
FRANCE
Lake Geneva
Geneva

Big Bang

Once data is obtained about fundamental particles and elementary forces, the Large Hadron Collider enables us to learn how the Universe was created just a tiny fraction of a second after the initial great explosion.

THE MOMENT OF COLLISION
During the collision, the highly energized particles that collide break into elementary particles that can "live" barely millionths of a second, a time during which they must be detected and analyzed.

CMS

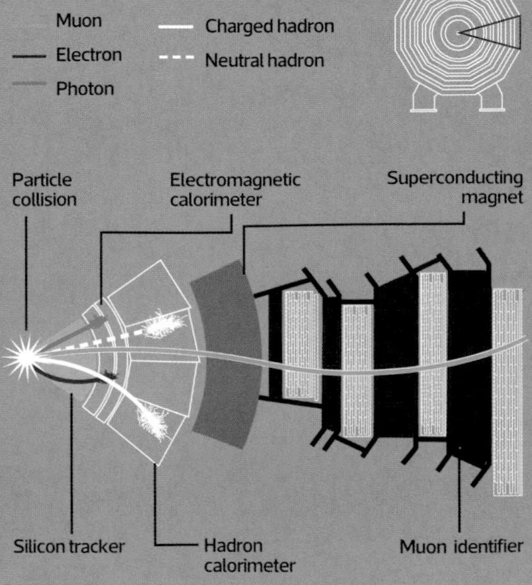
Muon
Electron
Photon
Charged hadron
Neutral hadron
Particle collision
Electromagnetic calorimeter
Superconducting magnet
Silicon tracker
Hadron calorimeter
Muon identifier

Other Famous Cosmologists

The achievements of Copernicus, Galileo, Newton, and Einstein have often been the culmination of research started by other great astronomers; on other occasions, they have been the starting point for new discoveries. Here are just some of the men whose contributions also greatly assisted the unraveling of the secrets of the cosmos and advanced our knowledge.

Tycho Brahe (1546–1601)

From Denmark, he was one of the last great astronomers prior to the invention of the telescope. He constructed various astronomical instruments and observatories, managing to measure the position of the stars and the planets with the greatest level of precision seen until then, in addition to tracking their movement.

Stellar map of Cassiopeia
In 1573, Brahe observed the appearance of a supernova in the Cassiopeia constellation, which contradicted the immutability of the heavens.

Johannes Kepler (1571–1630)

German astronomer and collaborator of Tycho Brahe. He established that the orbits of the planets around the Sun are shaped elliptically. He also discovered that the closer a planet is to the Sun, the faster it moves. He created the laws of planetary movement that made it possible to join together and forecast the movement of the stars.

KEPLER'S THREE LAWS

1 The planets move elliptically around the Sun.

2 The areas cleared by the planets' radii are proportionate to the time it takes them to travel the perimeter of these areas.

3 The square of the orbital period of a planet is proportional to the cube of its average distance from the Sun.

Edmund Halley (1656–1742)

The first scientist to calculate the orbit of a comet and forecast that the same comet would reappear toward the end of 1758. He developed a method to estimate the distance of Earth from the Sun with precision, using the phases of Venus. He identified the movement of several stars and drove the measurement of their parallax.

Halley's Comet
Photographed on May 18, 1910.

"If I have seen further, it is by standing on the shoulders of giants"
Isaac Newton

Walter Adams (1876–1956)

With the help of the spectroscope, he discovered the difference between giant and dwarf stars. He observed solar spots, measured the rotation of the Sun, and calculated the speeds and distances of hundreds of stars. He determined the luminosity and intrinsic brightness of stars, and demonstrated that the atmosphere of Venus was made up of carbon dioxide.

Mount Wilson observatory
Adams managed this observatory, which facilitated many of his discoveries between 1920 and 1940.

Edwin Hubble (1889–1953)

Made famous for his discovery that the Universe expands. He determined that galaxies are separated by a speed that is proportionate to their distance. His research made it possible to get an idea of the size of the cosmos and to set the groundwork for the development of the Big Bang theory.

Hubble Telescope
Named in honor of the American astronomer.

Stephen Hawking (b. 1942)

British physicist, cosmologist, and scientific commentator, whose work was centered on the basic laws that govern the stars. He discovered that black holes emit radiation and developed theories on the origin and future of the Universe. He is particularly well known as a scientific commentator, publishing several highly successful books.

Illness
Hawking has suffered a form of sclerosis since his youth, which has left him almost completely paralyzed over the years.

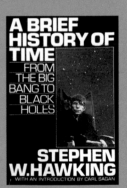

A BRIEF HISTORY OF TIME
FROM THE BIG BANG TO BLACK HOLES
STEPHEN W. HAWKING
WITH AN INTRODUCTION BY CARL SAGAN

SPACESHIPONE

The world's first private reusable
spacecraft, which has managed to fly
ten times higher than planes.

11

N328KF

ASTRONOMY AND DAILY LIFE

N328KF

The fruits of manned space programs, various technologies have been developed whose practical applications now form part of our daily lives: wireless devices, implanted defibrillators, and digital imagery, to mention just a few. What was until recently science fiction is now a reality. In 2004, SpaceShipOne became the first private manned vehicle to reach the proximities of outer space and remain outside the atmosphere for three minutes. Space tourism has taken off, and in the coming decades, it will become an affordable adventure. Today, all enthusiasts can even own their own equipment to catch a high-quality glimpse of the Universe from their own backyard.

Space Technology at Home

Space has served as a research and development laboratory for new technologies and methods, the application of which is reflected in our daily lives. Various devices, types of food, clothing, materials, and utensils have been tested in space under extreme conditions and have improved the quality of our lives.

Intelligent clothing

Clothes featuring computers and other technological elements are already a reality. Electronics can transform clothing into an intelligent biometric suit that responds to the environment in which the wearer is located and can measure his/her vital signs. Thanks to new fabrics, scientists are now discussing the development of garments to prevent illnesses.

MAMAGOOSE
Mamagoose pajamas can monitor babies while they sleep. They are equipped with sensors that monitor the baby's heartbeat and breathing. The pajamas detect and provide a warning of possible sudden infant death syndrome symptoms. The vital signs of astronauts are monitored using a similar system.

POLYCARBONATE
Compact polycarbonate sheets are used in the construction industry. They have a high impact strength, and have replaced glass in some applications, including goggles.

FIVE SENSORS
● Three on the chest
● Two on the stomach

Domestic uses

The popularization of space travel has resulted in the introduction of new technologies in our homes, such as microwave ovens and dried foods. Both have relatively recently taken a place in the daily lives of families at home.

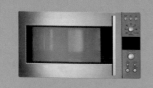

FOODS
Explorers have dry food stored in cool places. The menu includes dried fruits, smoked turkey, flour tortilla, soy milk cheese, and nuts.

MICROWAVE OVENS
Made popular in the U.S.A. in the 1970s, food can be cooked or quickly reheated thanks to the use of electromagnetic waves.

VELCRO
A hook–and–loop fastening system created by George de Mestral in 1941. He refined it in 1948 and patented it in 1955.

Air purifiers

These devices are designed to reduce the concentration of bacteria in the home and are beneficial for allergy and asthma sufferers. They are mobile and can be moved from one room to another.

1 **PHASE 1**
The purifier takes in air contaminated with allergens.

2 **PHASE 2**
A filter processes the contaminated air.

3 **PHASE 3**
The purifier returns pure air to the room.

Contaminated air → **Pure air**

KEVLAR
Synthesized polyamide, used in clothing for which resistance is essential, such as equipment for outdoor sports, bulletproof jackets, and covers.

PROTECTED CRAFT
To withstand the effects of extreme temperatures and impacts against meteorites, spacecraft must be protected by various layers. The outer shell is made of aluminum, which covers a screen for protection against high temperatures. The inside is equipped with a screen to provide protection against low temperatures. A layer of adhesive silicone is responsible for joining them together.

Screen for high temperatures
Offers protection against the adverse effects of the Sun.

Screen for low temperatures
Offers protection from extreme cold temperatures.

Silicone adhesive

Aluminum
To protect the spacecraft against impacts with meteorites.

SILICONE
Many polymers are made from silicone: it is used in lubricants, waterproof adhesives, kitchen molds, and medical devices.

TEFLON
The common name for polytetrafluoroethylene. Its special characteristic is that it is almost inert and does not react with other chemical substances, except under very specific circumstances. It is also renowned as being waterproof and nonstick. It is used in the lining of rockets and planes, and at home, in cooking pans.

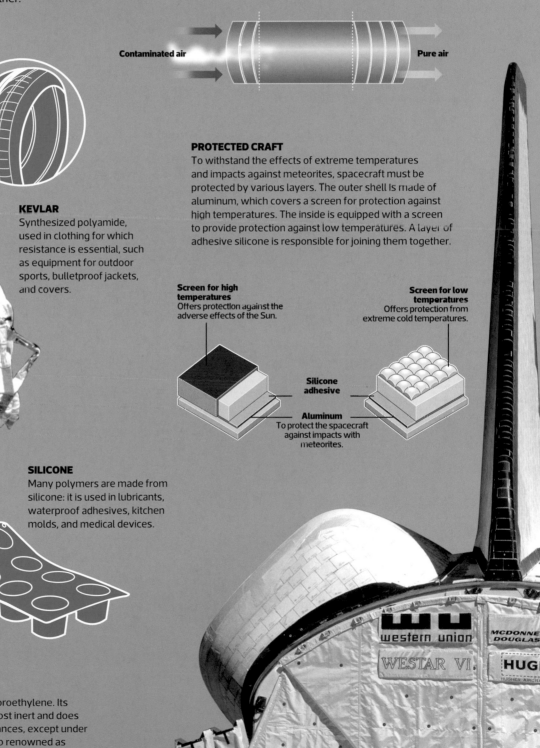

western union
MCDONNELL DOUGLAS
WESTAR VI
HUGHES
HUGHES AIRCRAFT COMPANY

GPS

The Global Positioning System (GPS) was developed by the U.S. Department of Defense and makes it possible to establish the position of a person, vehicle, or spacecraft anywhere in the world. To achieve this, it uses a constellation of two dozen NAVSTAR satellites. It was fully deployed in 1995 and, although it was designed for military use, it is now applied in various fields and forms part of our daily lives. The European Union is developing the Galileo System, similar to GPS, but comprising 30 satellites.

DISCOVERY FACT™

GPS satellites orbit twice in a day, and are arranged so that at least four are covering any point on Earth at any time.

Functionality

Using the electromagnetic waves sent by the satellite, receivers can convert the signals received to estimate positions, speeds, and times. To calculate an exact position, four satellites are required. The first three form a tripartite area of intersection, while the fourth works to correct the position. When the area scanned by the fourth satellite does not coincide with the previously established intersection, the position is corrected.

1 PHASE 1
The first satellite sends its coordinates. The navigational aid captures the signal, indicating its distance from the satellite within the scanned sphere.

2 PHASE 2
If a second satellite is added, an area is established within the intersection of both spheres in which the navigational aid is found.

SATELLITE A

SATELLITE A

SATELLITE B

COVERAGE AREA

INDICATOR
of latitude, longitude, and height.

CONTROL
To utilize the device's map.

Keep Right at Main Street
1/2 mi
1:30
15.5 mi
eta 13.17
11:47
500 ft

The receiver

It is equipped with all the controls required to precisely establish the location of a given point. It provides the user with all the coordinates needed.

POINT OF RECEPTION

Galileo System

The European Galileo project (whose first experimental satellite was put into orbit in 2005) is a satellite-based navigational system that will use a set of 30 satellites. These will orbit Earth at 14,300 miles (23,000 km) on three different planes to offer complete coverage. It is still not operational, but it is expected to be fully functional by 2020.

GALILEO

10 ft (3 m)

GALILEO'S ORBIT
The satellites' orbits ensure there is sufficient coverage to precisely calculate positions on Earth.

ORBIT
Around 55° on the equatorial plane

Equatorial plane

ELECTROMAGNETIC WAVES
Using the electromagnetic waves sent by satellites, the receiver calculates the distance and position of the point sought. The waves travel at 186,400 miles/sec (300,000 km/sec).

SATELLITE A

SATELLITE C

SATELLITE B

3 **PHASE 3**
Combining the three satellites, a common point can be established that indicates the exact position of the navigational aid.

GALILEO SATELLITE

First launch	2005
Orbital height	14,300 miles (23,000 km)
Orbital period	14 hours
Organization	European Union

SATELLITE A

SATELLITE B

SATELLITE D

SATELLITE C

4 **PHASE 4**
A fourth satellite is required to correct any possible positional error.

Environmental Satellites

Under the guidance of the French space agency CNES, Spot 1 was put into orbit in 1986; it was the first satellite of what is today a satellite constellation that can take very high resolution photographs of Earth. The latest version, Spot 6, was launched in 2012. Today, it is considered a commercial satellite par excellence, used by companies in the oil and agricultural industries. The U.S.A. originally launched Landsat in 1972, the latest version of which was launched in 2013.

Spot satellite constellation

The development of the Spot satellite constellation made it possible to commercially offer photographic monitoring of events linked to the environment. Based on the scanning system it uses, a Spot satellite can observe the same site two or three times a day. Its coverage capacity is immense: it can take photos of sections up to 73 miles (117 km) wide, right down to portions of just 8 ft (2.5 m). Depending on the areas, Spot Image can capture images guaranteed cloud-free.

SPOT SATELLITES
They work together, as a result of which it is possible to obtain an image from any point of the globe daily.

SPOT 5

Launch date	May 4, 2002
Orbital latitude	517 miles (832 km)
Orbital period	100 minutes
Maximum resolution	8 ft (2.5 m)
Organization	CNES

10.2 ft (3.1 m)

19 ft (5.7 m)

Landsat satellites

Landsat 7 was launched by NASA in April 1999 and is still in operation. It orbits Earth at a height of around 438 miles (705 km). It takes just 99 minutes to fully orbit the Earth and 16 days to take photographs of the entire surface of the planet. It is equipped with a digital camera that facilitates aerial views of more than 49 ft (15 m) transversally.

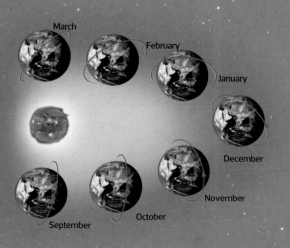

March
February
January
December
November
October
September

LANDSAT 7
It produces color images of Earth that are used to monitor changes in the climate and environment.

SUN-SYNCHRONOUS ORBIT
In order to compare observations of a given point captured on different dates, the images must be taken under similar light conditions. To this end, a Sun-synchronous orbit is used, which means it is possible to view the entire surface of Earth for a period of 26 days.

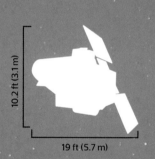

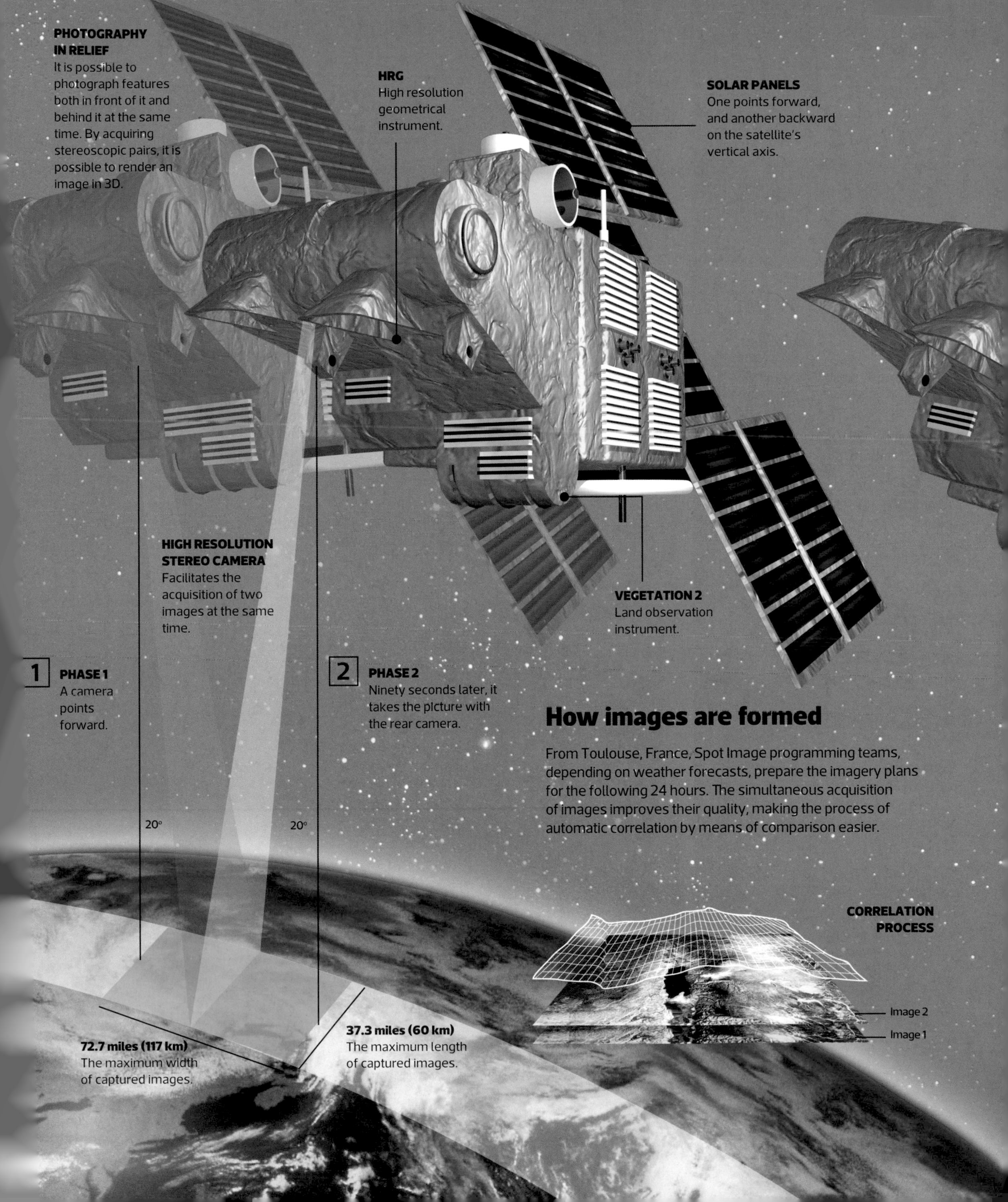

PHOTOGRAPHY IN RELIEF
It is possible to photograph features both in front of it and behind it at the same time. By acquiring stereoscopic pairs, it is possible to render an image in 3D.

HRG
High resolution geometrical instrument.

SOLAR PANELS
One points forward, and another backward on the satellite's vertical axis.

HIGH RESOLUTION STEREO CAMERA
Facilitates the acquisition of two images at the same time.

VEGETATION 2
Land observation instrument.

1 **PHASE 1**
A camera points forward.

2 **PHASE 2**
Ninety seconds later, it takes the picture with the rear camera.

How images are formed

From Toulouse, France, Spot Image programming teams, depending on weather forecasts, prepare the imagery plans for the following 24 hours. The simultaneous acquisition of images improves their quality, making the process of automatic correlation by means of comparison easier.

20°

20°

CORRELATION PROCESS

Image 2

Image 1

72.7 miles (117 km)
The maximum width of captured images.

37.3 miles (60 km)
The maximum length of captured images.

Satellite Imagery

The images taken by Spot 5 make it possible to view the relief of any region on the planet at different scales, from photographs that capture 8 ft (2.5 m) of terrain, to sections up to 37.3 miles (60 km) wide. The powerful definition of Spot 5 makes it possible to home in on very specific targets, from vegetation to port areas, from seas and geographical boundaries to fire areas.

Image resolution

The Spot satellite obtains a maximum definition of 8 ft (2.5 m) on Earth, a high resolution that makes it possible to cover very specific aspects of the target areas. It is also programmed to operate at resolutions of 16, 33, and 66 ft (5, 10, and 20 m). The images provided by Spot are used to control harvests, prevent natural disasters, and observe demographic growth.

ISRAEL
Latitude 32.98°
Longitude 35.57°

Satellite	Pixel size	Image
Spot 1 to 3	33 ft (10 m)	Color and B&W
	66 ft (20 m)	Color
Spot 4	16 ft (5 m)	Color and B&W
	33 ft (10 m)	Color
Spot 5	8 ft (2.5 m)	Color or B&W
	16 ft (5 m)	Color or B&W
	33 ft (10 m)	Color or B&W

3D imagery

The scanning method used by Spot 5 makes it possible to build images in three dimensions, for all types of terrain.

8 ft
(2.5 m)

is the maximum resolution that can be reached by Spot 5, capable of providing a detailed image of a boat in port.

Haifa ●

ISRAEL

● Gaza

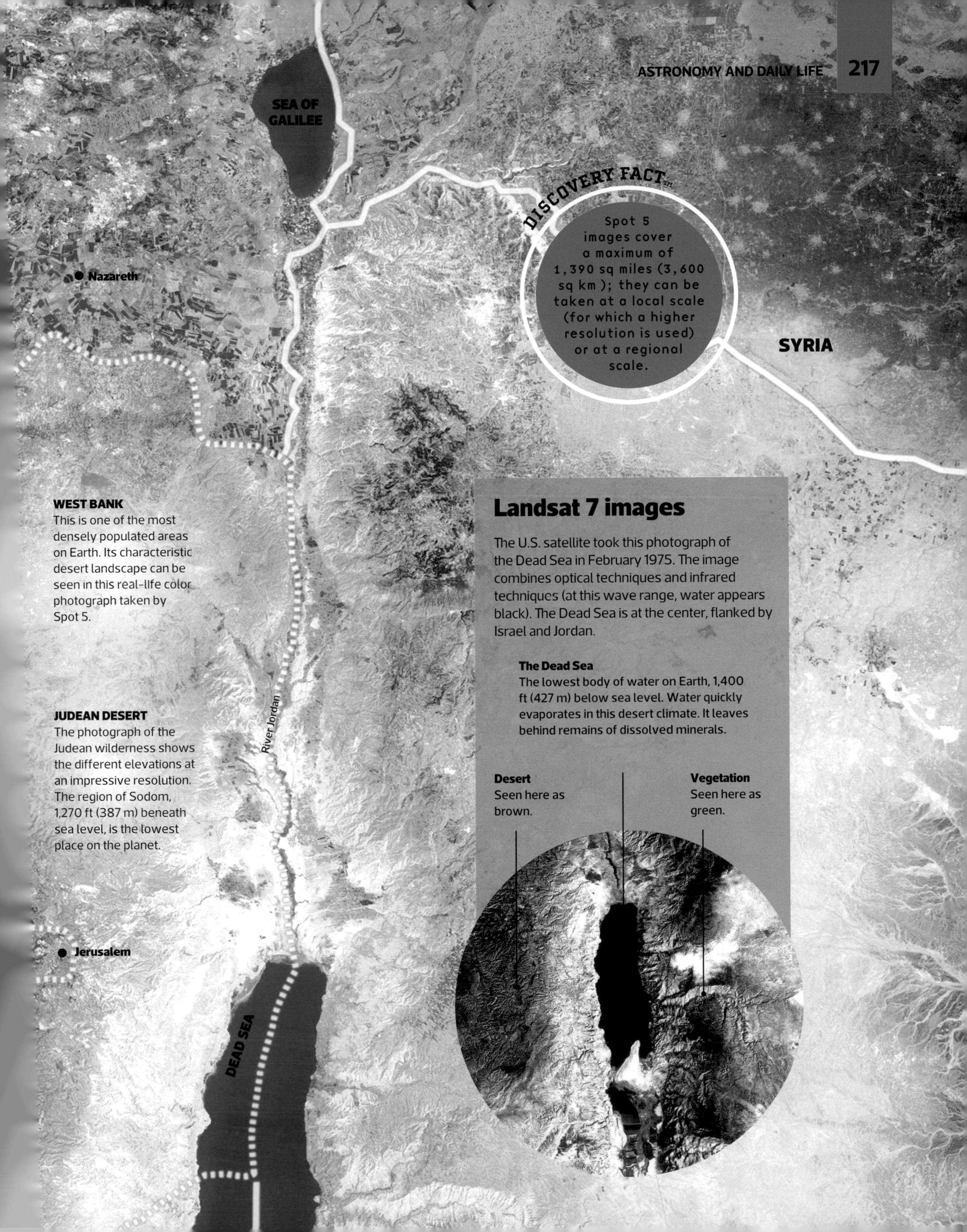

SEA OF GALILEE

● Nazareth

DISCOVERY FACT™

Spot 5 images cover a maximum of 1,390 sq miles (3,600 sq km); they can be taken at a local scale (for which a higher resolution is used) or at a regional scale.

SYRIA

WEST BANK
This is one of the most densely populated areas on Earth. Its characteristic desert landscape can be seen in this real-life color photograph taken by Spot 5.

Landsat 7 images

The U.S. satellite took this photograph of the Dead Sea in February 1975. The image combines optical techniques and infrared techniques (at this wave range, water appears black). The Dead Sea is at the center, flanked by Israel and Jordan.

The Dead Sea
The lowest body of water on Earth, 1,400 ft (427 m) below sea level. Water quickly evaporates in this desert climate. It leaves behind remains of dissolved minerals.

JUDEAN DESERT
The photograph of the Judean wilderness shows the different elevations at an impressive resolution. The region of Sodom, 1,270 ft (387 m) beneath sea level, is the lowest place on the planet.

River Jordan

Desert
Seen here as brown.

Vegetation
Seen here as green.

● Jerusalem

DEAD SEA

Space Vacations

In 2001, American multimillionaire Dennis Tito, the first space "tourist," was successfully sent to the International Space Station; he paid U.S. $20 million for an eight-day stay. Australian Mark Shuttleworth followed in his footsteps a year later. Later, SpaceShipOne, propelled by the plane White Knight, was created; in this craft, thousands of tourists will be able to travel into space at an affordable price. Several private companies are working on projects to offer trips into space.

The journey

Suborbital flights are less expensive than orbital flights. The journey lasts approximately two hours, at a maximum speed of 2,225 mph (3,580 km/h) and a maximum height of 62 miles (100 km). The visit to outer space lasts six minutes, from where the traveler can enjoy the globe's profile and experience the effects of low gravity.

115 ft (35 m)

269 ft (82 m)

8,090 lb (3,670 kg)

Weight of SpaceShipOne

MAXIMUM HEIGHT

Height (miles)

The spaceplane reaches a height of 62 miles (100 km), before falling back into the atmosphere. The crew feel weightless for around six minutes.

60

55

50

THE ENGINE
Is ignited for 80 seconds and reaches a speed of 2,225 mph (3,580 km/h).

45

40

35

TAKEOFF
After one hour in flight, at a height of 9.5 miles (15.24 km), the launch plane, White Knight, releases SpaceShipOne.

30

25

20

WHITE KNIGHT PLANE

Launch date	June 2004
Maximum height	9.5 miles (15.24 km)
First pilot	Mike Melvill
Company	Private

U.S. $200,000

Cost of the suborbital flight

4 days
training

2 hours
flight duration

REENTRY
The pilot configures the descent.

LANDING
The craft touches ground again.

GLIDING
The spaceplane descends toward the Earth's surface.

CREW
Seated at the rear of the plane. They wear pressurized suits and have undergone a rigorous training routine.

N318SL

SPACESHIPONE

Launch date	June 2004
Orbital height	62 miles (100 km)
First pilot	Mike Melvill
Company	Private

16 ft (5 m)

49 ft (15 m)

Propellant
Solid hybrid.

Boosters
Allow the plane to move up or down during flight.

Engine housing
with liquid fuel.

The cabin

Equipped with cutting-edge technology, allowing the pilot to maneuver the plane safely. It features 16 circular glass panels that facilitate a panoramic view of space.

Rudders
Managed electrically, they provide longitudinal stability.

CIRCULAR PANELS
The 16 glass panels provide great views.

HEIGHT GUIDE
Used during reentry into the atmosphere.

RUDDER PEDALS
While the plane turns, the rudder pedals prevent it from spinning around.

Flaps
Used to control the plane's height.

DISPLAY
Shows the position of the plane compared to Earth, the route to its destination and the amount of compressed air on the wings.

Movement of the nose
From one side to the other, around the center of gravity.

CENTRAL LEVER
Used to move the plane up or down.

Feathers
The wings and tail turn up to ensure a safe reentry.

ENGINE
Engaged using buttons, it burns fuel in 80 seconds.

REGULATOR
To control deviations from its flight path.

N328KF

Domestic Astronomy

Today, thanks to powerful domestic binoculars and telescopes, space can be seen at an acceptable quality and, with the help of a stellar map, it is possible to recognize galaxies, nebulae, star clusters, planets, and much more. It is important to become familiarized with the night sky first to make the most of observation time.

Basics

Before heading off to view the skies, make sure you have everything you need. The basic equipment for any budding observer includes binoculars and/or a telescope, star maps (planisphere) and a notebook. A compass is also handy for establishing the four directional points, in addition to a lamp.

Planisphere

Compass

Lamp with red cellophane to preserve dark–adapted vision.

BARREL

OPTICS TUBE

HOW TO SEE THE MOON
Observers can use instruments such as binoculars and telescopes to enjoy different views of astronomical objects. The Moon is a particularly good target for beginners to study, because it is generally very bright.

Moon. Normal view.

10 times larger. View with binoculars.

50 to 100 times larger. View with a telescope.

FOCUS WHEEL

FOCUS EYEPIECE

ADJUSTMENT NUT

TRIPOD ADAPTER

MOVING CONSTELLATIONS
Just as the Sun rises in the east in the morning and sets in the west in the evening, the stars and planets do exactly the same. However, it is not really the stars and planets moving, but the Earth spinning that creates this cosmic optical illusion.

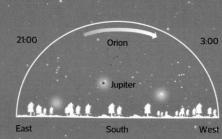

21:00   Orion   3:00

Jupiter

East   South   West

Viewable objects

In addition to stars and planets, communication and spy satellites, planes, comets, and meteors can all be seen in the sky. They are recognizable by both their shape and their movement.

METEORS
Very short bursts of light that last no longer than a fraction of a second.

MOON
The Moon is best observed when it is a crescent, using binoculars or a small telescope.

VENUS
Generally, it can be seen on the horizon at dusk.

COMMUNICATION SATELLITES
The largest shine brighter than some stars, and others take a long time to cross the night sky.

COMETS
Naked-eye comets can be seen every few years, and tend to be visible for a few weeks or months at a time.

LENS

Connecting the dots

A constellation is a group of stars that, when seen from a certain angle, appear close together and seem to take on a given shape. However, in reality, they are separated by huge distances.

PRISMS

OMEGA CENTAURI

16,000
light years from Earth

4.2
light years from Earth

ALPHA CENTAURI

Measurement methods

A celestial planisphere is a circular map of the constellations used to locate stars. To identify one in particular, your arms and your body can be used to measure the direction and height of an object against the horizon.

MEASURING DIRECTION

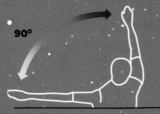

90°

45°

HORIZON

MEASURING HEIGHT

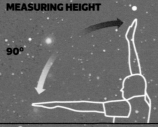

90°

45°

Planispheres indicate the cardinal direction of a star. Position your arms at 90°, using north or south as a starting point.

A star to the southeast may be located at 45°. Combine directional angles with height measurements using your arms.

Using the horizon as a starting point, extend one of your arms on this line and the other perpendicularly.

The easiest way to measure a 45° angle is to move your arm from the horizon to halfway through the 90° angle.

Index